RESTRUCTURING HEGEMONY IN THE GLOBAL POLITICAL ECONOMY

Has the idea of the free market triumphed over the interests of real social forces? Since the late 1970s, the spread of neo-liberalism and the failure of socialist economies and systems in Eastern Europe have resulted in a practically unchallenged hegemony of international capital across the globe. Neo-liberalism is now the dominant ideology, legitimizing the privatization of state-controlled economies and the substitution of the market for the social provision of basic welfare.

In *Restructuring Hegemony in the Global Political Economy* the authors argue that this process began with the defeat of the New International Economic Order, the Euro-Communist ascendency in Western Europe and the overthrow of the Allende government in Chile, and culminated in the collapse of East European and Soviet socialism. They assert that the victory of neo-liberalism is now so complete that its radical features have come to be accepted as the new normality. While tracing the development in individual countries, the book illustrates that these developments are part of an essentially transnational process. The social forces involved in this process, their international linkages, and their responses are discussed in their global context. This analysis is based on a common theoretical approach which transcends the limits of the state-centric discourse of (neo)-realism by taking the dialectical process of global class formation as its point of departure. *Restructuring Hegemony in the Global Political Economy* presents a timely appraisal of the process of transforming the world system as it has unfolded from the late 1970s. The contributors include some of the most stimulating and productive writers currently working in the area of international political economy.

Henk Overbeek is Senior Lecturer in International Relations at the University of Amsterdam. He has specialized in the international dimensions of British politics.

RESTRUCTURING HEGEMONY IN THE GLOBAL POLITICAL ECONOMY

The rise of transnational neo-liberalism in the 1980s

Edited by Henk Overbeek

ROUTLEDGE

London and New York

First published 1993
by Routledge
11 New Fetter Lane, London EC4P 4EE

Simultaneously published in the USA and Canada
by Routledge
29 West 35th Street, New York, NY 10001

© 1993 Henk Overbeek

Typeset in Scantext September by
Leaper & Gard Ltd, Bristol
Printed and bound in Great Britain by
T.J. Press (Padstow) Ltd, Padstow, Cornwall

British Library Cataloguing in Publication Data

*A catalogue reference for this book is available
from the British Library*

ISBN 0–415–05595–4

*Library of Congress Cataloging in Publication Data
has been applied for.*

ISBN 0–415–05595–4

CONTENTS

v

CONTENTS

FIGURES

TABLES

PREFACE

Gradually over the past two decades, the critical study of international political economy has gained for itself a certain autonomy within the larger discipline of international relations. The efforts to understand the dynamics of change in the global economy since the early 1970s have put a number of specific theoretical issues in the limelight. These issues are not new issues: they are questions as old as the first systematic attempts to think about the development of social (i.e. economic, political and ideological) relations at the global level. They are new only in the sense that they reappeared in a historically-specific guise as components of the intellectual attempt to understand the implications of the transformation of the global political economy, the contours of which were first becoming visible after the first internationally-synchronized recession of 1966–7.

One of the most complex and challenging theoretical problems to emerge concerned the adequate conceptualization of the 'internal–external' dialectic. From different corners, the early 1970s produced theoretical approaches investigating the importance of the global character of capitalism for understanding the development within distinct countries: in Latin America a number of *dependentistas* took up this question (Cardoso, Frank, Furtado, Villammil); in Germany the group working on the *Weltmarktbewegung des Kapitals* (world market movement of capital) did the same (von Braunmühl, Busch, Neusüss), and in France people such as Palloix and Andreff analysed the internationalisation of capital and of the capitalist labour process. Eventually, the world-system theorists following the lead of Immanuel Wallerstein captured the discussion and pushed the argument to its extreme limit, by declaring the world economy to be the determinant instance.

The second problematic arising out of essentially the same attempt to deal with the internationalization of capital was initiated when Robin Murray coined the phrase 'territorial non-coincidence'. Exploring the reality and the political implications of the non-coincidence between the territorial reach of capital and the boundaries of the nation-state formed the essence of the debates between Murray, Mandel and, in particular, Poulantzas on the nature of the nation-state and of international integration in the era of transnational capital. It was through Poulantzas' work and that of other French Marxists that the writings of Antonio Gramsci became known to a larger audience, prompting the first English translation of *Quaderni del Carcere (The Prison Notebooks)* in 1971. Gramsci's preoccupation with the ideological dimension, and particularly the consensual quality, of class rule in modern capitalist society seemed to provide a convincing answer to the questions thrown up in the 'revolutionary' convulsions of the late 1960s all over the Western world. In Britain, it was Bob Jessop who introduced Gramsci (through his concept of 'hegemonic projects'). In the 1980s, it was Robert Cox who introduced Gramsci's thought to the discipline of international relations theory, most comprehensively in his important *Production, Power, and World Order. Social Forces in the Making of History* (1987).

The third problematic appearing anew from the early 1970s onward is the question of structure and agency. In the context of the debate on the nature of class power mentioned above, this eternal problematic appeared as the question of the study of the fractioning of capital and of the bourgeoisie. Building on the work of others (Bode, Hickel, Fennema), it was Kees van der Pijl who formulated the most elaborate statement of what has sometimes jokingly been called the 'Amsterdam School' in *The Making of an Atlantic Ruling Class* (1984). Central in this approach was the analysis of the structural conflicts of interest within the ruling class arising out of the fractionation of capital along functional lines and the division of the bourgeoisie into blocs clustering around competing comprehensive concepts of control, and in particular the transnationalization of these conflicts as consequence of the transnational expansion of capital.

The contributors brought together in this volume share an interest in developing an approach to integrate the three problematics indicated. They are not a 'school' in a strict sense of the word: they do not work in the same place, they do not hold identical views on many (even centrally important) questions, and they do not aspire to present a uniform analysis. But they do agree that the nature of the neo-liberal revolution which has swept over the world in the 1980s, consummating its victory with the collapse of the Communist regimes in Eastern Europe and the Soviet Union, can only be understood if these elements are recognized:

1   the rise of neo-liberalism is to be explained as being determined by the restructuring of world capitalism in the 1980s;
2   it is therefore to be understood as a transnational phenomenon rather than as a series of basically unrelated national developments;
3   neo-liberalism is the concept of control of transnational finance capital (the coagulation of transnational money capital and globally-operating productive capital);
4   transnational neo-liberalism manifests itself at the national level not as a simple distillate of external determinants, but rather as a set of intricate mediations between the 'logic' of global capital and the historical reality of national political and social relations.

The neo-liberal project thus has a different face in each country. Yet, we hope that the present volume will present a convincing argument for highlighting the similarities rather than the dissimilarities, and for emphasizing the transnational character of contemporary capitalism.

This book is not the result of a concerted group effort. Nevertheless, the book would never have been realized were it not for the cooperation, endurance and mutual solidarity of the contributors. They had fewer problems in meeting their deadlines than did the editor. A word of thanks is also due to the people at Routledge. Alan Jarvis in particular has been very supportive and stimulating. Finally, I would also like to thank Malcolm Alexander for his support at a crucial moment in the editing process.

Henk Overbeek

CONTRIBUTORS

William K. Carroll is Associate Professor in Sociology at the University of Victoria, British Columbia, Canada. His publications deal with the structure of finance capital and the organization of hegemony in Canada. Carroll is the author of *Corporate Power and Canadian Capitalism*. Carroll's current research concerns the role of social movements in Canadian politics.

Alex Fernández Jilberto is Senior Lecturer in International Relations at the University of Amsterdam. His numerous publications deal with the politics of Chile and more generally the political economy of development in Latin America, including *Dictadura Militar y Oposición Política en Chile 1973–1981* (1985). His current research focuses on environmental issues in Central and South America.

Stephen R. Gill is Professor in Political Science at York University, Toronto, Canada. His publications, dealing with international political economy, include *The Global Political Economy* (1988, with David Law), *Atlantic Relations: Beyond the Reagan Era* (ed., 1989), *American Hegemony and the Trilateral Commission* (1990), and *Gramsci and International Relations* (ed., 1992).

Otto Holman is a Lecturer in International Relations at the University of Amsterdam. His research concentrates on European integration, and more specifically with the integration of Spain into Western Europe. His publications include *European Unification in the 1990s: Myth and Reality* (ed., 1992).

Ed Kaptein currently works as an independent consultant on issues concerned with formulating ecologically sustainable energy policies. He previously held positions both in business and in academia, most recently as Lecturer in Economics at La Trobe University in Melbourne.

His publications deal with (Australian) economic policy and environmental economics.

André Mommen is Senior Lecturer in Politics and Chief Librarian for Political Science at the University of Amsterdam. He has published extensively on the history of the Belgian labour movement and on the history of the Belgian ruling class, including *De Teloorgang van de Belgische Bourgeoisie* (1982) and *Een Tunnel zonder einde: het Neo-Liberalisme van Martens V en VI* (1987). He is currently preparing a manuscript dealing with the transformation of the Belgian political economy in the twentieth century, to be published by Routledge in 1993.

Henk Overbeek is Senior Lecturer in International Relations at the University of Amsterdam. His publications in the field of international political economy have in recent years focused on the international context of British politics: *Global Capitalism and National Decline. The Thatcher Decade in Perspective* (1990). His current research deals with the political economy of global migration and refugee policy.

Kees van der Pijl is a reader in International Relations at the University of Amsterdam. He has published widely on issues of transnational class formation, including *The Making of an Atlantic Ruling Class* (1984) and *Transnational Relations and Class Strategy* (ed., 1989). He is currently preparing the English edition of a history of international relations theory published in Dutch and German in 1992. Other projects include a study of Marxian thought on international relations, and a study of the rise and demise of the movement for a New International Economic Order in the 1970s.

Richard van der Wurff is a research assistant in the Department of International Relations at the University of Amsterdam. His postgraduate research concerns the politics of European environmental policy.

1

RESTRUCTURING CAPITAL AND RESTRUCTURING HEGEMONY

Neo-liberalism and the unmaking of the post-war order

Henk Overbeek and Kees van der Pijl

THE NEW NORMALCY

In one long revolutionary wave, the East European regimes of 'really existing socialism' have been swept away in the past two years. Communism as a living political movement no longer exists, and anti-communism is therefore no longer an essential element of bourgeois ideology in the West. Eastern Europe, the Soviet Union, and most of their former allies in the Third World (Angola, Ethiopia, Vietnam), are swiftly being reintegrated into the world economy, their social structures overturned to accommodate their insertion into the global capitalist class structure. In these formerly socialist countries, neo-liberalism has become the predominant ideology legitimating the privatization of the state-controlled economy and the substitution of the market for the social provision of basic welfare. For Europe as a whole this has set in motion processes of economic and political liberalization and mass migration on a scale unprecedented in the past century. The need for a 'New European Architecture' (Holman 1992) determines the shape of European politics to come.

In the West, the high tide of the 'Reagan revolution' and 'Thatcherism' seems to have receded with the political retirement of their namesakes, Ronald Reagan and Margaret Thatcher. Untrammelled international competition, the celebration of the market, of wealth and self, anti-communism and anti-unionism; all these are no longer propagated as 'revolutionary' in the sense of challenging a prevailing consensus of a different content, but they are now part of normal every

1

day discourse, self-evident, near impossible to contradict or even doubt. History conceived of as a struggle of ideologies has come to an end, as Fukuyama (1989) would have it. In short, the end of history appears to have resolved any remaining internal contradictions within international capitalism (other than straightforward competition), and to represent the triumph of the ideological tendency articulating these orientations, neo-liberalism. Its victory means that its radical tenets have themselves become the new 'normalcy'.

How can we account for such a process? Is it the outcome of a battle of ideas, or is it the product of the concrete agency of social forces? If so, does that then mean that social forces are capable of redefining the coordinates of what is considered 'normal', or is this apparent consensus merely a mental reflection of the real living and working conditions that people face, and do opinion leaders and politicians only 'ride the waves'?

The contributors to this collection have attempted to answer these questions by investigating a number of manifestations of what was essentially a transnational neo-liberal revolution. This transnational revolution took place against the background of the crisis of world capitalism of the 1970s which necessitated a far-reaching restructuring of the economic, social and political conditions for capital accumulation. Neo-liberalism, it will be argued in the chapters to follow, was the hegemonic project which guided this restructuring and shaped its trajectory. The social forces involved, their international linkages, and their responses to the structural obstacles facing them, are analysed for a number of less generally known cases. Reaganism and Thatcherism are the best known examples of course, and have as such been subjected to intense and often comparative scrutiny. Other cases have received less attention. This collection aims to show that the neo-liberal counter-revolution was indeed a transnational phenomenon, actually enveloping not just the heartland of world capitalism but also outposts such as Chile and Australia, and not just countries ruled by conservative political formations such as Britain but also countries ruled by Christian Democrats (Belgium, Germany) or by Social Democrats (Spain).

In this first introductory chapter, the conceptual framework which is common to the following chapters will be introduced. To say that there are certain commonalities in the theoretical approaches of the different authors is not to say that there are no differences of emphasis or even sometimes of opinion. On the contrary, the alert reader will have no trouble spotting some fairly important divergences. This indicates that their thinking has not (yet) become dogmatized, and that debate and even discord are positively valued. For all their differences, however, the contributors do share the theoretical view that class formation and class conflict are structured by what we have termed *comprehensive concepts of control*.

FRACTIONS OF CAPITAL AND CONCEPTS OF CONTROL

Comprehensive concepts of control are expressions of bourgeois hegemony reflecting a historically specific hierarchy of classes and class fractions. They express the ideological and in Gramsci's sense hegemonic structure of particular historical configurations of capital.

Capital fractions, as Hickel (1975) argues, are structures of socialization by which the fundamental contradiction between capital and labour is articulated in a concrete configuration of classes. Fractions of total capital are aggregates of capitalist interests which crystallize around a particular function in the process of capital accumulation.

Functions in this process give rise to common orientations, interest definitions, and collective experiences providing ingredients for a coalition of interests and a concept of control aspiring for comprehensiveness. 'In the continuous attempt (owing to competition) of individual capitals to make their particular interests appear as general interests at the level of the state', writes Hickel (1975: 151), 'resides the actual relevance of bourgeois fractioning.'

These functions are associated with distinct circuits of capital: circulation of money, circulation of commodities, exchange of money against labour in production. Closest to 'total capital' is *money capital*, which in its totality represents the total quantity of commodities, and which is at the same time the most general and abstract form of capital. *Productive capital*, even as an abstraction, always refers to tangible 'factors': human labour, raw materials, means of production. Bankers and industrialists, politicians and 'organic intellectuals' of the capitalist class, meet in a wide range of settings, from corporate boards of directors, private consultative and planning bodies, state and quasi-state institutions, to whatever informal channels are available (Fennema 1982, Gill 1990; see also Burch 1980). But the coherence of their eventual consensus derives its cogency from representing a particular, timely articulation of the general money capital perspective with a concrete deployment of productive capital.

The capacity of the resulting concepts of control to become

What is comprehensive becomes

comprehensive, that is, to be effectively applied as a policy expressing the general interest by governments or international institutions, is based on its objective comprehensiveness (i.e. coverage of labour process, circulation relations, profit distribution, and state and international power relations); and on the particular balance between the 'systemic' requirements of capital accumulation and its concrete, momentary needs. The former tend to reflect the money capital perspective (economic liberalism), and will be most easily and eagerly propounded by those familiar to it by trade or tradition; the latter will tend to the productive capital viewpoint, reflecting the particularities of non-market, non-value aspects of the productive process and its immediate social setting (cf. Jessop 1983).

If money capital represents the closest approximation of the general capitalist interest, so the functionaries of money capital (merchant and investment bankers, notably) tend to have a view of the world that is broadest within the limits of the capitalist world view, and at the same time most strictly confined to those limits. Their view is, to quote Polanyi

> The principle of economic liberalism, aiming at the establishment of the self-regulating market, relying on the support of the trading classes, and using largely *laissez-faire* and free trade as its methods.

> (Polanyi 1957: 132)

On the opposite side of the spectrum we find the principle of social protection, 'aiming at the conservation of man and nature as well as productive organization, relying on the varying support of those most immediately affected by the deleterious action of the market – primarily, but not exclusively, the working and landed classes – and using protective legislation, restrictive associations, and other instruments of intervention as its methods' (ibid.).

Concrete historical fractions will often be capable of capitalizing on a shift towards a particular concept, a redefinition of the general interest that is a recurrent feature of the political business cycle. Hegemony however is not simply prevailing through the application of power, but rather a qualitative coincidence between the particular concept it represents and the 'systemic' context in which it arises. Usually those groups assert themselves whose specific group interests at a given juncture most closely correspond with the objective state of capital accumulation and class struggle then prevailing (cf. Gossweiler 1975: 56; also Van der Pijl 1984: 33–4).[1] The notion of 'concepts of

4

control' thus provides a clue to understanding the nature of the relation between structure and agency: the structure defined by the process of the accumulation of capital, the agency of the concrete social forces which originate from the sphere of production relations and which struggle continuously over the direction of the accumulation process and over the role of the state.

It is this historical articulation which makes possible the political hegemony of a given empirical bloc of interests ('fraction of the bourgeoisie', Bode 1979; or 'historic bloc' in the terminology of Gramsci (1971) and Cox (1987)) on the basis of a combination of ideal-typical fractional positions (money/productive).

Clearly, the new normalcy which a newly hegemonic concept of control expresses is not a political ploy, but the objective 'general interest' as delineated by the current parameters of the prevailing mode of production and its class order. The susceptibility of different social classes and class fractions to capitalist logic varies, and increasingly so.

The process of socialization, deepening and widening the division of labour as well as the scope of accompanying normative structures as the result of capital accumulation, has expanded and differentiated the terrain on which the alternative principle of social protection is operative. In addition to the landed classes, who have historically opposed capitalist orthodoxy from the vantage point of a pre-capitalist critique of money capital (critique of usury and trade, 'anti-chrematism'), and productive capital properly speaking (the spokesmen of which have included both prominent industrialists like Ford and organic intellectuals of productive capital like Keynes), new strata have crystallized in the mean time. Located between the manual proletariat and the capitalist class proper these strata, while being of necessity functionaries of the capitalist order and subject to its normative and ideological constraints, have at the same time fostered the fulfilment of the technical requirements of production at the expense of property relations (Bihr 1989; for a more detailed exposition, see Chapter 2).

PARADIGMATIC SCALES OF OPERATION

To arrive at an understanding of how capitalist development has been guided by comprehensive concepts of control constructed from particular ideal-types activated by the momentary requirements of the mode of production, the spatial coordinates of capital accumulation have to be taken into account as well. For while money capital, abstractly as total capital, concretely as 'high finance', has operated on a cosmopolitan plane ever since the Middle Ages, production under its influence has operated on a gradually widening scale. When the typiccal, or 'paradigmatic' (in the sense of serving as a general frame of reference) scale of operation of industry coincided with the national state in the most important countries, a historically unique situation developed. Internationally operating money capital was subordinated to nationally operating productive capital (a development that reached its zenith in the 1930s and inspired Polanyi's dichotomy).

Prior to this stage of mobilizing the 'principle of social protection' in the context of the national state, industry operated on a subnational scale. Its output was marketed on a world market dominated by British industry, commerce and transport to such an extent that notions of universal free trade and harmony developed in Britain were also embraced in countries whose capacity to compete was undermined by unmitigated exposure. The era of the Pax Britannica spawned a comprehensive concept of control expressing and idealizing this state of affairs. Normalcy and the 'general interest' were predominantly defined therefore in terms of an abstract and cosmopolitan money capital perspective. The hegemonic concept of this era we call *liberal internationalism*.

In the period from the First World War to the 1950s the productive capital perspective (Polanyi's principle of social protection) was dominant at the national level; in this era, the hegemonic concept of control was that of *state monopolism*. Money capital was still principally engaged in international operations, but the crisis of the 1930s led to its curtailment by state authorities.

Gradually, and definitely following the Second World War, (US) industry expanded on an Atlantic plane, albeit in a highly regulated setting. A welfare state concept, the highest form of Polanyi's principle of social protection constructed around the productive capital viewpoint, combined aspects of expanding production with a measure of re-liberalization in the international sphere. Trade, however, held priority over money capital (in line with the hegemony of the productive capital view). The comprehensive concept defining the new normalcy and general interest at this stage was *corporate liberalism*.

In the crisis of the 1970s, finally, a struggle ensued which resulted in the triumph of *neo-liberalism*. Neo-liberalism reaches back to the abstract and cosmopolitan money capital perspective so prominent in liberal internationalism, but industry has meanwhile outgrown its national confines. The paradigmatic scale of operation of industrial capital today is global, at least in tendency. At the same time we

| paradigmatic scale of operation† | | hegemonic |
money capital	productive capital	concept
1820s–1870s	cosmopolitan*	local	liberal
1870s–1914	cosmopolitan*	national	internationalism
1920s	cosmopolitan	national*	
1930s	national	national*	state monopolism
1950s	national	Atlantic*	corporate
1960s and 1970s	cosmopolitan	Atlantic*	liberalism
1980s and 1990s	cosmopolitan*	global and regional	neo-liberalism

Figure 1.1 Paradigmatic scales of operation of capital and hegemonic concepts
of control in modern capitalism

*The asterisks mark the prevailing perspective (money or productive) in the hegemonic
concept of control.

†Although both 'cosmopolitan' and 'global' indicate that the paradigmatic
scale of operation encompasses the whole world, the difference is that money capital can
disengage itself almost completely from any form of nation-state control, whereas
productive capital, however globally operative, is always, at any particular moment
in time, bound to specific physical/geographical locations, and therefore subject
to state control.

witness a relative disintegration of the national framework into
multiple local and regional frameworks, leading some observers to
speak of 'globalization' as the typical trend of the new era. (See Figure
1 for a schematic representation of the paradigmatic scales of operation
of money and productive capital.)

We now turn to a discussion of these concepts in more detail, and
indicate some of the problems involved in employing this periodization
of international politics.

CONCEPTS OF CONTROL IN THE GLOBAL POLITICAL ECONOMY

Liberal internationalism

The heyday of historical liberalism coincided with the first industrial
revolution, the dominance in the state system of a power committed to
informal patterns of rule (the Pax Britannica), and the unhampered
freedom of high finance and trade. The liberal internationalism of the

w/ Pax B. what is essentially natl. production dominating on a world scale assumes a relation of the dominance of intl. trade and maintains its value internationally by dominance over gold and currency reserves.

British bourgeoisie, combining *laissez-faire*, an evasive approach to the domestic working class, and a Lockean concept of the state (the Night-watch State), of course favoured British capital, but by their success obtained the quality of a natural order of things.

> British predominance in world trade was at that time so overwhelming that there was a certain undeniable harmony between British interests and the interests of the world.
>
> (Carr 1964: 81)

The liberal internationalist concept, of which Polanyi's notion of economic liberalism constitutes the kernel, can be dissected into components referring to the labour process, circulation relations, the profit distribution structure, and state/international politics. These aspects, however, have to be understood in close interaction.

The ideal typical labour process of the early capitalist era was the extensive one, based on a low organic composition of capital. Workshop production with a strong craft element, only gradually shifting to larger establishments, and a regional concentration of industry were predominant in this long run-up to the twentieth century. Against the background of ample labour supply from the countryside, such industries as textiles, foodstuffs and the early machine industry providing the mechanized equipment for them, typiccally operated on a local scale, establishments often being 'distributed in much the same way as population itself', notably in food and construction (Estall and Buchanan 1966: 142; Andreff 1976: 27–8). At the same time, products of these industries, notably textiles, were inserted into commercial circuits flung far and wide; quite irrespective, in the case of Britain, of the limits of formal empire (Gallagher and Robinson 1967).

In the course of the later nineteenth century, this pattern gradually changed as finance and a new generation of industry became more prominent. At the national level, liberalism was superseded in an increasing number of countries by protectionism. But at the level of world order, the hegemony of the liberal internationalist concept remained effective. In Germany, for instance, domestic liberalism gave way to authoritarian nationalism from 1878 on, but it lasted until the eve of the First World War before the liberal internationalist concept was effectively challenged by a contrary view, viz., that 'the era of apparently peaceful competition of states (in the sense of Adam Smith) was definitively over' (Fischer 1984: 15).

The money capital perspective underlying liberal internationalism was corroborated by the continued prominence of high finance in the

natl. production

Liberal intlism is essentially a money capital perspective, finance capital.

international arena, where, in Polanyi's view, it 'functioned as a permanent agency of the most elastic kind'.

> Independent of single governments, even of the most powerful, it was in touch with all; independent of the central banks even of the Bank of England, it was closely connected with them. There was intimate contact between finance and diplomacy; neither would consider any long-range plan, whether peaceful or warlike, without making sure of the other's good will.
>
> (Polanyi 1957: 10)

In international politics, ascendant imperialism and rivalry implied that the informal cosmopolitanism of the Pax Britannica was confined to the British Empire and Commonwealth on the eve of the First World War. At the close of that war, Woodrow Wilson's dramatic intervention in world affairs aimed, among other things, at restoring the hegemony of the liberal internationalist concept of control on a truly international scale, with an eye to isolating the Bolshevik Revolution. The typical tenets of international harmony, premised on the notion that industrial competition was operative on a plane entirely different from that of inter-state conflict, both of them subject to informal control by international money capital, were reflected in the League of Nations system, with the International Chamber of Commerce and the International Labour Organization. These international organizations were the institutional forms of an incipient international quasi-state structure expressing the hegemony of the ruling class which is based on a particular concept of control; 'each international organization', Ernst Haas writes, 'owes its origin to some pattern of shared expectations, the "general interest" that must be specified' (Haas 1964: 130).

The League fell victim to forces supporting a contrary concept, however, one which was constructed around the productive capital perspective that had become hegemonic in the First World War.

State monopolism

Industry in the age of high finance passed through a transformation from first generation food, textile and machine industry to being centred on large-scale manufacturing, especially the iron and steel industry catering to the expanding railway and shipbuilding industries. These industries by their high organic composition of capital and fixed cost structure (intensive accumulation, Andreff 1976: 29–34) relied much more intimately on bank and state support for financing investments and foreign sales. Also, these industries, by their size and politically backed market power, could divide markets by cartel agreements, which proliferated from the turn of the century: the age of finance capital and imperialist rivalry had arrived.

In contrast to the liberal internationalism of pre-1914 vintage, the growing weight of the new industries was reflected in the emergence of a state monopoly tendency in the bourgeoisie. The state-monopolistic concept of control with its preference for the 'visible' over the 'invisible' hand (whether it concerned labour relations, markets generally, or international relations) reflected proclivities typical of productive capital. Its protagonists were to be found notably among the organizers of national and international trusts and cartels, often magnates from the fields mentioned and from the oil industry, and their investment bankers.

The First World War entailed the breakdown of the informal transnational networks of high finance and placed the new heavy industries in the foreground. The state role in establishing the iron and steel industry was decisive: especially in the industrial latecomer countries, such as Japan, Germany, Italy, or Holland, establishing an iron and steel industry was part of government policy, 'but there are few countries in which the iron and steel industry is without some form of government assistance' (Estall and Buchanan 1966, 166; also Martinelli *et al.* 1981: 39–40). The fact that the paradigmatic scale of operation of these industries was typically national, i.e. coincided with the national state, elevated commercial competition to the level of interstate rivalry. The second major element in this process of the 'nationalization' of social relations under capitalism was the rise of the organized labour movement in the latter decades of the nineteenth century. The victory of social democracy over anarchism in the First International – i.e. the strategic decision to aim to seize state power – focused the energies of working class organizations on the state (cf. Wallerstein 1984).

Until 1929–32, when the intricate network of high finance exploded in a series of events that began with the Wall Street Crash, the state-monopolistic bourgeoisie still coexisted with the financiers. The Dawes Plan inspired a hope that in spite of the distorted structure of international payments, the prosperity of the liberal era could be revived by means of international portfolio investment. After the Great Crash, coinciding with a shift from the steel industry to oil, chemicals and rayon, and electrical engineering industries as the standard-bearers of the state-monopolistic concept, the ruling class configurations in the various countries were typically oriented against internationalism and against cosmopolitan banking in particular. The internationally operating investment bank, the embodiment of *haute finance*, was put under state tutelage in all major countries in the course of the 1930s. In line with Keynes' prescription for the 'euthanasia of the rentier', priority was given to developing the internal market for industry (Keynes 1970, 376; Gramsci 1971: 293). Bank capital was still represented in the new configuration of forces supporting the 'Great Transformation': the oil-chemical-rayon-electrical industrial blocs of the 1930s were supported by the Chase National Bank in the US, Paribas, Worms, and BNCI in France, Deutsche Bank in Germany, and Midland Bank and Hill-Higginson in Britain. Significantly, these banks, with the Lazard connection an important link between several of them, handsomely survived a surge of social criticism of banking hitting the more exposed investment banks prominent in the period, such as J.P. Morgan, and others (van der Pijl 1984: Ch. 4).

The initial reaction to the Crash and the banking crisis of the early 1930s was largely based on the state-monopolistic concept of control. Even in the United States, protectionism, obligatory corporatism and other state controls characterized the early New Deal. The rise of the new industries of the 1920s such as oil, chemicals, and electrical engineering with their preference for cartelization and protection had inspired state-monopolistic policies. In contrast, the ascendancy of the automobile industry in the US necessitated a reconfiguration of the historic bloc and thus opened the way for an alternative concept which would eventually triumph in the New Deal, and which was transplanted to Europe in the Marshall Plan: corporate liberalism.

Corporate liberalism

Corporate liberalism as a concept of control captures the synthesis between an Americanized version of liberal internationalism and the state monopoly tendency with its national, productive emphasis, that was wrought in the New Deal and projected on to Western Europe through the Marshall Plan. The synthesis, pioneered by Henry Ford in the 1920s, combined the following elements.

In the first place, 'Fordism' meant standardized mass production. This corresponded to a trend in capital accumulation towards raising productivity in the production of consumer durables, and in producing the means of production for it. In this way, 'every push of the workers at the level of wages is translated into a push of capital towards the production of commodities necessary for the workers', resulting in the gradual incorporation of workers' consumption into the circuit of productive capital (Maurino 1974: 54–5; cf. Aglietta 1979). To sustain the intensification of the labour process required by production along these lines, a normative intervention into what formerly was private life was mandatory. Ford workers were spied on to encourage regular life-styles. Prohibition subsequently was meant to achieve the same nation-wide. '"Puritanical" initiatives,' Gramsci wrote in his seminal essay 'Americanism and Fordism' (1971: 303), 'simply have the purpose of preserving, outside of work, a certain psycho-physical equilibrium which prevents the physiological collapse of the worker, exhausted by the new method of production.'

Circulation relations between industries had to be reordered, and the rise of automobile production more in particular implied the subordi-nation of the iron and steel industry and its ancillaries to the steel consuming industry. Monopolistic and occasionally state enforced price controls in the US, nationalization in Britain, and the Coal and Steel Community in continental Western Europe served this purpose.

At the same time, the Fordist welfare assumptions necessary for sustaining the work-force were extended to the working population at large: the workers' purchasing power became as much a nodal point in the system as their labour power. Indeed, the reproduction of the worker came to be seen as a state task. As the Beveridge Report of 1942 (1968: 338) put it, 'The main feature of the Plan ... is a scheme of social insurance against interruption and destruction of earning power and for special expenditure arising at birth, marriage or death.'

New Deal and Beveridge-type social legislation testified to the productive capital, 'social protection' orientation underlying the corporate liberal concept. In profit distribution, Keynesian demand management was premised on curtailing investors' private whims and cutting money capital down to size. From the late 1930s to the 1970s, the share of profits accruing to the financial sector never exceeded 11 per cent (Economic Report of the President 1977: 279, tb. B-79).

The consequence of bringing in the workers and locking capitalism into national compartments and entrusting the state with its expansion under the hegemony of a technocratic alliance, inherent in state-mono-polism, was evaded by the second component of corporate liberalism, a revived liberal internationalism. In Europe, the enslavement of the working class by the corporatist order was the foundation for the Fascist mode of growth. In the US it was realized that foreign markets were essential if excessive dependence on domestic purchasing power was to be avoided. The state had to credit-finance sales abroad to allow, in corporation lawyer J.F. Dulles's words, 'foreigners to acquire goods for which domestic consumers otherwise would have to be found' (quoted in Gardner 1964: 35).

The capacity to reach a compromise between capital and labour in production had already been premised very much on internationalization. In the 1930s Ford could be classed among the internationalists along with electrical engineering, big oil after the international cartel agreement, and at a distance, other American car makers, who did not share the protectionist attitude of the typical state-monopolistic industries such as steel and chemicals (Ferguson 1984: 53 and *passim*). Foreign direct investment was one aspect of the internationalism by which union radicalism could be accommodated.

The multinational corporation was the expression *par excellence* of this international expansion of Fordism. Manufacturing multinationals in car production and electrical engineering displayed a flexibility which moved far beyond state-monopolism. Their global operations required the creation of a transnational quasi-state infrastructure which lent a new relevance to the informal networks of ruling class consultation, from the various 'European' elite networks and the Bilderberg Conferences, to the Trilateral Commission. Through the IMF and World Bank, the OECD and the 'European' institutions created in the course of the integration process, the transcendent 'liberal' perspective (albeit still subordinate to the pervasive productive capital orientation of the national welfare states) could be brought to bear on the individual national states.

Between 1960 and the early 1970s, world manufacturing output doubled and world trade in manufactures trebled. This surge in world production and world trade represented a tremendous development of the world productive forces and of the global socialization of labour. Characteristically, this development proceeded at a highly unequal pace in different core regions of the world economy, with an annual growth rate of Japanese manufacturing at 13.6 per cent against 5.3 and 5.4 for the US and West Germany throughout the decade (Dicken 1986: 28, tb. 2.6). By the early 1970s, the increasing strength of the metropolitan working classes, the revolt of the Third World clamouring for development, the rivalry among the major centres of 'multinational' expansion, and the defeat of the US in Vietnam, all undermined corporate liberalism. Capital embarked on a restructuration on a global scale, with money capital, freed from Keynesian controls since the late 1960s, playing a crucial role. The crisis of 1974–5 testified to the dismantling of the metropolitan, 'national' component of the corporate liberal synthesis: it particularly hit the industries characterized by an intensive, state-monitored mode of accumulation (Andreff 1982: 121), which had been at the core of the post-war 'Fordist' expansion.

THE RISE AND CONSOLIDATION OF NEO-LIBERALISM

Neo-liberalism as a hegemonic construct

The crisis of the latter half of the 1970s cannot be traced to any one single incident, or to any one isolated dip in the normal business cycle. It was a fundamental crisis of 'normality' affecting all aspects of the post-war order: social relations of production, the composition of the historic bloc and its concept of control, the role of the state, and the international order. Efforts to resolve this crisis necessarily acquired a comprehensive quality. As Stuart Hall has said,

> If the crisis is deep – 'organic' – these efforts cannot be merely defensive. They will be *formative*: aiming at a new balance of forces, the emergence of new elements, the attempt to put together a new 'historic bloc', new political configurations and 'philosophies', a profound restructuring of the state and the ideological discourses which construct the crisis and represent it as it is 'lived' as a practical reality: new programmes and policies, pointing to a new result, a new sort of 'settlement' – 'within certain limits'. These new elements do not 'emerge': they have to be constructed. Political and ideological work is required to disarticulate old formations, and to rework their elements into new ones.
>
> (Hall 1983: 23)

The new concept of control emerging out of this constructive effort to deal with the organic crisis of the 1970s we call *neo-liberalism*.

The precise meaning of the term neo-liberalism must now be elucidated, because it can easily lead to misunderstanding. An earlier meaning of the term was actually quite similar to the notion of corporate liberalism (cf. Harris 1972; also Cox 1987). A related cause for misunderstanding may be the renewed popularity of the term in the USA where 'liberalism' had the same connotations as corporatism in Europe, and where 'neo-liberalism' designates those political forces which try to revive the liberalism of the Kennedy era, but pragmatically incorporate many of the conservative criticisms of traditional American liberalism (cf. Rothenberg 1984).

The authors in this volume use the notion of neo-liberalism to describe the phenomenon which is also known as 'the New Right', neo-conservatism, or 'Thatcherism', characterized by the sometimes uneasy and contradictory fusion of liberal and conservative elements. In its liberal guise, neo-liberalism is the politics constructed from the individual, freedom of choice, the market society, *laissez-faire*, and minimal government. Its neo-conservative component builds on strong government, social authoritarianism, disciplined society, hierarchy and subordination, and the nation (Belsey 1986: 173).

The combination of the two is not nearly as contradictory as it sometimes seems. As a concept of control, neo-liberalism is the formulation of an identifiable fractional interest in terms of the 'national' or 'general' interest. Neo-liberalism is the fundamental expression of the outlook of *transnational circulating capital*.

But a project which consists only of liberalization, privatization and internationalization (not to speak of unemployment and falling real incomes), will have the greatest difficulty in becoming hegemonic, or even, particularly in parliamentary democracies, dominant. A hegemonic project needs a 'politics of support' as much as it needs a 'politics of power' (Gamble 1988: 208–41).[2]

Neo-conservatism provides the neo-liberal bourgeoisie with an effective 'politics of support': moral conservatism, xenophobia, law-and-order, the family, are the themes which provided the basis for a relatively stable electoral coalition, which even today seems to have relegated social-democracy to the past for good.

The precise mix of elements (free market ideology and neo-conservatism, destructive and constructive) varies from country to country, depending on the political conjuncture and the country's particular place in the world order of the 1970s. The rise and consolidation of the neo-liberal project – which involved disciplining labour through establishing a new core-periphery structure of labour relations, subordinating the global productive grid to profit criteria established by money capital, and confronting the Third World and the Soviet bloc with a new Cold War – were not realized at once. Even for its most ardent protagonists, neo-liberalism's 'rationality' transpired only gradually and through a process of trial and error. Furthermore, as will become clear from the following chapters, a hegemonic project is not absolutely and exclusively victorious. Elements which are alien to the hegemonic concept can and most likely will persist due to particular historical circumstances, as with the tenacity of liberal internationalism in Britain during the Fordist age, or with the persistence of corporate-liberal structures in the Germany of the neo-liberal 1980s and 1990s (cf. van der Wurff's chapter).

Restructuring global labour relations

The shift of Fordist industries to new production sites (steel and ship-building, notably) and the overall restructuring of capital of which it was part, interacted with a crisis of American imperialism and the apparent collapse of the post-1945, Cold War order. 'Rust belts' became apparent throughout the metropolitan economy, and the restructuring of capital once again required the restructuring of hegemony as well. Interacting with the partial breakdown of the system of fixed exchange rates pegged to the dollar, which increased direct competition between labour forces hitherto sheltered by nationally differentiated, counter-cyclical state policies (Mandel 1980: 12), an attack on established positions of the working class both on the shop-floor and in politics unfolded in the course of the later 1970s (e.g. the chapters in this volume devoted to Australia, Belgium, and Canada).

As the metropolitan states switched to increasingly synchronized deflationary economic policies, the concept of the welfare state became an anomaly to capital. Working-class autonomy in the mass-production plants turned factories into what Baudoin and Collin call 'fortresses of collective bargaining power' (*Le Monde Diplomatique*, February 1986; CSE 1980: 8). As Ross Perot, the computer services tycoon brought in to restructure General Motors, found, there were '... tens of thousands, maybe hundreds of thousands of people at General Motors who are quite insulated from the harsh realities of the competitive marketplace' (quoted in *Newsweek*, 17 June 1985).

The governments of the late 1970s, notably the Carter administration and Helmut Schmidt's and other European Social Democratic governments or coalitions, were still too strongly committed to the corporate liberal concept to be able to turn the wheel drastically (for various European experiences, see the chapters on Belgium, Germany, and Spain).

Carter's election campaign had still been conducted very much in the traditional Democratic vein and it took several years before the ascendant anti-inflation and anti-union orientation made itself felt (Burch 1980: III, 331–4). In Europe, regular patterns of government lent themselves even less to a mid-term shift of course, so that the late 1970s and early 1980s became marked by drastic interruptions of normal electoral and political procedures (cf. Sanguinetti 1982).

16

Ultimately, a new pattern of labour relations was established through 'historic' defeats of the trade union movement (mineworkers in Britain and Belgium, steelworkers in France, autoworkers in Italy) consolidated by high unemployment, increasing production automation, and the parallel growth of a new sweatshop economy. Essential in the return to liberalism in labour relations was the replacement of the 'shop communities' engendered by Fordist mass production, by the 'craft communities' of a type marginalized in the course of the New Deal (Piore and Sabel 1984). These could now be based on new 'core technologies' allowing a new phase in flexible production automation (van Tulder and Junne 1988). A new core-periphery structure of social relations of production was in the process of being established.[3]

The scope of production was both reduced and made part of the global productive grid. Production, although resuming particular forms belonging to the liberal era, is no longer 'local' in the sense of being isolated, but 'local' and 'global' at the same time, in the sense of being regionally concentrated (indeed often grafted on ethnic communities, Piore and Sabel 1984: 265–6) and belonging to integrated global circuits of productive capital. The analogy with the original liberal picture lies in the fact that productive capital often 'approximates the activity of a commercial enterprise or a consultancy firm, which selects the most advantageous components from the programmes of international producers' (Junne 1979: 74).

Replacing the corporate liberal concept by a neo-liberal one in labour relations relied also on a subordinate neo-conservatism. Whereas the former celebrates the market, the latter rather revolves around notions of violence and decline typical of the National Security culture, family, and religious fundamentalism (cf. Langille 1987; Hall 1983; also Overbeek 1990: 179–80).

Significantly, the propagation of a mere return to market liberalism was not judged effective as a means to mobilize a sufficient mass of interests. In a collection of essays first published in 1970, Irving Kristol already challenged the orthodox liberalism of Hayek and Friedman in this sense. Kristol, senior fellow at the right-wing American Enterprise Institute and a director in several corporations, argued that capitalism had always rested on particular 'ethics' complementing the functioning of the economy: the Protestant ethic for the lower classes, the Darwinian ethic for small businessmen, and the Technocratic ethic dominant in the recent, managerial era (i.e. corporate liberalism). A new 'ethic' for the 1980s should link its underlying conservatism with a professed striving for reform. Only a reformist, indeed 'revolutionary' profile would allow a new liberal trend to appear modern and turn Keynesianism and Socialism obsolete (Kristol 1971: 20, 26).

The new 'ethic' proved to have a strong appeal to new social strata such as the 'new middle classes' who were attracted by the newly professed morality of upward social mobility, as well as to such 'old' strata as the skilled working class, attracted by the ideology of the family and the nation. The defeat and disorientation of Social-Democracy throughout Europe seems terminal. Dahrendorf is quite right if he interprets the neo-liberal victory as the 'End of the Social-Democratic Century' (quoted by Gill 1991: 305).

The role of money capital in restructuring global production

A crisis of capitalism implies the restructuring of both the spatial and technical aspects of production and the social relations of production, in order to adjust production to consumption, and restore profitability by raising the rate of exploitation and the mass of surplus value. Generally speaking, money capital as capital-in-general plays a crucial role in shaping the new productive patterns.

In the crisis of the 1970s, international money capital, first of all the big commercial banks, initially failed to perform the role of capital-in-general. Their particular interests led them to use the space they had won upon the rescinding of Keynesian legislation in the late 1960s and early 1970s primarily for their own profit. Awash with funds once the dollar was no longer tied to gold and the proceeds from the oil price hike were recycled into the Atlantic financial system, the banks became the financiers not only of deficitary metropolitan countries but also of the long-term industrialization plans of Arab, Latin American, East Asian, and socialist states. Operating from a fractional rentier perspective negligent of the long-term interests of the capitalist class, the banks were in fact instrumentalized by the newly industrializing states of the capitalist periphery in their struggle to gain control of the runaway industrialization and emancipate from import substitution and multinational/metropolitan controls (cf. Frieden 1981).

Also, the key transnational institution supporting the Carter and bourgeois European administrations, the Trilateral Commission, still favoured conciliation with the forces of reform. The Club of Rome, committed to the same concept and bent on avoiding 'government by crisis, by incident',[4] sponsored a report on 'Reshaping the International Order' in direct response to the Non-Aligned Countries' meeting in 1973 where the programme for a New International Economic Order

(NIEO) was formulated (which was adopted as a United Nations document in March/April 1974).

In short, bank capital operated without a clear concept of control and hence lacked a class perspective, and the international NIEO coalition (for all its internal contradictions) in effect directed the flow of money capital.

Eventually, the 'general' capitalist interest was reasserted through the adoption of monetarism, the battering-ram of neo-liberalism.

Monetarism holds that by making money scarce, inflation can be combated effectively and sound micro-economic reasoning can be forced upon the state and society as a whole. Although unpopular since the 1920s, it had always continued to attract the support of economists, journalists, and government officials, particularly in the USA and Britain. After 1945, it was propagated by a series of transnational consultative and planning groups such as the Mont Pelerin Society, and as the crisis of the 1970s deepened, its voice grew louder and succeeded in winning over more and more influential bodies. The monetarists scored a decisive triumph when, following earlier instalments in Chile (see Ch. 3) and Britain, Paul Volcker was appointed chairman of the Federal Reserve. Two months after the shuffle, the Fed embarked on a policy of reducing the money supply in an attempt to bolster the value of the dollar, which in turn led to the high interest rates which triggered the debt crisis.[5]

For our purposes, the meaning of these episodes resides in their contribution to the emerging hegemony of the neo-liberal concept. Volcker, representing the collective wisdom of the most aggressively conservative groups such as the Pinay Circle, which met in his presence in 1979 in Washington (*Lobster* no. 17, 1988), considered it his task to frontally attack the accepted wisdom of the previous era and work against '20 years of government policies promoting inflation'. This pitted him not only against 'rust belt' industrial capital and labour but also against the commercial banks and caused bitter complaints from major Third World creditors such as Citicorp (*Newsweek*, 15 June 1987).

The high interest rates of the 1980s dealt the death blow to the NIEO movement by reversing priorities from developing production to securing profit and so subordinating the industrialization plans of the Third World to the discipline of capital. Spreading from the metropolitan countries, the loosening of state controls facilitated quick enrichment and reshuffled the class structure away from the corporate pattern to an individualist, rentier/'venture capitalist' one. Rentier incomes rose, stock ownership was popularized through privatization, and bank profits increased relative to those of industry. In the USA and Japan, the 1972 ratios between profits of non-financial and financial firms (5:4 and 3:2 respectively) were reversed in 1983; in West Germany it fell from 3:1 to 2:1 in the same period (OECD 1986).

Investment banking and financial services became the hottest industry, spreading a new acquisitive ethic throughout society. In contrast to the organized, regulated life of the corporate liberal era, neo-liberalism has ushered in the quest for profit at unprecedented levels of risk. As one observer saw it, 'where we saw in the sixties the notion of public service, in the eighties money is the thing'. The internalization of the money capital perspective under neo-liberalism goes so far that it turns 'the idea of the free market ... into a personal moral code' (*Fortune*, 8 December 1986).

The state and imperialism

The emerging transnational neo-liberal configuration did not confine its objectives to deconstructing the Keynesian Welfare State of metropolitan capitalism. It also confronted the transgressions into economic regulation in the Third World and, always in the background, the Soviet bloc.

By trying to use the established patterns of state sovereignty and international organization for their reformist ends, the NIEO movement challenged a vital, if often neglected, aspect of capitalist relations of production. As Krasner puts it, 'The South has been able to take two legacies of the North – the organization of political units into sovereign states and the structure of existing international organizations – and use them to disrupt, if not replace, market-oriented regimes over a wide range of issues' (Krasner 1985: 124).[6]

State sovereignty, 'internationalized' in a UN majority system, was incompatible with the free movement, indeed the sovereignty of capital. The threat to the capitalist system represented by the movement emanating from the NIEO coalition to put internationally operating capital under a UN-monitored regulatory regime is analysed in Chapter 2 of this volume. It led to a rapid mobilization of the forces resisting change and to a militant reaffirmation of the need for an open world.

The attack on the Third World – a counterattack in light of the defeats suffered by US-led imperialism in the previous decade – was partly realized by the imposition of a deflationary regime on the states committed to independent (if credit-financed) industrialization. The states themselves were hardly able to deal with their insertion into the emerging global productive grid once the UN role came under fire, being neither large enough to plan on a global scale, where that is needed, as in environmental controls and resource allocation, nor small enough to be accountable to people where they live.

This objective failure exacerbated the crisis of the authoritarian Third World state and eventually also of the Soviet-type state. As 'regional and local loyalties are becoming more intense, and antipathy to central authority is rising everywhere' (Barnet 1980: 306), an ostensibly democratic revolution began to spread as a consequence of the new liberalism. In very few cases did this 'democratization' represent a real (if perhaps only temporary) advance of popular forces: only where the development of the productive forces and the socialization of labour had made great strides in the previous decades (Southern Europe, and conceivably also such countries as South Korea and Brazil, cf. Fernandez and Holman 1990) were social forces able to assert themselves *vis-à-vis* the state. But most often 'democratization' just meant fragmentation and disintegration, most obviously so in Africa, but elsewhere too.

The role of the arms race was a final component of the realization of the neo-liberal concept of control. Concern about the world-political consequences of Soviet nuclear parity had already crystallized in the closing stages of the Vietnam war, and the January 1979, INF missile decision was one of the mid-term adjustments of the initially conciliatory Carter policy that reflected a new orientation.

The strategy to rekindle the arms race as a means to defeat the global reform movement (Gerbier 1987) became official doctrine under the Reagan administration. The young hawks recruited from the Committee on the Present Danger, such as Assistant Secretary for Defence Richard Perle, were committed to blow up the arms control infrastructure dating from the Nixon era and have 'the US engage in a massive build-up that the Soviets will be unable to match' (Brownstein and Easton 1983: 500).

The initial round of across-the-board rearmament, however, overburdened the US budget, distorted international capital flows and hampered American competitiveness in non-defence sectors. It also failed to connect the arms race to the new industries emerging from the restructuring of capital. By the mid-1980s the US electronics sector (IBM, Hewlett-Packard, Honeywell), succeeded in having the all-out arms race transformed from a course of quantitative to one of qualitative superiority through such organizations as Business Executives for National Security or by public statements. Ground lost to Japanese and European capital here was as important as the arms race itself: given the crucial role of the Pentagon in US industrial policy (Junne 1985), Star Wars and high tech conventional warfare provided more promising investment and research strategies than re-equipping battleships or continuing to build up missile arsenals.

In hindsight, the military thrust of the high tech revolution of the late 1970s and early 1980s exacerbated the creeping crisis in the Soviet Union, and threw the USSR back decisively and ousted it from the global productive grid:

> The challenge from the capitalist world, military in form, was economic in its consequences, whether it confronted the Soviet Union itself or a small peripheral aspirant to socialism. The arms race during the Reaganite phase of the Cold war was too much for an unreformed economy to sustain; and efforts to keep up with the arms race blocked economic reforms.
>
> (Cox 1991: 176)

The integration in the world economy of the socialist states was dramatically reduced: in 1973, CMEA states accounted for 22.7 per cent of machinery imports into the OECD area, but in 1985 this share had been reduced to 4.9 per cent (van Zon 1987: 11). In the 1990s, the former socialist states of Central and Eastern Europe are struggling to return to the world market. The conditions that are being imposed are very harsh indeed, and it is doubtful whether these countries will all be able to make the transition.[7] For the former Soviet Union or most of its successor states, any thought of the world market is overshadowed by the much more immediate need to feed, clothe and house the population. The second Cold War has been won by the West, through economic warfare at least as much as through a battle of ideas as Fukuyama would have it. But, as these final lines are written in March 1992, prospects for the victor are not without shadows either. In 1991, industrial production fell in eight of the thirteen biggest OECD economies, unemployment was up in ten out of thirteen, and the inflation rate had crept up to over 4 per cent in seven out of thirteen (*The Economist*, 22 February 1992). Must we conclude that the failure of neo-liberalism is at hand?

This would certainly be the case if we were to take the neo-liberals' own goals as our yardstick: the world economy in recession, unemployment no lower than when they came into office around 1980, and, worst of all from their own perspective, inflation accelerating. And what is more, the two economies that have provided world capitalism with its necessary stability in the 1980s (Japan and Germany) are showing increasingly worrying signs that they too might go into a real recession within a year, if not sooner. And then, who is going to bail out the USA?

THE PLAN OF THIS BOOK

The global context of the crisis of the 1970s and the challenge of the NIEO movement is dealt with in the second chapter, where Kees van der Pijl looks at the attempts to regulate the activities of multinational corporations to illustrate the general development of the global neo-liberal counter-offensive.

Of central significance in the rise of global neo-liberalism was the overthrow of the Unidad Popular government of President Allende in Chile and the neo-liberal experiment which was carried out in this unfortunate country after 1975. Alex Fernández Jilberto analyses these developments and the restructuring of Chile's class structure in Chapter Three.

In the next two chapters, the rise of neo-liberalism in two English-speaking countries on opposite sides of the globe is analysed. In Chapter Four, Ed Kaptein takes a closer look at the case of Australia which in the early 1970s had a fairly left-wing Labor Party government, but ended up in the late 1980s with an extremely radical neo-liberal Labor government. In Chapter Five, Henk Overbeek discusses the transformation of Britain's international posture under the Thatcher reign.

Next, three cases in Continental Europe are considered. Otto Holman looks at the case of Spain, where neo-liberal type economic policies were implemented by a Socialist-led government, posing important questions with regard to the limits of the notion of concepts of control (Chapter Six). Richard van der Wurff provides an analysis of the German political scene and attempts to identify two projects which aim to formulate an alternative for outright neo-liberalism in Germany (Chapter Seven). André Mommen studies the rise of neo-liberalism in Belgium, interesting both because of the particular role of the Christian Democrats and because of some of the central figures in recent Belgian politics, such as former Prime Ministers Vandenboeynants and Wilfried Martens (Chapter Eight).

To conclude the book, we take a look at developments in North

America. William Carroll discusses the reconfiguration of Canadian capital under the impact of the neo-liberal counter-revolution and the conclusion of the Canada–US free trade agreement (Chapter Nine). Finally, Stephen Gill evaluates the transformation of US hegemony in the world system in the era of neo-liberalism, showing the shift from direct American hegemony towards a US-centred transnational hegemonic order, a shift comprising as it were the different national shifts analysed in earlier chapters.

NOTES

1   This view of the structural underpinnings of concepts of control should answer the critique of voluntarist pluralism which is levelled against the closely related notions of accumulations strategies and hegemonic projects propounded by Jessop (1983) (cf. Clarke 1983, 1988).
2   Several of the contributions to this volume provide illustrations of the relevance of this notion, but more implicitly the same question also lies at the heart of the contributions on Continental Europe. And in a very different setting, the Junta in Chile faced the same problem which it was in the end unable to overcome.
3   Cf. Cox 1987, Ch. 9; Cox does not primarily refer to a new geographical structure but rather to a new social structure involving the segmentation of labour forces into established and non-established workers, with age, gender, ethnicity and national origin making the equation a complex one to grasp.
4   Interview with co-founder and OECD planner Alexander King, *De Volkskrant*, 21 November 1987.
5   This road from bank liberalization to monetarism to the debt crisis has been the subject of several excellent studies (Greider 1987; Naylor 1987).
6   The NIEO challenge was particularly strong, and hit an especially sensitive cord, in the sphere of the control over natural resources, first of all energy. And nor was OPEC the only instance of this challenge to the established position of transnational oil capital. In the Netherlands, the Christian–Social Democratic coalition of 1965–6 had already been broken up on the issue of control over Holland's natural gas just then discovered. The Minister of Economic Affairs at that time (Joop den Uyl) later became Prime Minister in 1973 and played a prominent role in resurrecting the Socialist International. In Australia, a similar battle was forced upon the reformist Labor government of Gough Whitlam, as Kaptein shows us in his contribution to this book.
7   Stephen Gill speaks of 'disciplinary neo-liberalism' as the 1990s East-European version of the conditionally imposed by the IMF upon Latin America during the 1980s. German unification, he argues, can be seen as an extreme example of this phenomenon (Gill 1991: 302).

REFERENCES

Aglietta, M. (1979 [1976]) *A Theory of Capitalist Regulation. The US Experience*, London: Verso/NLB.

Andreff, W. (1976) *Profits et Structures du Capitalisme Mondial*, Paris: Calmann-Levy.

Andreff, W. (1982) 'Regimes d'accumulation et insertion des nations dans l'économie mondiale', in J. R. L. Reiffers (eds.) *Economie et Finance Internationales*, Paris: Dunod.

Barnet, R. J. (1980) *The Lean Years. Politics in the Age of Scarcity*, London: Sphere Books.

Belsey, A. (1986) 'The New Right, social order, and civil liberties', in R. Levitas (ed.) *The Ideology of the New Right*, Cambridge: Polity Press.

Beveridge, W. (1968) 'The Beveridge Report 1942', in S. B. Clough, T. Moodie and C. Moodie, (eds), *Economic History of Europe: Twentieth Century*, New York: Harper & Row.

Bihr, A. (1989) *Entre Bourgeoisie et Proletariat. L'Encadrement Capitalists*, Paris: l'Harmattan.

Bode, R. (1979) 'De Nederlandse bourgeoisie tussen de twee wereldoorlogen', *Cahiers voor de Politieke en Sociale Wetenschappen*, 2 (4): 9–50.

Brownstein, R. and Easton, N. (1983) *Reagan's Ruling Class*, New York: Pantheon.

Burch, Ph. H., Jr. (1980) *Elites in American History*, 3 volumes, New York and London: Holmes & Meier.

Carr, E. H. (1964 [1939]) *The Twenty Years' Crisis 1919–1939*, New York/Evanston: Harper & Row.

Clarke, S. (1983) 'State, class struggle, and the reproduction of capital', *Kapitalistate* 11/12: 113–30.

Clarke, S. (1988) *Keynesianism, Monetarism, and the Crisis of the State*, Aldershot: Edward Arnold.

Cox, R. W. (1987) *Production, Power, and World Order. Social Forces in the Making of History*, New York: Columbia University Press.

Cox, R. W. (1991) ' "Real Socialism" in historical perspective', in R. Miliband and L. Panitch (eds) *Communist Regimes: The Aftermath, Socialist Register 1991*, 169–93. London: The Merlin Press.

CSE Microelectronics Group (1980) *Microelectronics. Capitalist Technology and the Working Class*, London: CSE.

Dicken, P. (1986) *Global Shift. Industrial Change in a Turbulent World*, London: Harper & Row.

Economic Report (1977) *Economic Report of the President*, Washington: Government Printing Office.

Estall, R. C. and Buchanan, R. O. (1966) *Industrial Activity and Economic Geography*, London: Hutchinson.

Fennema, M. (1982) *International Networks of Banks and Industry*, The Hague: Nijhoff.

Ferguson, Th. (1984) 'From Normalcy to New Deal: industrial structure, party competition, and American public policy in the Great Depression', *International Organization*, 38 (1): 41–94.

Fernández, A. and Holman, O. (1990) 'Authoritarian breakdowns in Brazil and

Spain: social invertebration versus regional integration', in *After the Crisis*, Conference papers vol. 1: 83–110, University of Amsterdam.

Fischer, F. (1984) *Griff nach der Weltmacht*, Dusseldorf: Droste, or. 1961.

Frieden, J. (1981) 'Third World indebted industrialization: international finance and state capitalism in Mexico, Brazil, Algeria, and South Korea', *International Organization*, 35 (3): 407–431.

Fukuyama, F. (1989) 'The End of History?', *The National Interest*, Summer: 3–18.

Gallagher, J. and Robinson, R. (1967) 'The imperialism of free trade' , in E. C. Black (ed.), *European Political History, 1815–1870. Aspects of Liberalism*, New York: Harper.

Gamble, A. (1988) *The Free Economy and the Strong State. The Politics of Thatcherism*, London: Macmillan.

Gardner, L. C. (1964) *Economic Aspects of New Deal Diplomacy*, Boston: Beacon.

Gerbier, B. (1987) 'La course aux armements: l'impérialisme face au Nouvel Ordre International', *Cahiers de la Faculté des Sciences Economiques de Grenoble*, 6: 117–46.

Gill, S. (1990) *American Hegemony and the Trilateral Commission*, Cambridge: Cambridge University Press.

Gill, S. (1991) 'Reflections on global order and socio-historical time', *Alternatives*, no. 16, 275–314.

Gossweiler, K. (1975 [1971]) *Großbanken, Industriemonopole, Staat. Oekonomie und Politik des staatsmonopolistischen Kapitalismus in Deutschland 1914–1932*, Berlin: DEB.

Gramsci, A. (1971) in Q. Hoare and G. N. Smith (eds), *Selections from the 'Prison Notebooks'*, New York: International Publishers.

Greider, W. (1987) *Secrets of the Temple. How the Federal Reserve Runs the Country*, New York: Simon & Schuster.

Haas, E. B. (1964) *Beyond the Nation-State. Functionalism and International Organization*, Stanford: Stanford University Press.

Hall, S. (1983) 'The great moving right show', in S. Hall and M. Jacques (eds) *The Politics of Thatcherism*, 19–39, London: Lawrence and Wishart.

Harris, N. (1972) *Competition and the Corporate Society*, London: Methuen.

Hickel, R. (1975) 'Kapitalfraktionen. Thesen zur Analyse der herrschenden Klasse', *Kursbuch*, 42: 141—52.

Holman, O. (1992) 'Introduction: Transnational Class Strategy and the New Europe', in O. Holman (ed.) *European Unification in the 1990s: Myth and Reality, International Journal of Political Economy* 22 (1), Spring 1992: 1–22.

Jessop, B. (1983) 'Accumulation strategies, state forms, and hegemonic projects', *Kapitalistate*, 10/11: 89–111.

Junne, G. (1979) 'Internationalisierung und Arbeitslosigkeit', *Leviathan*, 7 (1).

Junne, G. (1985) 'Das amerikanische Rüstungsprogramm: Ein Substitut für Industriepolitik', *Leviathan*, 13 (1).

Keynes, J. M. (1970 [1936]) *The General Theory of Employment, Interest and Money*, London and Basingstoke: Macmillan.

Krasner, S. D. (1985) *Structural Conflict. The Third World Against Global Liberalism*, Berkeley: University of California Press.

Kristol, I. (1971) '"When virtue loses all her loveliness" – some reflections on capitalism and "the free society"', in I. Kristol and D. Bell (eds) *Capitalism Today*, New York: Mentor Books.

Langille, D. (1987) 'The Business Council on national issues and the Canadian State', *Studies in Political Economy*, 24: 41–85.

Mandel, E. (1980 [1977]) *The Second Slump*, London: Verso.

Martinelli, A., Chiesi, A. M. and Dalla Chiesa, N. (1981) *I grandi imprenditori italiani*, Milano: Feltrinelli.

Maurino, J. D. (1974) *Procès d'internationalisation et développement des luttes de classes*, Université des sciences sociales de Grenoble, CERES (mimeo).

Naylor, R. T. (1987) *Hot Money and the Politics of Debt*, London: Unwin Hyman.

OECD (1986) *National Accounts 1972–1984*, Paris: OECD.

Overbeek, H. W. (1990) *Global Capitalism and National Decline. The Thatcher Decade in Perspective*, London: Unwin Hyman.

Pijl, K. van der (1984) *The Making of an Atlantic Ruling Class*, London: Verso.

Piore, M. and Sabel, Ch. F. (1984) *The Second Industrial Divide*, New York: Basic Books.

Polanyi, K. (1957 [1944]) *The Great Transformation. The Political and Economic Origins of Our Time*, Boston: Beacon.

Rothenberg, R. (1984) *The Neo-Liberals. Creating the New American Politics*, New York: Simon & Schuster.

Sanguinetti, G. (1982 [1979]) *Over het terrorisme en de staat*, Bussum: Wereldvenster.

Tulder, R. van and Junne, G. (1988) *European Multinationals in Core Technologies*, Chicester: Wiley.

Wallerstein, I. (1984) *The Politics of the World-Economy*, Cambridge: Cambridge University Press.

Zon, H. van (1987) *Planeconomieën en de Wereldmarkt in de Jaren Tachtig*, (mimeo) University of Amsterdam.

2

THE SOVEREIGNTY OF CAPITAL IMPAIRED

Social forces and codes of conduct for multinational corporations

Kees van der Pijl

The issue is one of survival. At stake may well be not only the survival of the MNC but the continued existence of the private enterprise market system that has served us so well for so long.

(F. Perry Wilson, Chairman and CEO,
Union Carbide Co., 1976)

INTERNATIONAL SOCIALIZATION AND THE LIMITS OF REGULATION

In this chapter, we will analyse the perceived threat to capitalist relations of production posed by the drive for a New International Economic Order (NIEO), which in the course of the 1970s mobilized a fraction of the capitalist class into what would eventually become a neo-liberal counterrevolution. More particularly, our attention will focus on the nature of the emerging class coalition that embodied this threat and on a key element in the actual reform project, the regulation of 'multinational' private capital.

Our thesis will be that the regulatory drive expressed a logic of socialization to which capital itself is subject but which also generates a class effect of its own in capitalist society. This effect, i.e. the formation of a capitalist cadre class subject to the contradictions of the mode of production but tendentially unified (Bihr 1989; Konrád and Szelényi 1981), not only is a product of socialization but adds a regulatory moment to it which has a transformative quality.

The crisis of imperialism in the 1970s enhanced this transformative

28

potential and turned the cadre class into a critical factor in a mass of interests including Third World state classes and the Soviet leadership which for different reasons wanted to revamp the liberal world economy to a more equitable and state-directed, 'authoritative' order (Krasner 1985). Regulating multinational capital, however timidly, had implications ultimately jeopardizing the sovereignty of capital *vis-à-vis* public structures. In the course of the later 1970s and the 1980s, an unreconstructed liberal fraction in the capitalist class was able to restore full sovereignty to private capital in this sense. For reasons to be explained below, the renewed subordination of the radicalized and autonomized cadre class was a prime objective in the eventual neo-liberal counteroffensive.

The development and international combination of the productive forces by capital in the twentieth century has generated a world-wide division of labour which has inserted local production into global capital accumulation. Giant private corporations have connected formerly isolated locations into integrated product chains. These product chains are moments of a process of socialization, not just of the productive forces and of capital itself, but of the entire reproductive sphere of human society. Raw materials, semi-finished products, and final products, but also engineers, education, marketing and advertising, and indeed, the domain of cultural expression in its totality, have become available and to a considerable extent, interchangeable, on a world level to be combined on the most profitable basis by the multinational corporation. To be able to cast their nets on so vast a scale, and to marshal the funds necessary for it, individual firms have had to insert themselves into networks of co-operation, information and strategic planning. While the growth of large-scale firms through concentration and centralization of capital is already an instance of socialization of the productive forces, the coalescence of large corporations into looser capital groups (or 'financial groups'), tends to make competition less and less immediately subject to real cost and quality advantages and more subject to market 'power'; that is, the capacity of networks of interlocked banks and industrial corporations to structure the context of competition and the nature of markets (Fennema 1982: Ch. 2).

The concept of the 'multinational corporation' itself was a temporary phenomenon. It marked the profound imbrication of the internationalization of capital and the projection of national state power that characterized the pattern of capitalist and imperialist relations in the post-war era. Much of the criticism of multinationals' operations was formulated from the vantage point of national sovereignty. It was not primarily against capital that this national sovereignty was defended; rather, the threat was defined in terms of the extraterritorial jurisdiction of the mother country of the multinational corporation. The presence of the MNC, whether in Chile or in France, was felt as an extension and lever of US power in 'private' guise (Baade 1980: 13).

With the further internationalization of capital, this 'national' identity of the multinational corporation (which was also thrown into relief by foreign direct investment practices evoking the image of industrial empires spreading across existing economic boundaries) had to be abandoned. The restructuring of capital towards an accumulation regime centring on new core technologies also involved the termination of highly bureaucratic and omnivorous corporate empire-building. In the words of two authors on the subject,

> the very concept of what a multinational corporation is may have to change. The development of [new technologies] makes it possible that one single headquarters in one country can direct and control far-flung activities in many countries around the globe without owning any of the productive units any longer – eventually even without possessing any formal assets abroad.
>
> (van Tulder and Junne 1988: xii)

The restoration of competition, that is, the restoration of capital as the comprehensive principle governing the process of social production and reproduction in its totality, *total capital*, under these conditions became a necessity. But the question of whether the equally necessary regulatory structures, which on the national level are summarized in the capitalist state, could be reproduced on the international level without succumbing to the trend to bureaucratization and democratization then under way, was entirely open in the later 1960s. In this period, the foreign output of multinational corporations grew at twice the rate of growth of world Gross National Product and 40 per cent faster than world exports (Dicken 1986: 61 quoting J.H. Dunning). With the crisis of the early 1970s, this pace slackened; but simultaneously, socialization of the productive forces and of capital became entwined with political arrangements, politicizing the overall socialization process. The increased dependence on oil from non-OECD sources led to the prominence of a cartel of oil-producing countries, the Organization of Petroleum Exporting Countries (OPEC) in addition to the existing cartel of Anglo-American oil companies ('The Seven Sisters'). OPEC was to become an important lever in politicizing capitalist world market strategies and ultimately, also in questioning the sovereignty of capital as such. Its drive to gain full control of oil sources activated state-monopolistic tendencies in EEC countries which were (with the exception of the Netherlands) largely excluded from the networks of control operated by the 'Seven Sisters'. The smaller oil companies in the EEC, often state-owned or partially state-owned already, in 1976 proposed to link up with the Arab countries to obtain oil from them directly, bypassing the Anglo-American oil majors (van der Pijl 1981: 4). This led to a tentative *rapprochement* between the EEC and the Middle East countries, backed up by various industrial-financial cross-participations of which the Libyan participation in FIAT, and Iran's in Krupp and Eurodif (France's uranium enrichment project) were the most spectacular (Bourrinet 1979). Since the Libyan deal with FIAT was part of a triangular transaction which also included the Soviet Union (Friedman 1988), the momentum of this type of arrangement tended to create a drift of continental European society into networks of interest and power contradicting its postwar Atlantic moorings.

This contributed to a further politicization of the socialization process, i.e. a reinforcement of the political-institutional forms of inter-national collusion in matters concerning the international division of labour. Thus, the environment in which private capital had to operate became pregnant with countervailing arrangements of a public nature, inviting social forces critical of the operations of multinational corporations, or simply outside their control, to formulate their interests in terms of these public arrangements. As Kurt Waldheim, Secretary-General of the UN, put it in 1975, the consequences of international productive investment were so vast that 'such a dynamic phenomenon could not, and should not, remain outside the purview of international institutions which had effectively developed means of monitoring, and to some extent regulating, other aspects of economic intercourse' (IMDI 1976: 35).

Eventually, as the remaining chapters of this collection will demonstrate, it was the cumulation of public-institutional solutions to problems raised by the international socialization of the productive forces that the neo-liberal offensive would seek to undo. Among these public-institutional solutions to the internationalization of production, the codes of conduct for multinational corporations were of prime importance. For in these codes, the question of whether the social forces of production would be directly subordinated by capital, or be controlled by public institutions in which heterogeneous interests are articulated, and where interest articulation is more transparent and subject to democratic checks, was epitomized. Even the most fragile attempts at regulating the movement of capital would entail an impingement of the implicit notion of the sovereignty of capital, which is an essential element in the normative structure of the capitalist mode of production; a normative structure which the capitalist class consciously seeks to uphold in the process of internationalization (Hinkelammert 1985: 52).

The idea that capitalist socialization may become subject to a logic of socialization *per se*, contradicting its specific capitalist nature, is a key aspect of Marx's critique of capitalism. As Marx saw it, the socialization of the productive forces is bound to drive beyond the confines of capitalist relations of production, as the dialectic of socialization and regulation on a world scale creates favourable conditions for the planned moment to prevail over the workings of the 'invisible hand'. Still in this perspective, the regulation of multinational corporations could assume, its timid manifestations notwithstanding, truly revolutionary qualities. If we extrapolate Marx's conclusions on factory regulation in *Capital*, control of multinational corporations, too, 'ripens, with the material conditions and the social combination of the production process, the contradictions and antagonisms of its capitalist form, hence simultaneously the constructive elements of a new, and the moments of a transformation of the old society' (MEW 23: 525–6).

In the 1970s, this line of analysis resurfaced in various analyses of the European Left, but these on the whole tended to stop short of conceptualizing the arena of global transformation by their emphasis on the single state (Collectif PCF 1971; Basso 1975). Even the most influential study of the so-called 'regulation school', Aglietta's *Theory of Capitalist Regulation*, was conceived as the preface to a more sophisticated theory of state monopoly capitalism rather than as replacing it by a broader theory of international capitalism from which the author expressly abstracted (Aglietta 1979). This preoccupation with the national level may be explained from the state's prominence in guiding and containing processes of rapid social change taking place, notably in France and Italy; as well as from the fact that these countries at the time were witness to a breaking-up of the traditional political alliances of big capital and the old middle classes and their replacement by tentative coalitions of big capital and certain segments of the wage-earning classes, particularly those active in advanced production processes subject to internationalization (Farhi 1976). The capitalist cadre class, in the drive for regulating the multinational corporation, allied with these new social forces and even merged with it as far as its 'private' fraction was concerned. The typical national, *Etatist* orientation of this coalition was at the root of both the regulation movement as such and the failure adequately to co-ordinate it on the international level.

The remainder of this chapter will consist of (1), a brief overview of the different social and political forces that formed the NIEO coalition and the basis of their desire for regulating the world economy; (2) the role actually played by these forces in the attempts to develop codes of conduct for multinational corporations; and (3) the reaction of the capitalist class to these attempts in the period before a full-fledged neo-liberal offensive against the reform movement as such (which will be detailed in the remaining chapters of this collection) was undertaken. We will not consider the liberation movements in the Third World. Although they added a critical challenge to the rule of capital in the period, they were not specifically engaged in the struggle over codes of conduct for multinational corporations.

SOCIAL FORCES IN THE NIEO COALITION

The cadre class in advanced capitalism and social democracy

The foremost social force in the drive for regulating the capitalist world economy in the 1970s in our view was the capitalist cadre class in developed capitalism. Its preference for regulation over liberal capitalism was a function of its own role in advanced capitalist society and in the course of a century had matured into a set of explicit doctrines, such as reformism, managerialism, technocracy, and the 'end of ideology'. The socialization of work inside the plant, and the socialization of the productive forces and of capital itself, have had a profound effect on the class structure and class consciousness. From the turn of century, scientific management and 'rationalization' of production spread the illusion among the workers that work was organized along lines of objective, technical necessity, while tendentially removing the more visible forms of subordination of labour to capital. Socialization also created a space in the class structure that was occupied by a new category of intermediary functionaries ranging from managers (who, in Frederick Taylor's words, 'assume the burden of gathering together all of the traditional knowledge which in the past has been possessed by the workmen and then of classifying, tabulating, and reducing this knowledge to rules, laws, and formulae' (quoted by Braverman 1974: 112), to actual clerical workers, whose number increased as a

33

consequence of the need to calculate, standardize, and control 'claims to ownership to value' (Braverman 1974: 304). The growth of state intervention in the capitalist economy was a key aspect of socialization and also added to the growth of the managerial/clerical stratum.

The tendential 'organization' of capitalism that results from socialization and which represents a dialectical 'moment of regulation' in the socialization process, is not just a subjective preference on the part of the social forces shaped by it. To the degree socialization advances, productive processes become impermeable to market forces, so that within capitalism, ever-greater areas of production are in fact operated under different laws. These laws are subsumed under 'the unity of measurement of labour and machinery in their productive application', and to the 'continuous flow of production' reduced to what Marx already called 'economy of time' (Sohn-Rethel 1978: 29–31). The regulation of the economy away from its subordination to market forces hence becomes a necessity, and definite social forces assume the role to execute and propagate this necessity.

Alain Bihr's study on the capitalist cadre class (1989) constitutes the most recent analysis of the particular social class acting as the product and agent of socialization. This class has also been labelled 'new middle class', 'professional-managerial class', 'intelligentsia', etc. Wright's criticism that a social function does not by itself generate a social class remains valid, but his solution to rank the managerial class among the 'contradictory class locations' in the class structure (Wright 1978: 11) lacks the necessary historical dimension. That the cadre class remains subject to the push and pull of the struggle between capital and labour does not imply that it does not represent a moment of its own in this struggle. In a sense, its vacillations are inherent in the function of intermediary that unifies the cadre class; this in turn follows from its being an agent of socialization. The cadre class is oriented to the state as the privileged arena for imposing on the actual working class the 'equilibrium of compromises' through which the capitalist class rules in modern capitalism (Bihr 1989: 283). Both inside and outside the state, the cadre class tends to arbitrate between antagonistic positions, deriving a certain neutrality from its role and mystifying that role to the degree the solutions found are necessarily compatible with the interest of capital first.

However, as socialization progresses and hence, the state becomes more salient relative to society, management to capital, and organized social forces to individuals, the weight of the cadre class will increase. Its three-fold preference for the modernization of capitalist society, the rationalization of capitalist development, and the democratization of capitalist power (Bihr 1989: 252) will become more prominent in the class struggle. In the early 1970s, in the context of growing state intervention, a crisis of imperialism, and profound imbalances in the system of international production highlighted by the dollar and oil crises, these preferences and the 'moment of regulation' that arises from its generic links to organized capitalism and state intervention, tended to radicalize the cadre class. At that time, Sohn-Rethel's conclusion was particularly apposite that 'the market economy has lost its regulating power over social production, but its continued existence prevents the modern law of production from becoming the regulative of social economy' (Sohn-Rethel 1978: 31–2).

Social Democracy after the war became the dominant political expression of the regulatory impulses of the capitalist cadre class. As Bahro (1980: 157) writes, 'Social Democracy in power is the party of the compromise of interest between the layer of specialists drifting to "transcending the system" and the part of management oriented to "system reform"' even though they find their 'common language only in the confrontation with the conservative fraction of the bourgeoisie'.

With the extrapolation of the New Deal to Europe, the enhanced role of the state and the surge in the concentration and centralization of capital also contributed to reinforcing the cadre class element in the different parties, notably in Social Democracy. 'Revisionism ... did not originate in the Marshall Plan years ... but it was greatly encouraged by the vast programme of social engineering launched under Marshall Aid', the author of a recent study on the Plan's effect on labour concludes. 'The discovery of the key to sustained economic growth and commitment to it by national governments was an intrinsic part of the post-war value system of capitalism. It inspired and in turn fed on managerialist thinking, a growing productivity consciousness and the powerful notion of the "end of ideology"' (Carew 1987: 240–1).

In the 1950s and 1960s, programmatic reformulations replacing the anti-capitalist orientation of Social Democracy by a platform of social reform (the Godesberg Programme and its equivalents in other countries), further facilitated the rise of the cadre class in the former working class parties. When in 1969, Social Democrats carried government responsibility in fourteen countries, this signified the prominence of the cadre class rather than a victory of socialism (see also data on the social composition of Social Democratic parties in Raschke 1981).

Its electoral basis in the working class involved Social Democracy in the late 1960s in the global drift to the left, and reformism revived accordingly. The Godesberg spirit which between 1958 and 1962 seemed to have purged Western European Social Democracy of the idea of socialism, was challenged by rank-and-file militancy. In Austria, Scandinavia, and Britain, the notion of a transformation of society resurfaced at party congresses in 1972–3. The Socialist-led Brandt government, revealing (not unlike the Roosevelt Administration during the class struggles in the early New Deal) the priority of its links with the cadre class over those with the working class, aggressively countered the radicalization among the rank-and-file with the *Berufsverbote* campaign launched in 1972. Yet, the growing influence of the German trade union and Social Democrat tradition in the EC already was felt to be a nuisance by international capital. Thus Henry Ford II complained in 1976 that 'today, the multinationals' freedom of decision is threatened by restrictive legislation and by the efforts of some elements of organized labor and well-intentioned but uninformed critics to participate in the shaping of business decisions' (IMDI 1976: 11).

The NIEO movement, however disparate and incoherent, threatened to amplify the consequences of the regulatory impulses of Social Democracy on a global scale. The Dutch economist Jan Tinbergen had been appointed chairman of the Council for World Development Policy of the Socialist International in 1972. In 1974, he led a group of specialists to write a report for the Club of Rome. The report was financed by the Dutch Social Democratic Minister for Development Cooperation, Jan Pronk, a former collaborator of Tinbergen. It stressed the need for an overhaul, not just of the world economic chaos 'created by the relentless operation of market forces', but of the entire normative structure created by post-war capitalism. Hence, the report preferred to speak of a comprehensive New International Order and not just of its economic component (Tinbergen 1977: 5, 15). Pronk was also instrumental in launching the so-called Brandt Commission in 1976–7 by the then World Bank President McNamara. This Commission, which was to produce several reports, brought out the need for enhancing the 'moment of regulation' favoured by the cadre class as the preferable way out of the crisis. Brandt's ideas (as he himself explained in several meetings with representatives of the capitalist class) did not envisage the overthrow of capitalism but only its stabilization by extensive infrastructural supports and regulation, or *Ordnungspolitik* to use the German term (Brandt 1971: 271). Tinbergen in turn explained that 'planning' should not be taken too literally as 'detailed global planning' but rather in the sense of a loose planning framework curbing unstable markets (interview in *Wirtschaftswoche*, 31 March 1978). Social

Democracy at this point enjoyed a clear hegemony over the greater part of the Left as well as over the moderate element in the capitalist class, represented at the time by the Trilateral Commission (Gill 1990).

Building on established patterns of bi- and tripartite collective bargaining, this legitimacy allowed the cadre class in Social Democracy to play the paramount role in the drive for regulating multinational capital.

The state classes in the Third World

Although the state classes in the Third World constituted the most salient and vociferous component of the NIEO coalition, their role in the actual implementation of controlling multinational corporations was less important. Like the cadre class in advanced capitalism, the ruling groups in peripheral capitalism were primarily subordinate to the metropolitan bourgeoisie. Only in the crisis of the 1970s, they became exposed to popular demands and radicalized. Yet the origin of most Third World ruling strata in the compromise that was decolonization predisposed them to follow a strategy of negotiation as the road to economic betterment, and multilateralism was their preferred framework for doing so.

To the ruling groups in the Third World, the 'moment of regulation' was even more vital than to the cadre class. As Krasner (1985: 40) notes, their quest for controlling the world economy through international organizations was motivated by their being subject, externally as well as internally, to forces outside their control. This lack of control was rooted in the segmentation of society between a part controlled by international capital and a part marginalized by it, but Third World societies are already much less cohesive to begin with. The *Hobbesian state* is the attempt to weld together the heterogeneous social basis by confiscating civil society, albeit to varying degrees (Lamounier 1989). The often decisive foreign content in their economic power structure forced the Third World 'political state classes' (Fernández 1988: 55; Cox 1987: 235) to use the crisis of imperialism to stress the rights inherent in national sovereignty, notably voting rights in international organizations, and make an attempt to extend the Hobbesian subordination of society to the state to the international level (Krasner 1985: 124; Chesneaux 1988: 29).

This ambition was highly contradictory as to its socio-political content. Whereas on the international level, the NIEO movement represented a democratic force, on the state level the need to hold on to state power as well as the aspirant bourgeois nature of the state class in the confrontation with metropolitan capitalism, narrowly circumscribed the possibilities for domestic democratization. The states most prominent in the NIEO revolution are the product of what Löwy (1981) calls 'unfinished bourgeois revolutions': Mexico, Brazil, Algeria, India. Inherently unstable, the Hobbesian state classes wielding power in them continuously face the dilemma whether to 'cross the Rubicon between the "Algerian" and the "Cuban" roads, that is, between a Bonapartist capitalist "normalization" or a deepening toward socialist revolution' (Löwy 1981: 165).

The NIEO strategy, meant to stabilize raw material prices and more generally, to regulate the world economy away from its liberal framework (which included the regulation of multinational corporations' foreign activities) was one way of postponing this choice. Industrialization and persistent poverty of the large mass of the population necessarily led to attempts to control the external economic environment. Thus, as Kolko writes, 'Much of Brazil's internally generated capital for state-sponsored development has been gathered by taxing the masses and increasing inequality. In Latin America, the advocacy of a hemisphere-wide Latin American Free Trade Alliance has been a way around the small size of internal markets, and it reflects the chimera of nationalism and its basic dilemma' (Kolko 1989: 45).

Where internal developments were on a leftward drift, international multilateralism must be seen as an attempt to mitigate the violent implications of an entirely domestic and hence, more radical change. Allende in Chile pointed to this combination of domestic gradualism and internationalism in his message to the Chilean Congress in May 1971 (Allende 1973: 49). The Chilean experiment was stopped short by a US-monitored coup in 1973, but the oil crisis and the 1974–5 recession created acute difficulties for the state classes in other countries, too. In India, Indira Gandhi's government had to resort to a National Emergency to avoid radical choices at home (Roy 1986: 43). The typical pattern was one of modernizers intent on improving foreign economic balances but impatient with domestic democratic forces, and hence, like the Peruvian progressive military in the late 1960s, imbued with 'a strong antipathy toward working-class or revolutionary socialist politics' (Petras 1970: 132). In the discussions on a code of conduct for multinational corporations, matters concerning trade union rights accordingly would create sharp divergences between the Third World representatives and those of the metropolitan cadre class.

The Soviet bloc

The role of the Soviet bloc in the NIEO movement was based on the objective convergence of Soviet and Third World interests in a reorganization of liberal capitalism and on certain similarities of state/society structure that can be summarized in the concept of the Hobbesian state. This convergence became apparent soon after the Russian revolution was forced to seek a common ground with non-revolutionary allies abroad. As a Soviet author notes, already at the International Economic Conference in Genoa in 1922, the Soviet delegation proposed a NIEO package of equal rights for all peoples, non-interference, arms reduction, planned international arrangements in matters of trade, transport and raw materials, in addition to demanding the representation of the colonial peoples at international conferences (Kannapin 1984: 6–7).

In 1973, the crisis of imperialism by default reinforced the international weight of the USSR, and its enhanced prominence was also reflected in the United Nations. In that year, Secretary-General Waldheim for the first time invited the Soviet Union to take part in negotiations on the establishment of a UN peace-keeping force in the wake of the Arab-Israeli war, and throughout this period, the number of Soviet nationals working in the UN Secretariat increased substantially. This did not lead to a consistent Soviet commitment to the organization. Although the US position was weakened and the West was time and again outvoted by Third World representatives, the Soviet attitude, like the Chinese one, was one of indifference (Shevchenko 1985).

The support the USSR gave to the Third World in the UN, UNCTAD, and NIEO context mainly was a reflection of its own domestic priorities. Thus, in the period preceding the spectacular increase of credit-financed trade that followed the oil price hike of 1973, the emphasis was still on nationalization and autocentric development. In his speech to the 24th Congress of the CPSU on 30 March, 1971, Leonid Brezhnev, after having stressed the priority of Soviet relations with the CMEA countries and the quest for a definitive agreement on European borders (which would later result in the Helsinki Agreements), devoted considerable attention to the trend towards nationalization in the Third World. Among the countries having chosen the 'non-capitalist road', he mentioned with approval the share of state-owned industrial production in the United Arab Republic, Burma, Algeria, and a number of smaller African countries (XXIV. Parteitag 1971: 32–3). In Latin America, the Chilean experiment, followed at a distance by Peru and Bolivia, was mentioned by the Soviet leader as an example of the transformation of the struggle for national liberation 'into a struggle against the foundations of the exploitative order itself' (ibid.: 35).

Once the increased price of oil made Brezhnev's vision of 'importing efficiency' by multi-billion dollar deals prevail over Kosygin's and Podgorny's caution with respect to preserving irreplaceable raw material sources (Shevchenko 1985: 284), the NIEO concept was more emphatically embraced. At the 1976 Conference of Communist Parties, the NIEO theme even permitted Western European 'Eurocommunist' and Soviet-bloc parties to come to common conclusions. Soviet specialists, meanwhile, were pessimistic about the chances for an NIEO to materialize even if the USSR supported it in public (Hough 1986: 99).

On the whole, the USSR for obvious reasons preferred regulation and planned interdependence to wildcat liberalism in international economic affairs and therefore tended to side with the reform forces in the question of regulation of multinational corporations as well. Simultaneously, it jealously guarded its sovereignty and economic state monopoly against any attempt to extend such regulation to Soviet enterprises.

CODES OF CONDUCT VS. THE SOVEREIGNTY OF CAPITAL

We will now investigate how the social forces identified above played their part in the debates on a code of conduct for multinational corporations.

The problem of regulating international capital movements and synchronizing related national legislation has a long history that is part of the tendency of state forms to assume an international format. Originally, the unification of capital into 'total capital' was confined to the single state, and the establishment of conditions of equal competition and fair treatment was a national affair. Abroad, the state backed its 'national' capital with all means at its disposal. Only when capital became international itself through direct productive investment, the legal conditions on which its operation is premised, had to become international too. This entailed a conflict between the state role in establishing the conditions of equal competition and the function of supporting national capital in world market competition (Knieper 1976: 47). The result was a tendential integration of national and international regulation, in which the International Chamber of Commerce in Paris played an important role as the centre of business consultation and planning. The protection of property rights abroad, international business taxation, anti-trust regulation, and other aspects of public monitoring of capital movements became part of a web of international legal arrangements which in turn were subject to a tendency towards the establishment of quasi-state structures on the international level. Yet the corollary growth of an international bureacratic-administrative culture with important roots in the British Commonwealth and later reproduced in the League of Nations framework on the whole left the sovereignty of capital intact. As Picciotto writes, 'Due to its narrow political base, international coordination has been treated as a technical and specialist matter, and has favoured secretive and informal procedures' (Picciotto 1989: 15).

Rivalry between the United States and Western Europe (and Canada) by the mid-1960s shattered this informality and tended to politicize questions of international business regulation, such as the measures taken by the US to stem the outward flow of capital. France notably became embroiled in several conflicts over the primacy of national vs. international capital, opting for Western European solutions if international mergers were inevitable. In 1965, the EEC installed a Committee on Medium Term Economic Policy under R. Marjolin in apparent support of the Gaullist approach. However, when France proposed to adopt uniform legislation in the EEC to stimulate EEC-wide mergers, which would have realized the ideas prevalent in the Marjolin Committee, the Commission reacted by proposing a European Company Statute, which ran counter to French conceptions of state support and national planning (Holland 1975: 323–9). Other French proposals to control foreign capital movements failed likewise (Meynaud and Sidjanski 1967: 82, 73). Thus the Hobbesian legacy of the French state (see Cohen-Tanugi 1987) was effectively blocked from informing the emerging Western European quasi-state. But the question of multinational capital's violations of national sovereignty had been placed firmly on the agenda. The social forces emerging in the subsequent global reform movement and entitled to participation in the recognized fora of international negotiation, all would take up the issue.

Cadre class – trade unions – social democracy

The Social Democratic International Congress of Free Trade Unions (ICFTU) raised the idea of a code of conduct for multinational corporations in 1969. In that year, the ICFTU suggested to the ILO that it undertake a review of labour relations issues raised by multinational corporations, and a year later, it proposed that the UN develop a code of conduct with trade union participation. In 1972, it was decided that the ICFTU would work out a code of its own with the International Trade Secretariats (ITS), which resulted in the 'Multinational Charter' of 1975, which asks for binding regulation of multinationals (de Kemp 1985: 42–3).

The chemical workers' ITS through its Secretary-General Charles Levinson was virulently opposed to ICFTU/ITS co-operation in this matter as it preferred international corporatism over state regulation. It also rejected the proposals of the International Metalworkers' Federation to work out a 'comprehensive code of international corporate law' jointly with 'progressive political forces' (Etty and Tudyka 1974: 360). The question of whether the organized workers' weight should be brought to bear through state or quasi-state regulation or on capital directly, through established patterns of collective bargaining and representation, remained a source of contention exposing the trade union position to divisive counter-strategies.

At the EEC level, the two strategic lines intertwined. Following the rejection of the dirigiste French orientation, the codetermination tradition developed in West German labour relations served as the starting point for regulating the internationalization of capital in the EEC. The draft European Company Statute published by the European Commission in 1970 included a codetermination clause allowing labour to appoint one-third of the outside directors. However, this one-third labour representation was judged insufficient by the European Trade Union Congress (ETUC). When the European Parliament debated the issue in 1974, a majority also rejected the codetermination set-up as too limited. The employers meanwhile rejected codetermination at the EC level and the 1972 directive on company structure in which this question was tackled, remained a source of contention (Bundesverband 1980: 1–2).

In its 1974 ten-point programme (Hellman 1976: 93), ETUC expressed its hopes that the EC might provide the framework for introducing an effective code of conduct monitoring multinational corporations and enhancing workers' rights. Rather than reflecting working class interests as such, the support of the national trade union federations and ETUC for a reinforced European Commission and a directly elected European Parliament (foreseen for 1978) were significant as an expression of the preference of the cadre class for public regulation and formal democratization. However limited, such democratization clearly went beyond the reproduction at the EC level of 'total capital' by safe-guarding conditions for equal competition (e.g. through EC anti-trust law upheld by the European Court of Justice; see Hogenhuis n.d.: 5–6). The support by the EC institutions for capital resisting US domination – reciprocated by US Supreme Court decisions against European companies, and by a trend to protectionism (then expressed in the Burke-Hartke bill, supported by the American trade unions) – should also be distinguished from the forms of control favoured by the European trade union bureaucracies and Social Democracy at the time.

Eventually, these were defeated. The attempt in 1980 by Social Democratic EC Commissioner Vredeling to require companies active in the EC but irrespective of their country of origin, to inform workers about company plans with respect to all issues affecting the workers (Vredeling 1980) led to conflict within the European Commission. It also came at a moment when the regulation movement was losing momentum and the neo-liberal counter-offensive to restore the sovereignty of capital had gained the upper hand. At the overall international level, the trade union bureaucracy brought its influence to bear on the UN and its specialized agencies. In the ILO, reflecting demands on the part of the trade union representatives from the mid-1960s on and following a unanimous resolution in 1971, a 'Tripartite Meeting on the Relationship between Multinational Corporations and Social Policy' was held in 1972. The recommendation to undertake further study into the desirability of guidelines for multinationals was adopted by the ILO in early 1973 (de Kemp 1985: 50–2). In October 1975, the World Congress of the ICFTU in Mexico adopted the 'Multinational Charter'. This Charter was meant to guide ICFTU actions in the context of the UN and asked for explicitly binding regulation (ibid.: 72). This testified to the continued interest of the trade union bureaucracy in subordinating capital to public arrangements, and supported the drive by the Third World states in that process. As to the ILO itself, the organization adopted a 'Tripartite Declaration of Principles concerning Multinational Enterprises and Social Policy' in 1977.

This Declaration only contains non-binding recommendations and cannot be considered an infraction of the sovereignty of capital by any means. But the trade union/Social Democratic orientation was not to stress the question of formal status too much, and to emphasize a pragmatic way of implementation based on transparency. As one TUC official put it, 'Central to any implementation machinery is an effective international system for information disclosure and for consulting on this information' (Pursey 1980: 279).

The Socialist International (SI), organizing the (mainly West European) Social Democratic Parties, envisaged the NIEO movement as a chance for reinforcing the regulatory structure of international capitalism. In the discussions between Brandt, Palme, and Kreisky that preceded the eventual reorganization of the SI in 1976, Kreisky wanted a revamped SI to work closely with the statistical and planning infrastructure of the Western world, represented by the EC, OECD, and the Club of Rome, but also with the UN (Günsche and Lantermann 1977: 143). In 1977, the SI Study Group on Multinationals was set up by the Rome meeting of the SI. Its report was approved in September 1978. It recommended, among other things, to support the Group of 77 position and make an eventual UN code of conduct legally enforceable. 'If only voluntary codes can be obtained at the international level', the report stated, 'they should at least be accompanied by an effective complaints and supervision machinery which allows governments and trade unions to submit individual cases where the code has been infringed' (SI Report 1978: 169).

Within the OECD, this position was reflected in the support for binding regulation on the part of the Dutch and Swedish governments (de Kemp 1985: 87). The SI Report also recommended that

> Each country should as a priority establish a special MNC monitoring agency which would gather information for national and international use from MNCs, other governmental bodies and trade unions. The national agencies should be given the power, the ability and the duty to obtain information on all relevant activities of MNCs within their boundaries and should monitor all flows of inward and outward investment.
>
> (SI Report 1978: 169)

This approach, coming from a political tendency enjoying full legitimacy and participating in the governments of several important countries, must have been felt as a particularly threatening one. When in 1979, the Committee dealing with the application of the OECD Guidelines (for Multinational Enterprises, adopted in 1976) recommended setting up national liaison offices ('contact points') with approximately the task as recommended by the SI Report, the business advisory committee to the OECD warned that these offices 'should not assume the function of a judicial or quasi-judicial forum' since this 'would run counter to the concept of voluntary guidelines' (quoted in de Kemp 1985: 153).

It must be noted at the same time that following 1974–5, the manoeuvring space for Social Democratic governments was step by step being reduced, which among other things was apparent in the replacement, often in mid-term, of prominent Social Democratic government leaders (Brandt, Whitlam, Wilson). The 1977 British Labour government project for a Code regulating investment in South Africa, which followed the promulgation of the principles by the American vicar, Reverend Sullivan, earlier in the year, served as a legitimation for, rather than an obstacle to, investment in the apartheid economy (de Kemp 1985: 102).

In hindsight, the threat posed by projects for regulating multinational corporations' international activities can easily be belittled. Especially if we take into account that a degree of regulation was necessary also from the point of view of capital itself, the democratic content of it as proposed by trade unions and Social Democracy can hardly amount to much. Yet at the time, there was real concern on the part of prominent capitalists (cf. the collection of views in IMDI 1976, from which we also took the Wilson quote at the beginning of this chapter). Why this was so, becomes clear when we turn to the simultaneous pressure on this issue exerted by the Third World states in the context of the UN.

The Third World state classes

The role of multinationals (ITT, but also the US copper corporations) in the destabilization of the Unidad Popular government in Chile (Sampson 1974) acted as a catalyst for raising the issue of regulation of multinational corporations in the context of the UN. Building on prior discussions in ECOSOC since 1968, UN reports on Chile and the UNCTAD III Conference in Santiago in 1972 turned regulation into a general Third World concern. Some countries, like Brazil and Mexico, had a 30 to 40 per cent foreign share in manufacturing industry (Dicken 1986: 64) and they were in the front line of the drive for regulation.

The tone of their demands was bold and threatening, although hardly anti-capitalist. Foreign investment was welcomed, according to the Programme of Action adopted by the UN General Assembly in its sixth special session, 'both public and private, from developed to developing countries in accordance with the needs and requirements ... and determined by the recipient countries' (quoted in Commission 1980: 5). From the beginning, the emphasis in this strategy of directing the flow of investment funds was on equipping the planned export industries of the Third World states (ibid.), which has to be seen in the context of the refusal and/or incapacity to devise a strategy of industrialization based on developing the internal market, referred to above.

The fear that with the multinational corporation, the host country invited the extraterritorial jurisdiction of the corporation's home state, was one factor in favouring foreign lending over direct investment (Frieden 1981). But in that case, state corporations operated by the Third World state classes had to obtain advanced means of production in the free market. This led to their quest for gaining control over production technology. In the first instance of Third World control of the flow of investment, the Andean Common Market, by its Cartagena Agreement in 1969, covered both aspects by drafting a common system regulating foreign investment and the transfer of technology (Commission 1980: 25). UNCTAD III set up an expert committee to investigate the possibility of guidelines for multinational corporations, with special reference to the transfer of technology (de Kemp 1985: 54–5).

The first problem upsetting the NIEO coalition in matters concerning regulation of the multinational corporation derived from the different class perspective of the Third World state classes from that of the cadre class in metropolitan capitalism. In the second half of 1973, the Group of Eminent Persons appointed by ECOSOC started its activities. The political representatives (in contrast to experts) were mainly from the Third World. The employers' organizations also were represented, but trade unions were not. Therefore, the ICFTU and the Christian Democratic WFL boycotted the hearings. Only the AFL-CIO and the Communist WFTU testified (de Kemp 1985: 57; Ruhwedel 1976: 263).

The US was very critical of the Group's 1974 report. From the capitalist point of view, the selection of the multinational corporation was the consequence of political incapacity of the Third World states. 'The tendency of local governments to look outward to explain internal troubles', Walter Wriston of Citicorp wrote, 'has made the world corporation a scapegoat and object of concern' (IMDI 1976: 32).

The Third World states also scored a victory over the Social Democratic governments like the Dutch (which wanted the successor Commission on Transnational Corporations – CTC – to be an experts' body), when they succeeded in establishing an intergovernmental commission instead. This triumph was confirmed by a solid Third World majority in the eventual CTC: thirty-three members from the Third World, ten from the advanced capitalist countries, and five from the Soviet bloc. For the Third World states with their two-thirds majority in the CTC, the Commission was seen as a key lever for bringing closer the realization of an NIEO. The first session of March 1975 was clear testimony to this (de Kemp 1985: 61–4). The trade unions, on the other hand, who had observer status in the first CTC session, were to find out that the export-led industrialization strategy of the Third World state classes did not envisage a broadening of trade union rights. The ICFTU, which had itself been prominent in trying to secure a code of conduct including such rights, thus were confronted by the fact that the Third World state classes, as an aspirant fraction of world capital, did not reciprocate the concerns the trade unions and European Social Democracy had expressed with respect to the need for Third World development.

While national sovereignty was the starting point for the Third World states, the envisaged UN regulation was preceded by regional arrangements on which national legislation should be modelled. Thus the Andean Pact adopted its 'Decision 24' to create a common regulatory framework for foreign investment to be followed by the different member states (UNCTC 1986: 5). The Pacific Basin Economic Council, too, issued its own 'Charter on International Investments' (IMDI 1976: 23). Especially following the crisis of 1974–5, the attitude towards multinational corporations in some cases hardened into economic nationalism. In Brazil, an 'Administrative Council of Economic Defence' in 1976 began monitoring the activities of the subsidiaries of foreign companies and fined several of them for price-fixing (*Newsweek*, 10 May 1976).

When the preparation of a draft code was begun by the intergovernmental working group of the CTC in 1977, the advanced capitalist countries were already in a position to demand that any code would have to be balanced by the establishment of standards for the treatment of MNCs in addition to standards for their conduct (UNCTC 1986: 6). This idea, accepted by ECOSOC in its 'Mexico Declaration' in 1980, signified the reversal of the regulatory drive and the challenge to corporate sovereignty. Initially, national sovereignty prevailed over the sovereignty of capital in the 'Action Programme', pertaining to natural resources as well as 'all economic activities'. In order to exercise effective control and safeguard resources, a state was entitled to any means suitable, 'including the right to nationalization or transfer of ownership to its nationals, this right being an expression of the full permanent sovereignty of the State' (quoted in Commission 1980: 7).

By 1980, the internationalization of capital itself began to undermine the position of the Third World state classes. Their aspiration to insert their national economies as integral industrial locations in the emerging world economy was overtaken by the rise of Asian island- and city-states as export-industrial locations and more generally, by the tendency of capital to carve out export enclaves non-coincident with state territories and outside their jurisdiction, the so-called export processing zones. Thus in Mexico, a key state in the NIEO drive, a Border Industrialization Programme allowing US capital to produce in Mexico under offshore conditions was inaugurated in 1965 in direct competition with US investment in Asian export locations. Between 1974 and 1981, the number of workers employed in border EPZs doubled to 130,000 in 630 plants (Dicken 1986: 175). Other countries originally prominent in the regulation drive of the Group of 77 had become home bases of their own multinational corporations and began to adopt a different posture on the question of binding regulation. Brazil was the most important example (de Kemp 1985: 118, 179; for an overview of the current state of the UN Code project, see UNCTC 1986).

Thus, even disregarding political developments, the internationalization of capital itself worked to undermine the posture of the Third World state classes and their regulation project which had caused the greatest concern in 1973–6. Ultimately, the only regulation project to emerge from the Third World drive in the UN, the 'Set of Multilaterally Agreed Equitable Principles and Rules for the Control of Restrictive Business Practices' of 1980, has to be understood as an extension of existing anti-trust legislation in the US and the EC. It contributes to the establishment of the conditions for 'total capital' on a world scale in the most classic sense, i.e. as a way of guaranteeing maximum competition and the interdiction of non-economic arrangements interfering with it (de Kemp 1985: 123).

The Socialist countries

Seen in this light, it is clear that one major issue for the socialist countries was the question of whether their state enterprises would be subject to the liberal strand of regulation that was emerging out of the debates initiated by the NIEO movement. At first, the socialist states, notably the USSR, declared themselves vehemently opposed to the extension of such liberal regulation, equivalent from their point of view to deregulation. In the ILO and, between 1976 and 1979, in UNCTAD, this position was stubbornly defended. Ultimately, the Soviet bloc had to give in on this issue as far as the UNCTAD restrictive business practices code was concerned (de Kemp 1985: 51, 113).

On the other hand, in the discussions in ECOSOC on a general code of conduct, the USSR tried to conciliate the Third World and the trade union positions by stressing the need for solidarity with the under-developed countries and the need to defend workers' interests. In spite of the occasional instances of anti-imperialist invective, the socialist countries in the period under review had fully accepted the reality of international capital (Hellman 1976: 82).

The need to restrict the application of extraterritorial jurisdiction was particularly important to the socialist countries. If this was interdicted by a code of conduct or otherwise, the US could not force its subsidiaries to conform to COCOM export restrictions to socialist countries (de Kemp 1985: 38).

THE RESPONSE OF CAPITAL

Since the other chapters in this book deal with other aspects of the neo-liberal offensive, I will deal here only with those actions on the part of the international bourgeoisie that were taken in the context of the code of conduct debate.

The essence of the response of capital was that as long as regulation remained confined to internationalizing 'total capital', i.e. internationalizing anti-trust legislation, creating the conditions for equal competition, standardizing procedures, etc., it went along with such regulation. As soon as the sovereignty of capital was impaired, however, whether by enhancing trade union rights, state class jurisdiction, or otherwise by subjecting the actions of private capital to public scrutiny and democratic procedure, the capitalist class effectively blocked the way to such regulation. To international capital, the proliferation of controls was viewed with mounting apprehension. What the employers feared most was not the idea of a code of conduct in itself, but the dynamic it might set in motion. Thus Lawrence McQuade (Procon, W.R. Grace) at the time expressed his 'worry whether such an international code might gradually evolve into a mechanism which would unduly limit and restrict ... the activities which constitute the core responsibilities of business' (IMDI 1976: 44).

Collaboration on the part of the capitalist class and the major capitalist states in the development of codes of conduct was therefore practically confined to guiding the regulatory impulse into channels of desirable synchronization and international standardization. Even then, caution prevailed. The OECD in 1977 acknowledged that its own (largely pre-emptive) Guidelines, 'though voluntary in origin, may ... in the course of time ... pass into the general corpus of customary international law even for those multinational enterprises which have never accepted them' (OECD, quoted in Baade 1980: 9).

In addition to the existing treaty structure protecting foreign investment and the multilateral arrangements in that field, the elaboration of a quasi-state structure specifically dealing with international investment was begun in the 1960s. The World Bank in 1965 set up an International Center for the Settlement of Investment Disputes, from the point of view that stability and confidence in matters of foreign investment would facilitate the flow of such investment to developing countries. But, as a regulatory device, this was seldom used (IMDI 1976: 38; UNCTC 1986: 4).

In 1972, the International Chamber of Commerce adopted a code of conduct which was an obvious attempt to reorient the democratic regulation movement to a format compatible with the sovereignty of capital. Compared to the ICC code of 1949, which still was oriented to protecting foreign investments, the 1972 code was meant to placate the host countries as well. In the Introduction to the Code, it was stated that the aim was to 'create a climate of mutual confidence', and that it was hoped that 'these guidelines will be helpful to the United Nations' and other organizations in their efforts to 'promote constructive discussions' of the problem (quoted by de Kemp 1985: 55).

The recognition of the need for regulation and quasi-state structures on the global level at this point began to transpire in several statements. It was clear that the restructuring of capital itself, from a regionally concentrated Atlantic setting to a world-wide deployment, and coinciding with a technical restructuring that rearticulated different modes of accumulation into a new regime centring on high-tech production and communication, required an adjustment of particular regulatory instances. As long as the metropolitan capitalist class was on the defensive, and its own, corporate liberal, concept of control proved counterproductive by its tendency to invite antagonistic social forces to press particular compromises further to their advantage, regulation was seen in almost apocalyptic terms (cf. Wilson quote in the motto of this chapter). Only when the perspective on successful restructuring brightened, the more perceptive elements in the capitalist class dared to encourage their fellow capitalists to go along with regulation in the confidence that they would hold their own in the transition.

The sights of this fraction were set on a reaffirmation of international liberalism and minimal regulation along these lines. In the US, the Chamber of Commerce of the United States undertook an effort to lay the foundations for what was significantly termed a 'GATT for Investment' by setting up a task force on International Investment Codes in 1974. Encouraged by the work in the OECD and other international organizations, members of the Chamber of Commerce, too, 'were beginning to feel that some form of international regulation was inevitable', as Chamber President Richard Lesher put it in 1976 (IMDI 1976: 23). Since existing codes and code projects were seen to be too universal, it was decided to write a model on which individual companies could base a code of their own (IMDI 1976: 24).

In the ECOSOC Eminent Persons group of 1973–4, Senator Javits, the US member, attacked the report as based on hypotheses rather than facts, while the US stuck to its right to 'take legal action against activities outside the geographical confines of the United States which threaten its vital national interests', thus countering the rejection of extraterritorial jurisdiction by the Group (de Kemp 1985: 59). Yet Javits argued in favour of accepting the principle of a Code:

> Rather than drag its heels on this subject, the United States should put forward its own proposals and assume an active role in the discussion of a code of conduct, lest the final product be drafted by nations whose views differ so sharply from our own as to make the code ineffectual.
>
> (IMDI 1976: 38)

Indeed, in 1975–6, negotiations in ECOSOC, UNCTAD, and the ILO were accelerated under the influence of external political pressure and the OECD states at this point made haste with their Guidelines project to let it function as a model and keep the Third World states from launching more ambitious projects. Within the cadre class, pro-business voices now became louder by reference to these anticipatory codes. Thus in his comments on the RIO Report to the Club of Rome, Social Democratic Unilever manager Pieter Kuin stressed that regulation was not to be understood as a disciplinary measure against capital, but as support for the multinationals' global reach. In his view, multinational corporations had done more than governments in establishing a true world economy and in the main had shown a great sense of responsibility by their manner of doing business and by the initiation of, or subscription to, codes of conduct such as the ICC or the (1976) OECD codes (P. Kuin in Tinbergen 1977: 354).

The stress on the sovereignty of capital against public structures gradually became the central axis of capital's response to the regulation drive. Thus the International Chamber of Commerce criticized the ECOSOC Eminent Persons' report in 1975 for wanting to increase the state role in the economic process at the expense of the market mechanism (de Kemp 1985: 60). Only by showing confidence and by boldly maintaining that sticking to the essentials of the capitalist system was the ultimate form of social responsibility, this system could be defended. At the twenty-fifth ICC Conference in Madrid, a Committee on Social Responsibilities chaired by Ian McGregor (then of the ICC's US Council and AMAX) and with Rupert Murdoch of World News Corporation as Rapporteur, in its first point mentioned 'making profits' as the key to social responsibility. ICC Secretary-General C.-H. Winqwist, Director-General of the Swedish Moderate Party and director of Skandinaviska Enskilda Banken, quoted the Committee's recommendation to use the free press more self-confidently as a means to educate the public in the basics of capitalism, such as the 'true role of profit'. If not,

> the attitude of government and society toward the business community, already highly critical in many nations, could become downright hostile. And that might mean the end of the free economic system as we know it today.
>
> (IMDI 1976: 30)

In the CTC, the new self-confidence of the metropolitan capitalist states was expressed in confronting the Third World states with a list of demands seeking to protect the multinationals against discriminatory regulation by reference to existing codes of the ICC and the OECD (de Kemp 1985: 65).

The EC apparently showed itself more willing to make concessions. When the US adopted a more flexible posture in the issue of technology transfer in 1975, this was partly caused by the flexibility which the EC had shown towards the Third World in the Lomé Treaty earlier in the year (de Kemp 1985: 70). But the general resilience of the capitalist order to infractions of the existing, Lockean pattern of international relations transcended these differences. One way of upholding this pattern against excessive regulation was to keep codes of conduct separate from, or explicitly subordinate to, existing international law. UN Secretary General Waldheim had explicitly referred to 'international law in this field [as] sketchy and very controversial' (IMDI 1976: 36). But even the publicly undisputed EC South Africa code was not issued as a Regulation or a Directive, which would have given it legal status, but as a declaration by the Foreign Ministers. In the ILO and in the OECD, the respective regulatory codes were likewise issued through 'unconstitutional' acts turning them into non-binding gestures (Baade 1980: 6). This is important, because since multinational corporations themselves lack international personality, 'their compliance with codes of conduct or guidelines, whether voluntary or not, cannot in and of itself give rise to customary international law' (ibid.: 11).

Even so, such codes as were promulgated stressed their being non-binding, or conformed entirely to the type of regulation necessary to assure the sovereignty of capital on a global scale. The OECD Declaration on International Investment and Multinational Enterprises, or Guidelines, was explicitly non-binding and the OECD was not even allowed discussion of individual companies. A company could only be invited, if the monitoring committee was unanimous on it, to express its views. After 1979, even this arrangement was watered down and the 'invitation' procedure dropped (de Kemp 1985: 88).

The OECD guidelines of 1976 proved crucial in setting the tone for further regulatory projects. Thus the 'Tripartite Declaration of Principles concerning Multinational Enterprises and Social Policy' of 1977 showed that in the ILO, the original ICFTU proposals made one year before had been overruled by the counter-proposals of the employers. Declaratory statements apart, the actual content of the ILO document was practically identical to the OECD guidelines. Any observance of compliance, as demanded by the labour representatives, was rejected by the USA (then about to leave the organization) in order not to create 'a tribunal against MNCs' (de Kemp 1985: 98). In the question of regulating restrictive business practices, the capitalist states likewise had their way. That this instance of regulation was a success, primarily derived from the fact that it was first of all a form of deregulation. The capitalist states had several times before tried to work out anti-trust legislation for the international sphere, and the eventual Restrictive Business Practices code 'was a reflection of existing anti-trust legislation existing in the EEC and the United States' (de Kemp 1985: 123).

CONCLUSION

The 'moment of regulation' which expressed itself in the drive for developing codes of conduct for multinational corporations in the early 1970s marked the intersection of several lines of development in contemporary capitalism. One was the process of restructuring of capital from an Atlantic pattern characterized by a Fordist regime of accumulation to a global one centred on production organized around new core technologies (see van Tulder and Junne 1988). In this process, quasi-state regulation necessary for the operation of 'total capital' had to be broadened from the national and regional to global levels.

Secondly, a crisis of political control occurred, partly expressed in the breakdown of corporate liberalism in the Atlantic heartland of capitalism, partly in the failure to sustain the transition from colonial to neo-colonial patterns of imperialist control of the periphery. In the metropolitan areas, a workers' revolt contained by corporate liberal capitalism tended to overload the compromise format of prevailing class relations to the detriment of the ruling class, constraining its capacity for governing. In the periphery, US-led neo-colonialism ran upon economic nationalism and multilateralism (Chile, OPEC, the NIEO movement), failed to complete the transition from European colonialism (Vietnam), or even failed effectively to begin the transition, as in Portuguese Africa.

Thirdly and finally, within the reform coalition that temporarily appeared to successfully press for a New International Order, the cadre class in capitalism, which is the product of the socialization of labour and in turn, is oriented to maintaining social cohesion, anticipated the 'moment of expropriation' and hence sought to prevent imbalances and excesses that might set in motion a true revolutionary development. Yet from the point of view of capital, this anticipatory action was dangerous in itself. Ultimately, the intiatives of the cadre class, expressed through Social Democracy at the EC, national government, party or trade union levels were defeated as part of a more general defeat of the tendency of the cadre class to autonomize under the influence of the groundswell of democratic social forces that characterized the 1970s. Of the broad array of regulatory proposals, ultimately only those survived that were compatible with the sovereignty of capital on a world scale. Yet the threat and the transformative potential of the code of conduct challenge were sufficiently well perceived to fuel a vehement counteroffensive along a much broader front.

REFERENCES

Aglietta, M., (1979 [1976]) *A Theory of Capitalist Regulation. The US Experience*, London: New Left Books.

Allende, S., (1973) *Chile. Volkskampf gegen Reaktion und Imperialismus – Aus Reden des Präsidenten der Republik Chile Salvador Allende Gossens*, Berlin: Staatsverlag der DDR.

Baade, H. W., (1980) 'The legal effects of codes of conduct for multinational enterprises', in N. Horn (ed.) *Legal Problems of Codes of Conduct for Multinational Enterprises*, 3–38 Deventer: Kluwer.

Bahro, R. (1980 [1977]) *Die Alternative. Zur Kritik des real existierenden Sozialismus*, Reinbek: Rowohlt.

Basso, L. (1975) *Gesellschaftsformation und Staatsform*, Frankfurt a/M: Suhrkamp.

Bihr, A. (1989) *Entre Bourgeoisie et Proletariat. L'encadrement Capitaliste*, Paris: L'Harmattan.

Bourrinet, J., (ed.), (1979) *Le dialogue Euro-Arabe*, Paris: Economica.

Brandt, W. (1971) *Bundeskanzler Brandt. Reden und Interviews*, Hamburg: Hoffmann & Campe.

Braverman, H. (1974) *Labor and Monopoly Capital*, New York/London: Monthly Review Press.

Bundesverband der Deutschen Industrie (1980) *Überblick über den Stand der europäischen Gesellschaftsrechts* (mimeo) May.

Carew, A. (1987) *Labour under the Marshall Plan. The Politics of Productivity and the Marketing of Management Science* Manchester: Manchester University Press.

Chesneaux, J. (1988) 'Which fight for what liberation?', in Lelio Basso International Foundation (eds) *Theory and Practice of Liberation at the End of the XXth Century*, 27–45, Brussels: Bruylant.

Collectif PCF (1971) *Le capitalisme monopoliste d'Etat*, Paris: Ed. Sociales.

Cohen-Tanugi, L. (1987) *Le droit sans l'état*, Paris: PUF.

Commission on Transnational Corporations, (1980) *Progress made towards the establishment of the new international economic order: the role of transnational corporations*, Report of the Secretariat, New York: UN/ECOSOC.

Cox, R. W. (1987) *Production, Power, and World Order. Social Forces in the Making of History*, New York: Columbia University Press.

Dicken, P. (1986) *Global Shift. Industrial Change in a Turbulent World*, London: Harper & Row.

Etty, T. and Tudyka, K. P. (1974) 'Wereldconcernraden: vakbonden en hun "kapitaalgerichte" strategie tegen multinationale ondernemingen', *Te Elfder Ure*, 21: 357–93.

Farhi, A. (1976) 'Europe: Behind the Myths', in T. Nairn (ed.) *Atlantic Europe? The Radical View*, Amsterdam: Transnational Institute.

Fennema, M. (1982) *International Networks of Banks and Industry*, The Hague/Boston/London: Nijhoff.

Fernández Jilberto, A. E., (1988) 'El debate sociologico-politico sobre casi dos siglos de estado nacional en America Latina, un intento de reinterpretacion', *Afers Internacionals*, 12/13: 41–75.

Frieden, J. (1981) 'Third World indebted industrialization, international finance and state capitalism in Mexico, Brazil, Algeria, and South Korea', *International Organization*, 35 (3): 407–31.

Friedman, A. (1988) *Agnelli en het netwerk van de Italiaanse macht*, Baarn: Anthos.

Gill, S. (1990) *American Hegemony and the Trilateral Commission*, Cambridge: Cambridge University Press.

Günsche, K.-L. and Lantermann, K. (1977) *Kleine Geschichte der Sozialistischen Internationale*, Bonn: Neue Gesellschaft.

Hellman, R. (1976 [1974]) *Controle op multinationale ondernemingen*, Utrecht/Antwerpen: Spectrum.

Hinkelammert, F. (1985 [1981]) *Die ideologischen Waffen des Todes. Zur Metaphysik des Kapitalismus*, Freiburg/Münster: Exodus/Liberacion.

Hogenhuis, N. (n.d.) *Een Vergelijking van Codes voor Multinationale Ondernemingen*, Den Haag: Bibliotheek en Documentatiedienst Tweede Kamer.

Holland, S. (1975) *The Socialist Challenge*, London: Quartet Books.

Hough, J. (1986) *The Struggle for the Third World, Soviet Debates and American Options*, Washington: The Brookings Institution.

IMDI (1976) *Corporate Citizenship in the Global Community*, E. C. Bursk and G. E. Bradley (eds), Washington: International Management and Development Institute.

Kannapin, K. (1984) *Imperialistische strategie gegen die Neue Internationale Wirtschaftsordnung*, Berlin: Dietz.

Kemp, A. de (1985) *Internationale Regulering van Multinationale Ondernemingen*, Nijmeegse Studies, no. 6, Nijmegen: University of Nijmegen.

Knieper, R. (1976) *Weltmarkt, Wirtschaftsrecht und Nationalstaat*, Frankfurt: Suhrkamp.

Kolko, G. (1989) 'Varieties of third world elites. A framework for analysis', in P. Limqueco (ed.) *Partisan Scholarship, Essays in Honour of Renato Constantino*, 36–50, Manila: Journal of Contemporary Asia Publishers.

Konrád, G. and Szelényi, I. (1981 [1978]) *Die Intelligenz auf dem Weg zur Klassenmacht*, Frankfurt: Suhrkamp.

Krasner, S. D., (1985) *Structural Conflict. The Third World Against Global Liberalism*, Berkeley: University of California Press.

Lamounier, B. (1989) 'Brazil, inequality against democracy', in L. Diamond, J. J. Linz and S. M. Lipset (eds.) *Democracy in Developing Countries – Latin America*, 111–57, Boulder: Lynn Rienner.

Löwy, M. (1981) *The Politics of Combined and Uneven Development. The Theory of Permanent Revolution*, London: Verso.

MEW, *Marx-Engels Werke* (1973) 23 Berlin: Dietz.

Meynaud, J. and Sidjanski, D. (1967) *L'Europe des affaires*, Paris: Payot.

Parteitag der KPdSU, XXIV, 30 March/9 April 1971, APN, Moscow.

Petras, J. F. (1970) *Politics and Social Structure in Latin America*, New York/London: Monthly Review Press.

Picciotto, S. (1989) 'Slicing a shadow. Business taxation in an international framework', in L. Hancher and M. Moran (eds) *Capitalism, Culture, and Economic Regulation*, 11–47, Oxford: Clarendon Press.

Pijl, K. van der (1981) 'De E.E.G. als kader voor kontrole', *Tijdschrift voor Diplomatie*, 7 (10) June: 568–601.

Pursey, S. K., (1980) 'The trade union view on the implementation of codes of conduct', in N. Horn (ed.) *Legal Problems of Codes of Conduct for Multinational Enterprises*, 277–90, Deventer: Kluwer.

Raschke, J. (ed.) (1981) *Die politischen Parteien in Westeuropa*, Reinbek: Rowohlt.

Roy, A. (1986) *Contemporary India – A Perspective*, Bombay: Build.

Ruhwedel, K. (1976) 'Der Europäische Gewerkschaftsbund und die westeuropäische Integration', in F. Deppe (ed.) *Arbeiterbewegung und westeuropäische Integration*, 228–75, Köln: Pahl-Rugenstein.

Sampson, A. (1974) *The Sovereign State of ITT*, Greenwich: Fawcett-Crest.

Shevchenko, A. N., (1985) *Breaking with Moscow*, New York: Ballantine.

SI Report on Multinationals (1978) in *Socialist Affairs*, November/December, 168.

Sohn-Rethel, A. (1978 [1976]) 'The dual economics of transition', in R. Panzieri a.o., *The Labour Process and Class Strategies*, 26–45, London: CSE Books.

Tinbergen, J. (Co-ordinator) (1977) *Naar een Rechtvaardiger Internationale Orde*, Amsterdam/Brussels: Elsevier.

Tulder, R. van and Junne, G., (1988) *European Multinationals in Core Technologies*, Chichester: Wiley.

UNCTC (1986) *The United Nations Code of Conduct on Transnational Corporations*, New York: United Nations.

'Vredeling plan for MNCs gets green light "in principle"' (1980) *Industrial Relations Europe*, 8(88) April.

Wright, E. O. (1978) 'Intellectuals and the Working Class', *The Insurgent Sociologist*, 8(1) (Winter): 5–20.

3

CHILE: THE LABORATORY EXPERIMENT OF INTERNATIONAL NEO-LIBERALISM

Alex E. Fernández Jilberto

The relation between social actors and models of development can be expressed, on the basis of an examination of the latter, as the result of a correlation of social forces benefiting in unequal degrees from the process of development. At the same time, models of development are largely defined by the economic and political characteristics of the elite which directs the process of social transformation. In Latin American Sociology of Development, this relation has been expressed in terms of two approaches: the logic of objective structures and the logic of the ideology of social actors (cf. Touraine 1987). Both approaches are based on the concept of social class, insofar as the socio-economic structure defines the position and the nature of the political orientations of the said actors. In the first case, the actors' behaviour is related to the functioning of the economy. In the second case, their behaviour is guided by the ideological values of social classes advocating radical or conservative changes in the existing correlation of social forces. Both approaches can be found in the most diverse theories that have inspired the debate on development in Latin America. The conflictual relation between economic rationality and political voluntarism, and the search for an equilibrium between the two, has been a constant point of reference of the various theories of development in Latin America.

In this context, the most diverse theories of Latin American development put emphasis on the active role of social actors. Theories of modernization assigned a special role to the principle of co-operation and social alliance between the middle and the popular sectors, which found expression in the populist period (cf. Garcia and Martins 1985;

58

ECLAC 1986; Sigal 1982; Tokman 1982); in the studies of dependency and the debate on unequal exchange, social classes became the significant actors (cf. Ominami 1986; Evers 1979; Frank 1978). As for the debate on what came to be known as 'the other development', the studies did not so much focus on the identification of actors as on the idea of a development geared to the demands of social actors. The new impetus given to the concept of 'communitary development' was particularly significant for the countries which experienced the 'new authoritarianism' and can be seen as a form of resistance against the State (see Sunkel 1979).

The situation of Chile is not substantially different from these images generated by Latin American Sociology, and the changes on socio-occupational structure as well as the social participation profile merely confirmed what has been said before. The establishment of the military dictatorship and the monetarist policy of economic restructuration radically altered the situation and attempted to reduce social actors to the role of consumers closely regulated by economic mechanisms and lacking any form of political mediation to resist the consequences of the neo-liberal utopia in a society self-regulated by the market. This failed attempt and the difficulties which the neo-liberal transformation of social relations created for a democratic transition is the central question examined in this paper. To this end, we have divided the paper into four parts. First, we shall give an account of the debate on these neo-liberal dictatorships and discuss the place which they have assigned to social actors. In the second part, we shall examine the consequences for the preceding social structure of the change in the economic and political functions of the democratic State. In the third part, we shall give an interpretation of the effects of the economic crisis which started in 1981 on the transition to the model of 'protected democracy' put forward by the authoritarian regime. Finally, we shall conclude with a discussion of the difficulties which stand in the way of a genuine transition to democracy.

SOCIAL ACTORS AND NEO-LIBERAL DICTATORSHIPS

The sociological and political debate on social actors, the State and civil society has been dominated by studies of authoritarian regimes and neo-liberal dictatorships. The first attempt to present this discussion in a systematic way was made by David Collier in a work which has now become a classic (Collier 1979). It was this work which gave currency to the term 'bureaucratic authoritarian State' formulated by Guillermo O'Donnell (O'Donnell 1977, 1979). This concept combines the logic of objective structures with the ideological logic of social actors in order to explain the emergence of authoritarianism. The stagnation of industrialization and the exhaustion of the Keynesian economic policies that had supported it were the result of a policy of import substitution industrialization combined with the absence of specialization in a context of a very narrow internal market. These were the conditions which required a deepening of the industrialization process and an integration of economic development which were supposed to lead to the emergence of an industrial apparatus, capable of producing capital goods. At the same time, the establishment of authoritarian regimes was also the result of a defensive reaction of the State to the constant political pressure generated by the populist movement. This 'mass praetorianism', in the words of O'Donnell, was intent upon carrying income distribution policies further, creating difficulties for the process of capital accumulation. This required a break with the populism associated with the development model that had been followed until then, and the principal actor involved in this break was the military bureaucracy.

O'Donnell emphasized on the fact that the policies of income concentration had facilitated the creation of an internal market for consumer durables (especially in the automobile sector), which called for authoritarian policies designed to contain the demands of the popular actors. There have been several critiques of the concept of Bureaucratic Authoritarian State. Albert Hirschman indicated that there had been a confusion between the economic consequences of a political process and the economic determinants of an authoritarian State (Hirschman 1979). On the other hand the Brazilian economist José Serra has pointed out that various Latin American countries, including Colombia, Venezuela and Chile during the Frei regime, had attempted to resolve the problem of industrial stagnation by democratic means. This was done by a policy of export promotion supported by limited devaluations. Thus the establishment of bureaucratic authoritarian states was not an inevitable development (Serra 1979). Serra goes even further by showing that the economic recovery experienced by Brazil from 1967 had consequences that were opposed to 'deepening' industrialization:

> a large part of the powerful effects derived from a higher investment rate and a lower level of spare capacity was directed

abroad. In addition to the damaging effects this had on a part of the existing capacity for accumulation, it had the result of limiting the expansion of capital goods and increase its relative technological backwardness.

(Serra 1974)

This is the argument which puts into doubt the explanation of the economic crisis in terms of a stagnation of the process of import substitution industrialization. On the other hand, the idea of crisis on a more global scale has been proposed, in which case studies of the authoritarian State based on the logic of economic systems must be replaced by the study of the formation of economic policy.

Paul Cammack (Cammack 1985) has put forward the most systematic theoretical and methodological critique of the concept of Bureaucratic Authoritarian State. In his view, this concept is based on an extreme simplification of the relation between stages of economic development and the emergence of a given political regime. But it was the work of Pilar Vergara (1984, 1986) and Manuel Antonio Garreton (1983), as well as the studies made by CIEPLAN in Chile (Foxley 1982) and by A. Canitrot (1981), and Juan Corradi (1985) in Argentina, which provided the decisive arguments against an economic explanation of military regimes. These studies showed that the main result of the monetarist policies conducted by the authoritarian regimes of Chile, Uruguay and Argentina, which subordinated the national economy to the principle of comparative advantages, was to provoke deindustrialization. Since it was more a financial and monetary policy, its results had nothing to do with a process of deepening of industrialization (cf. Cortazar et al. 1984; also Fernández Jilberto 1987). Only a study of these economic policies made it possible to go beyond the economic determinism on which O'Donnell's interpretation was based.

It is for these reasons that we prefer to use the concept of neo-liberal dictatorships giving rise to a general process of restructuration of society. This involves a change in the form of the State, in the type of insertion of the economy in the world market, in the model of development, in the relation between State and civil society and in the system of social relations associated with the preceding period. According to the neo-liberal vision, the restructuration of society on the basis of a new economic organization of free markets would open the way for a neo-liberal utopia of a society self-regulated by the market. Social actors would bear the impact of these transformations in the form of a 'cultural revolution' which would alter its subjectivity (logic of ideology), in accordance with the requirements of stability and efficiency for the new social order. The transfer of the function of regulating social and economic inequalities from the populist State to the markets would displace the focus of socio-economic demands from the political arena to the markets. This would bring about the depoliticization of social actors in relation to development problems.

The formation of the new power block involves, on the one hand, a powerful front of business groups linked with the external rearticulation of the economy, capped by a financial fraction which ensure its cohesion and its direct access to the international financial system and, as part of the same process, the transformation of the Armed Forces into a military bureaucracy, that is into a State corpus, with its own social, economic and political interests. The crystallization of these two fractions which make up the power block belong to the same matrix, but their structure, interests and position within the State are different, although they converge in the task of structuring an export economy.

CHANGES IN THE ECONOMIC FUNCTIONS OF THE STATE AND ITS IMPACT ON SOCIAL CLASSES

Structural transformations and the weight of the social classes are derived from changes in the economic and political functions of the State (see Moulian and Vergara 1979; Vergara 1982), which result from a fusion of the military bureaucracy with a neo-liberal policy of economic restructuration. From this follows a substitution of the model of development based on industrialization by another model based on diversified primary exports, which constitutes the material basis of the changes in the structure of social classes.

Studies by Javier Martínez and Ernesto Tironi (1982, 1983, 1984, 1986) indicate that the middle classes have been most directly affected by the transformation of the structure of the labour force which resulted from the reformulation of the role of the State as economic agent as well as from the reduction in the size of the state apparatus. The policies designed to reduce the influence of the State in the economic process, as is already known, were the outcome of a transfer of public sector companies and banks to the private sector. Of 533 State enterprises in existence in 1973, there were only twelve left in 1981. In addition to this, there was a reduction in the role of the State as financial intermediary. In 1970, the Banco del Estado accounted for 51.9 per cent of domestic currency deposits while the corresponding figure for the private sector was 48.1 per cent (this does not take into account the nationalization of the banking system which took place between 1970 and 1973). By 1981, the private sector accounted for 73.6 per cent of these types of deposits while the Banco del Estado's share had dropped to 26.4 per cent. The reduction in size of the State also took the form of a reduction in public sector expenditures. In 1973, public expenditures as a proportion of the Gross Domestic Product amounted to 44.1 per cent; by 1979, this figure had dropped to 22.9 per cent. In addition, public sector employment dropped by 25 per cent between 1973 and 1979, a reduction of 95,000 jobs during this period which were lost at an average annual rate of 4.6 per cent. In spite of the fact that this loss was not made up by the private sector (Marshall and Romaguera 1981; Marshall 1981), this was a process that came to be known as the 'privatization of the middle classes'. For the middle classes, the change in the role of the State has meant the loss of a privileged source of employment and of a channel of upward social mobility. This is even more obvious if we consider that the image built up by Latin American Sociology of Development, of a modern middle class associated with employment expansion and increasing State expenditures and economic functions since the 1930s, closely fitted the Chilean case. The idea of a privatized middle class had always seemed irrelevant.

Initially, the effects of the economic restructuration on the middle classes gave rise to two interpretations which were not verified in reality. The first interpretation emphasized the idea of 'social extinction' which would result from the elimination of support from the State. The second opened up the prospect of a process of proleterianization of the middle classes and their progressive economic marginalization. Various statistical sources show that their participation in employment was in the order of 40 per cent during the 1970–80 period. On the other hand, workers' participation in employment dropped from 20.2 per cent to 17.6 per cent during the same period while the corresponding figures for non-salaried manual workers were 29.6 per cent and 22.9 per cent respectively for the same period (Filgueira and Geneletti 1981). This shows that the changes which they have experienced are not so much related to their levels of income nor to quantitative measures but to the fact that they have moved from the public to the private sector while remaining salaried employees. They found a place in the modern services sectors, in commerce, in the financial sector and mainly in independent economic activities. This had significant effects on their role as political actors and on the means of upward mobility to which they had access. The privatization of the middle classes and their expulsion from the State apparatus which had turned them (during the populist period) into a political class of the State, deprived them of the capacity to exercise political pressure on the State. The mechanisms of upward social mobility give a decisive advantage to the sectors of independent activities and limit the mobility of the salaried sectors. Those who showed the greatest degree of adaptability to the new model were the middle classes associated with independent economic activities (Martínez and Tironi 1986).

Moreover, prestige and social status come to depend on access to consumption of modern consumer durables and consumer credit comes to replace public employment and expenditure as instruments of social mobility. The result of these processes of change is an accentuation and a deepening of the heterogeneity of the middle classes which facilitates the breakup of the homogeneity which its previous political behaviour had demonstrated. The effects of this heterogeneity (incomes, educational levels occupational situation, etc.) were to be overshadowed by the homogenizing effects of modern consumption. However this homogenization does not rest upon the middle classes as political actors in the modernization of society, but on the middle classes as modern consumers. It is because of this that the economic crisis which started in 1982 brought about a new restructuration, caused by the contraction of credit and the lack of growth of the modern tertiary sector.

The working class does not only suffer the structural impact of a reduction and an end to the role of the State as economic agent, it is also hit by the uncontrolled opening of the economy to the international system. The effect of this was to stimulate the process of de-industrialization and reduce industrial employment. This negative impact on the growth of the industrial sector reduced the structural influence of the working class on the national society (Martínez and Tironi 1983). It is confronted with the fact that it is decreasing in size, that its strategic importance in the economy is diminishing and that its internal homogeneity is being lost. This simply confirms a tendency towards a reduction in the participation of salaried sectors in the secondary sector of the economy started in the 1960s, which several Latin American sociologists had forecast (cf. Slavinsky 1965; also Cardoso and Reyna 1968; Nun 1972). In the case of Chile, the industrial working class in 1980 accounted for 16 per cent less of the economically active population than it had in 1952 and 18.7 per cent less than it had in 1960. During this latter decade, workers were confronted with a reduction in their participation in industrial employment to the tune of 103,000 persons who were pushed towards the informal sector or became officially unemployed. This was accompanied by a loss on the part of the trade unions of their capacity to exercise pressure on the economy (see Frias 1983; Larrain 1987; Ruiz-Tagle and Urmeneta 1985).

This would explain why informal employment in the 1980s was comparable to what it was during the 1950s. According to studies by Raczynski (1978), informal employment which in 1952 amounted to 23 per cent of the economically active population, had dropped to 19 per cent by 1970. On the basis of the definitions used by Raczynski, Martínez and Tironi came to the conclusion that informal employment had reached 26.5 per cent of the economically active population by 1980. On the other hand, given that official unemployment had tripled over the previous ten years in relation to historical rates of unemployment, reaching an average of 17 per cent, we must conclude that this has been the most important social mutation to have taken place in Chile in the past forty years.

The political implications of all these processes gave rise to a debate on the question of the 'growing expansion of the working class' which had provided support for its political behaviour and for a revolutionary transformation (socialist) of dependent capitalism. This debate, within the Chilean left, was waged mainly between socialist and social democratic alternatives.

At the same time, agricultural workers were confronted by a series of transformations which gave rise to a new agrarian structure. This has been widely examined by various authors whose studies have highlighted three parallel processes (e.g. Cox Urrejola 1979; Gomez 1980; Gomez et al. 1981). The first of these has to do with the nature of the agrarian structure characterized by the end of the latifundio, as a result of the various agrarian reform initiatives taken since the 1960s. In 1965, farms of eighty or more basic irrigated hectares accounted for 55.4 per cent of agricultural land; by 1976, this had dropped to 2.9 per cent. However, this did not mean that the agrarian structure had become stabilized, as we can see from the dynamism of the market for agricultural land between 1977 and 1980. The second process has to do with the emergence of a new social sector known as the 'smallholders of the agrarian reform'.

In 1979, a total of 491,015 basic irrigated hectares had been assigned, corresponding to 54.8 per cent of agricultural land (Vega and Ruiz-Tagle 1982). The emergence of smallholdings coming out of the previous agrarian reform processes, created a new social sector which occupied the best agricultural land (Jarvis 1985). Yet this sector was confronted with difficulties stemming from the high cost of credit, insufficient initial capitalization and the problems associated with incorporating the required technology (agricultural machinery). This led to the sale of many agricultural properties, to the introduction of various forms of sub-tenancy, on the part of the recipient smallholders, to the benefit of small- and medium-scale farmers and traders. The recipient smallholders of the agrarian reform were reduced to the condition of poor peasants (cf. Bengoa 1984; also Cereceda and Dahse 1980). The third process has to do with the growing pauperization of traditional 'minifundistas' and small peasants which became more serious when the relative prices of agricultural products experienced variations. Various studies conducted by the Grupo de Investigaciones Agrarias (GIA) know that the purchasing capacity for these products dropped by 40.9 per cent in 1979 in relation to a base of 100 for 1970.

During the period 1973–80, this new type of social relations in the agricultural sector was characterized by a rational and impersonal organization of work and by the spread of employment, which involved the elimination of the 'inquilinaje' system with its payment in kind and systems of material compensation (CEPAL 1982). Contrary to the traditional social order in Chilean agriculture where power was associated with the ownership of the latifundio and with sociocultural control exercised over the various peasant strata (Salazar 1985), power in the new system was held by social sectors which exercised control of marketing, of the sources of technical and financial assistance and of the industrial transformation of agricultural production.

As regards the Chilean entrepreneurial sector, it should be noted that they constituted, at least initially, the most stable social and political support base of the military regime. This support was expressed through their business organization as well as through the political presence of the National Party. What is surprising, however, is the speed with which they joined the currents that were critical of State participation in economic activities at the national level. This vision was further strengthened at a later stage with the rising ideological influence of the neo-liberal technocracy within the military regime. This contradicted the historical experience of Chilean entrepreneurs whose modern existence was due to unlimited support by the State. According to studies conducted by Petras (1969), during the period 1940 to 1965, 35 per cent of the large firms and 14 per cent of the medium sized ones were established with State support. This had even favoured the process of industrial concentration to the point where at the beginning of the 1960s, nine firms accounted for 25 per cent of the capital invested in the manufacturing sector (Nolff 1965).

This rapid assimilation of an ideology critical of State participation in economic activities was due fundamentally to the economic and political impact of the prolonged process of agrarian reform which took place in 1970 and 1971. The fact that these industrial and agrarian sectors both regarded State intervention as a threat is not only a consequence of those processes. It can also be explained by the high degree of integration between the two sectors resulting from the agrarian origins of the Chilean industrial bourgeoisie as shown by Kirsch's research (Kirsch 1977). Moreover, in the work already quoted, Petras showed that in the mid-1960s, almost half of all Chilean entrepreneurs owned agricultural properties or had family ties with landowners.

The reduction of the State, the reformulation of its role as economic agent and the opening to the international system, all these implied a profound restructuring of the entrepreneurial sector (Campero 1984). In the first place, from the beginning of the 1975–6 recession, there is a clear acceleration of the process of economic concentration. At the end of 1978, the so-called 'economic groups' controlled the largest 250 firms in the country, 82 per cent of bank loans and 64 per cent of loans made by non-banking institutions. In 1982, 574,200,000 pesos corresponded to 4.2 per cent of debtors to the banks (see Sanfuentes 1984; also Cerri 1979; Dahse 1979; Meller *et al.* 1984; Muñoz 1986a; Foxley 1982; and Ramos 1986). Secondly, this process of economic concentration was accompanied by many bankruptcies in the industrial sector; these amounted to 1,116 between 1976 and 1980. Finally, we must point out the process of re-localization of the entrepreneurial sector which, in the work of Martínez and Tironi, was measured in terms of the location of the occupational category 'employers', according to branch of economic activity. From this, it can be seen that between 1977 and 1981, there was a significant shift of employers from the productive to the tertiary sector. There is no doubt that the external commercial opening of the economy on the prices of non-transitable goods stimulated this shift.

If we equate the concept of entrepreneur to that of bourgeoisie, several authors have asked whether the change in the model of development has given rise during this period to a 'new bourgeoisie'. The work of Ricardo Lagos has established that the most powerful economic groups are of recent origin and, contrary to the traditional sectors, their control over a large part of the productive apparatus is based on the fact that they dominate the financial system (Lagos 1981). This contrasts with traditional entrepreneurial groups who extended their interests in the financial sector through activities associated with the production of goods. In addition to the support it derived from the new model of development, this 'new bourgeoisie' was strengthened by a highly ideological entrepreneurial technocracy, stemming from the transfer of social and economic functions from the State to the operation of the market. They constituted the most dynamic of the privatized middle classes under the economic model.

THE EFFECTS OF THE CRISIS ON THE TRANSITION TO THE MODEL OF 'PROTECTED DEMOCRACY'

The onset of the economic crisis which began during the second half of 1981 was surprising and unexpected for the dictatorship. The political system created by the military bureaucracy, which guaranteed both the reproduction of the economic model and that of political authoritarianism, was based on a presumed success of the economic policy. According to the neo-liberal technocracy (the 'Chicago Boys'), two phases could be distinguished (Tironi 1986). The first, an authoritarian phase, was to set down the bases of a sufficiently prosperous market economy, while the second, permanent one, would correspond to the establishment of a solid democracy supported by pragmatic citizens, fully satisfied and devoted to their own personal success and enrichment. The failure of the model and the economic crisis prevented the gradual transition towards the model of 'protected democracy' from taking place in the way the military regime had envisaged. This was a result of the large scale social mobilization which erupted during the political crisis (1982–4) when civil society shed its immobilism. At different levels, and showing different degrees of restructuring, a wide variety of groups re-emerged to take part in public life: political parties, the trade union movement and other representative organizations, the slum dwellers, the student movement, as well as new actors such as highly radicalized youths from the marginalized communities and a pluralistic women's movement. The publication of many magazines and other opposition publications opened up new political space. Successive mass mobilizations were almost exclusively urban and have remained so, as peasant participation was limited and regionally defined. These mobilizations did not constitute a single centralized movement but were the point of convergence of several sectoral mobilizations, each showing a different degree of organization, spontaneity and combativeness. Their collective actors neither emerged nor reconstituted themselves simultaneously but succeeded each other through various modalities which expressed their ever changing and hetero-geneous social composition: from the first day of protest convened by the Copper Workers' Federation, through those organized by the trade unions and/or political parties, to the Civic Assembly led by the profes-sional organizations.

It is essential to specify the real political dynamics of these mass mobilizations and to examine them through the complex political process which their eruption provoked and, in turn, the way in which this reverberated upon them, giving rise to their present political logic.

While the regime was trying to cope with this process of disaggrega-tion of the power bloc, it was also confronted with difficult negoti-ations over the international debt and was conducting an erratic economic policy. The political logic of the social mobilizations directly threatened the existence of the regime. This period of political crisis was marked by a triple objective: departure of Pinochet, provisional Government and setting up of a Constituent Assembly.

In the face of this situation, the dictatorship decided in 1983 to take the political initiative and to accelerate the process of 'transition'. The regime named Sergio Onofre Jarpa as Minister of the Interior, thus handing over to a civilian right-wing politician who had been an active participant in the overthrow of Salvador Allende, the task of defusing the political conflict through a crucial but short-lived political opening.

The failure of this approach, which was confirmed in November 1984 when the regime declared a State of Siege, was the result of the impossibility of achieving two alternative objectives. The first had to do with the capacity to reconstitute the support base of the government which would allow it successfully to wage open political warfare against the opposition; the second, with the possibility of reaching a minimum agreement with the Christian Democrats which would guar-antee their support for the 1980 Constitution in return for concessions regarding the timing of the return to democracy.

The successive inadequacies of the political and civilian support base of the regime (neo-liberalism and the Jarpa cabinet) in the face of the crisis led the military bureaucracy to take direct responsibility for the recomposition of the ruling classes and the restructuring of a power bloc through an open and/or tacit delegation by entrepreneurial organ-izations of their economic and political interests. It was the only way to save the regime. Simultaneously, the regime moved towards a policy of intimidation on a large scale, concentrating on disarticulating any potential autonomous social regroupings. It abandoned all populist pretence that might have been costly and come into conflict with the objective of restructuring the ruling classes. The State of Siege, declared in 1984, gave rise to a wave of repression in the form of actual military operations including large-scale troop mobilization. In one year, 156 people were killed and two-thirds of the victims were under twenty-four years old.

It was also during this period that the political parties began to re-emerge, restructured and reorganized and with new linkages with their traditional social base. The political leadership was the same as in 1973, although with new types of divisions and forms of regrouping (see Bajoit 1986). No new parties emerged except for very small groups that have not become significant to the present day. From 1983, the opposition parties fell into two blocs (the Democratic Alliance and the Popular Democratic Movement), with very different strategic outlooks. The composition of the political leadership became even more complex when the Catholic Church began to play a direct and central political role (cf. Smith 1982). The Church's political involvement was direct (providing political cover for the opposition, large-scale assistance to the poorest sectors of the population, staunch defence of human rights) and, as an ancient political soulmate of the State, it entered the political scene to ensure that the economic, social and political crisis should not create a crisis of the State which would give rise to a social explosion that might destroy it or lead to civil war. Its political project consisted of organizing negotiations between the regime and the opposition to open the way for a new type of regime which would deactivate the social and political polarization provoked by the military regime. Its first development in this direction was the failed negotiations, organized between Minister Jarpa and parts of the opposition. The second instance culminated in the National Accord which was prepared by a commission nominated by the Cardinal.

Another factor to be taken into account in surveying the Chilean political scene, was direct political intervention by the United States through their representatives at various levels. While their approach was obviously pragmatic, leading them to adapt their pressures to the changing requirements of the situation, there were nevertheless certain constant features to their intervention. They had nothing but praise for the regime's economic policy designed to restructure the dominant classes, and they protected their interests both in relation to the management of the external debt and by assigning important sectors of the economy to United States capital; however, they also considered that support for the regime involved some political risks because of the social and political polarization that had been building up. Even to the present day, they are not confident that the government will be in a position to implement the new political regime dictated by the 1980 constitution which will only be viable if it incorporates the democratic opposition, to serve as a safety valve against the enormous social and political pressures that have accumulated. Neither do they trust the Christian Democrats, or any other democratic bloc that might emerge under its leadership, as a viable alternative to the present regime if it is not supported by the military bureaucracy. That is why they have been putting pressure on the regime and the Christian Democrats to enter into an arrangement that would be in both parties' interest. At the same time, United States intervention is limited by the danger of provoking a crisis within the Armed Forces, the consequences of which could be unmanageable. For obvious reasons, they exclude the possibility of any Communist Party participation in a new political regime. Cynically, they present their objectives and their interests as the expression of a deep preoccupation for the human rights situation in Chile.

DIFFICULTIES OF THE TRANSITION TO DEMOCRACY 1983–9

When the difficulties associated with a transition to democracy were debated among the social and political forces that advocated such a transition, the most commonly held idea was that of a restoration of the kinds of democratic practices which had characterized Chilean society between the 1930s and the beginning of the 1970s (some contributions to this debate were Aldunate *et al.* 1985; Walker *et al.* 1986; Urzua Valanzuela 1986; Muñoz 1986b; Arrate 1985; Lagos 1985). What came to be known as the 'Chilean democratic arrangement' (1930–70), unquestionably a very solid arrangement in a Latin American context, was based on a consensus within the Chilean political class regarding the need to find an equilibrium between democracy, participation and industrialization. This consensus ensured an increasingly solid economic development, a gradual reduction of social and economic inequalities and a genuine broadening of political participation by civil society. The numerous crises which affected Chilean society during this period did not alter this historical tendency until 1973.

Nevertheless, prospects for a transition to democracy in Chile present two variants. The first is the 'really existing' transition inspired by the dictatorship which seeks the institutionalization of the authoritarian and exclusionary features of the regime (cf. Garretón 1985) as a maximum objective, or the maintenance and defence of capitalist achievements as a minimum objective, in a context of crisis and weakening of the authoritarian regime. For the centre right opposition, democracy is a set of juridical and political institutions associated with the system of liberal representation. It is characterized by the division of powers, political pluralism, individual freedom and human rights on the basis of the rule of law and popular sovereignty. In addition to these characteristics, democracy for the centre left opposition also involves being sensitive to popular demands through the transformation of social and economic structures generated during the authoritarian period, in order to give rise to 'real or substantive democracy'.

Various structural and political processes created obstacles to a 'real' transition to democracy. The first of these is the involutionary nature of economic development and the changes in the social structure Chilean society had shown until 1970. In this context, the modernization processes which took place during the military regime constituted a generally regressive process. An example of this is the fact that in the last decade, the average per capita GNP growth rate has been zero and was accompanied by a reduction in the productive infrastructure.

The involutionary character of the economic modernization implemented by the authoritarian regime has exhibited three characteristics in the Chilean social structure, which studies by Martínez, Tironi and Touraine have pointed out: (a) the nature and magnitude of social, economic and political exclusion created by the process of authoritarian restructuration; (b) the lack of organic connection among the social classes and sectors that have managed to survive this process; and (c) the impermeability and lack of absorptive capacity shown by the new economic, social and political structure with respect to the increase in the economically active population (cf. Martínez and Tironi 1986; Touraine 1987). These three characteristics have led to a deep destructuration of Chilean society while the impact of the monetarist restructuration on the previous social classes has not led to a consolidation of new social structures. The results of this impact continue to be seen by civil society as temporary and associated with the presence of the authoritarian regime. The destructuration of society contributes to a prolongation of the authoritarian system and a postponement of the democratic transition, but it does nothing to consolidate a new type of society which could guarantee the autonomous reproduction of the authoritarian political system and of the economic transformation which it has carried out. It is this articulation which explains in part the fact that the opposition parties have enormous difficulties in establishing relations with their social base and with civil society in general.

Finally, there are political/ideological reasons affecting the perception of the social and political conflict that characterized the period preceding the authoritarian regime, which generate a certain political immobilism and help prolong the dictatorship (cf. Foxley 1987 and Tironi 1986). This has taken the form of a debate on the kind of social and political concertation that could lead to a restoration of democracy and to its consolidation on the basis of a project for a viable governing regime. There are two variants which place the emphasis on the need for a social pact. The first of these emphasizes the need for a pact between workers and employers, regarding the formulation of a new alternative development model and the functions which the State should exercise in the future. The second gives more importance to the need for an agreement among political actors which would garantee the stability of the future democratic political system, beyond the corporative demands of the social actors. Both variants present difficulties (as was shown by e.g. Pinto 1983; Foxley 1985; and Tironi 1984). The idea of a pact between employers and workers comes up against the latter's low level of social representativeness, given the importance of the sectors that have been excluded from the process of economic development. Similarly, the idea of a pact among political actors is problematic because of the low level of representativeness of the party leaderships, the problem of the exclusion or incorporation of the Communist Party and that of the future role of the Armed Forces in the new democratic system.

Both alternatives are also confronted with another significant obstacle associated with factors of an ideological/political nature. The first of these has to do with the interpretation of the 1973 crisis generated by the exhaustion of the democratic arrangement that had characterized Chilean society between 1940 and 1973. This was expressed by the sense of being under threat which entrepreneurial sectors experienced as a result of the nationalizations which took place between 1970 and 1973, and by similar feelings among victims of the authoritarian regime who were confronted with a policy of large-scale social and political genocide. The second factor which stands in the way of the two alternatives already mentioned, has to do with fear that the victims of the authoritarian regime and the excluded sectors might wreak revenge upon their oppressors. For those who have collaborated with the regime, the main problem is how to distance themselves from a situation where they are regarded as accomplices to the act of political genocide. For the civilians who have supported the military regime, the problem is how to reconcile and to give public credibility to their new democratic vocation with their gratitude towards a regime that has allowed them to renegotiate credits or handed them back plants that had been nationalized. The third factor relates to the question of how to demilitarize Chilean politics after a period of fifteen years during which the regime has considered dissidence or opposition from civil society as a military problem. Finally, there is a central problem of how civil society could, in a stable manner, recover its political sovereignty, faced with a State which, in the past forty years, has played a crucial role in generating changes that have transformed society.

REFERENCES

Aldunate, A., Flisfisch, A. and Moulian, T. (1985) *Estudio sobre el Sistema de Partidos en Chile*, Santiago de Chile, FLACSO.

Arrate, J. (1985) *La Fuerza Democrática de la Idea Socialista*, Santiago/Barcelona: Ediciones Documentas/Ornitorrinco.

Bajoit, G. (1986) 'Mouvements Sociaux et Politiques au Chili 1983–1985', Problèmes d'Amérique Latine, 79: 5–27 Paris: La Documentation Française, Paris.

Bengoa, J. (1984) *El Campesinado Chileno después de la Reforma Agraria*, Santiago de Chile: SUR.

Cammack, P. (1985) 'The political economy of contemporary military regimes in Latin America: from bureaucratic authoritarianism to restructuring' in P. O'Brien and P. Cammack (eds) (1985) *Generals in Retreat. The Crisis of Military Rule in Latin America*, 1–34, Manchester: Manchester University.

Campero, G. (1984) *Los Gremios Empresariales en el Período 1970–1983: Comportamiento Sociopolítico y Orientaciones Ideológicas*, Santiago de Chile: Estudios ILET.

Canitrot, A. (1981) *Orden y Monetarismo*, Buenos Aires: Estudios CEDES.

Cardoso, F. H. and Reyna, J. L. (1968) *Industrialización, Estructura Ocupacional y Estratificación Social en América Latina*, Cuestiones de Sociología del Desarrollo, Santiago de Chile: Editorial Universitaria.

CEPAL (1982) *Las Transformaciones Rurales de América Latina: Desarrollo Social o Marginación?*, Santiago de Chile.

Cereceda, L. E. and Dahse, F. (1980) *Dos décadas de cambio en el agro Chileno*, Cuadernos del Instituto de Sociología, Santiago de Chile: Pontificia Universidad Católica.

Cerri, R. (1979) *Antecedentes acerca de la Concentración y Centralización Patrimonial en Chile*, Memoria de Prueba, Facultad de Ciencias Económicas y Administrativas, Santiago de Chile: Universidad de Chile.

Collier, D. (1979) *The New Authoritarianism in Latin America*, Princeton: Princeton University Press.

Corradi, J. E. (1985) *The Fitful Republic: Economy, Society and Politics in Argentina*, Boulder and London: Westview Press.

Cortazar, B., Foxley A. and Tokman, V. (1984) *Legados de Monetarismo, Argentina y Chile*, Buenos Aires: Ediciones Solar PREALC/OIT.

Cox Urrejola, S. (1979) 'Les depossédés de la campagne. Communautés indigenes, petits agriculteurs et paysans sans terre au Chili pendant le gouvernement militaire', thèse présenté pour le doctorat du troisième cycle à l'Université de la Sorbonne Nouvelle, Paris.

Dahse, F. (1979) 'El poder de los grandes grupos económicos nacionales', *Documento de Trabajo*, no. 18, Santiago de Chile: FLACSO.

ECLAC (1986) 'Development and Crisis in Latin America: 1950–84', in A. Maddison (ed.) (1986) *Latin America, The Caribbean and OECD. A Dialogue on Economic Reality and Policy Options*, 28–66, Paris: OECD.

Evers, T. (1979) *El Estado en la Periferia Capitalista*, Mexico: Siglo XXI Editores.

Fernández Jilberto, A. E. (1987) 'América Latina: la herencia estructural de los Estados Autoritarios', *Revista Sistema*, 79, July: 73–85.

Filgueira, C. and Geneletti, O. (1981) 'Estratificación y movilidad occupacional en América Latina', *Cuadernos CEPAL*, no. 39, Santiago de Chile.

Foxley, A. (1982) 'Experimentos Neoliberales en América Latina', *Colección Estudios CIEPLAN*, no. 7, Santiago de Chile.

Foxley, A. (1985) *Para una Democracia Estable*, Santiago de Chile: Editorial Aconcagua.

Foxley, A. (1987) *Chile y su Futuro. Un País Posible*, CIEPLAN, Santiago de Chile.

Frank, A. G. (1978) *l'Accumulation Dépendante*, Paris: Editions Anthropos.

Frias, P. (1983) 'Orientaciones y prácticas del movimiento sindical Chileno bajo el régimen militar (1973–1982)', dissertation doctorale en Sociologie, Université Catholique de Louvain.

Garcia, M. A. and Martins, A. J. A. (1985) *Autour du développement Latino-Américain. Etat Integration Société*, Institut du Sociologie, Brussels: Université Libre de Bruxelles.

Garretón, M. A. (1983) *El Proceso Político Chileno*, Santiago de Chile: FLACSO.

Garretón, M. A. (1985) *Dictaduras y Democratización*, Santiago de Chile: FLACSO.

Gomez, S., Arteaga, J. M. and Cruz, M. E. (1981) 'Cambios Estructurales en el Campo y Migraciones en Chile', *Documento de Trabajo*, no. 128, Santiago de Chile: FLACSO.

Gomez, S. (1980) 'Depués del Latifundio qué? (El caso Chileno)', *Documento de Trabajo*, no. 92, Santiago de Chile: FLACSO.

Hirschman, A. O. (1979) 'The turn to authoritarianism in Latin America and the search for its economic determinants', in D. Collier (ed.) (1979) *The New Authoritarianism in Latin America*, 66–98, Princeton: Princeton University Press.

Jarvis, L. (1985) *Chilean Agriculture under Military Rule*, Berkeley and Los Angeles: University of California Press.

Kirsch, H. W. (1977) *Industrial Development in a Traditional Society. The Conflict of Entrepreneurship and Modernization in Chile*, Gainesville: University Press of Florida.

Lagos, R. (1981) 'Le secteur emergent de la bourgeoisie', *Revue Amérique Latine*, no. 6, Paris.

Lagos, R. (1985) *Democracia para Chile. Proposiciones de un Socialista*, Santiago de Chile: Editorial Pehuen.

Larrain, C. P. (1987) *Estado y Fuerza de Trabajo en Chile 1974–1985*, Programa de Economía del Trabajo, Santiago de Chile: Academia de Humanismo Cristiano.

Maddison, A. (1986) *Latin America, The Caribbean and OECD. A Dialogue on Economic Reality and Policy Options*, Paris: OECD.

Marshall, J. and Romaguera, R. (1981) 'La evolución del empleo público en Chile, 1970–1978', CIEPLAN, *Notas Técnicas*, no. 26, Santiago de Chile.

Marshall, J. (1981) 'El gasto público en Chile: 1969–1979', *Estudios CIEPLAN*, no. 5, Santiago de Chile.

Martínez, J. and Tironi, E. (1982) 'La clase obrera en el nuevo estilo de desarrollo: un enfoque estructural', *Revista Mexicana de Sociología*, Vol. XLIV, no. 2: 453–80.

Martínez, J. and Tironi, E. (1983) 'Clase obrera y modelo económico. Un estudio del peso y la estructura del proletariado en Chile, 1973–1980', *Documento de Trabajo*, Santiago de Chile: SUR.

Martínez, J. and Tironi, E. (1984) 'La estratificación social en Chile', *Revista Pensamiento Iberoamericano*, no. 6, 133–45.

Martínez, J. and Tironi, E. (1986) 'Las clases sociales en Chile. Cambio y estratificación, 1970–1980', Santiago de Chile: Ediciones SUR.

Meller, P., Livacich, E. and Arrau, P. (1984) 'Una revisión del milagro económico Chileno (1976–1981)', *Estudios CIEPLAN*, no. 15, Santiago de Chile.

Moulian, T. and Vergara, P. (1979) 'Estado, ideología y políticas económicas en Chile: 1973–1978', *CIEPLAN*, Santiago de Chile.

Muñoz, O. (1986a) 'El papel de los empresarios en el desarrollo: enfoques, problemas y experiencias', *Estudios CIEPLAN*, no. 20, Santiago de Chile.

Muñoz, O. (1986b) 'Chile y su industrialización. Pasado, crisis y opciones', *CIEPLAN*, Santiago de Chile.

Nolff, M. (1965) 'Industria manufacturera', in *Geografía Económica de Chile*, 508–48, Santiago de Chile: Editorial Universitaria.

Nun, J. (1972) 'Sobrepoblación relativa, ejército industrial de reserva y masa marginal', *Revista Latinoamericana de Sociología*, no. 2, 47–65.

O'Brien, P. and Cammack, P. (1985) *Generals in Retreat. The Crisis of Military Rule in Latin America*, Manchester Latin American Studies, Manchester: Manchester University Press.

O'Donnell, G. (1979) 'Tension in the bureaucratic authoritarian state and the question of democracy', in D. Collier (ed.) (1979) *The New Authoritarianism in Latin America*, 285–318, Princeton: Princeton University Press.

O'Donnell, G. (1977) 'Reflexiones sobre las tendencias de cambio del Estado Burocrático Autoritario', *Revista Mexicana de Sociología*, XXXIX, 1: 325–39.

Ominami, C. (1986) *Le Tiers Monde dans la Crise*, Paris: Editions La Découverte.

Petras, J. (1969) *Politics and Social Forces in Chilean Development*, Berkeley/ Los Angeles: California University Press.

Pinto, A. (1983) 'Concensos, disensos y conflictos en el espacio democrático popular', *Revista Mensaje*, no. 319, Santiago de Chile.

Raczynski, D. (1978) 'El sector informal urbano: controversias e interrogantes', *Apuntes de CIEPLAN*, no. 13, Santiago de Chile.

Ramos, J. (1986) *Neoconservative Economics in the Southern Cone of Latin America 1973–1983*, Baltimore and London: Johns Hopkins University Press.

Ruiz-Tagle, J. and Urmeneta, R. (1985) *Los Trabajadores del Programa del Empleo Mínimo*, Programa de Economía del Trabajo, Academia de Humanismo Cristiano, Santiago de Chile.

Salazar, G. (1985) *Labradores, Peones y Proletarios*, Colección de Estudios Históricos, Santiago de Chile: Ediciones SUR.

Sanfuentes, A. (1984) 'Los grupos económicos: control y políticas', *Estudios CIEPLAN*, no. 15, Santiago de Chile.

Serra, J. (1974) *Desarrollo Latinoamericano. Ensayos Críticos*, Fondo de Cultura Económica, México.

Serra, J. (1979) 'Three mistaken theses regarding the connection between industrialization and authoritarian regimes', in D. Collier (ed.) (1979) *The New Authoritarianism in Latin America*, 99–163, Princeton: Princeton University Press.

Sigal, S. (1982) 'Sociologie du développement et sociologie des sociétés péripheriques', *Revue Tiers Monde*, XXIII(90): 397–406.

Slavinsky, Z. (1965) 'Los cambios estructurales del empleo en el desarrollo de América Latina', *Boletín Económico para América Latina*, X(2): 27–54.

Smith, B.H. (1982) *The Church and Politics in Chile, Challenges to Modern Catholicism*, Princeton: Princeton University Press.

Sunkel, O. (1979) 'The development of development thinking', in H. Villamil (1979) *Transnational Capitalism and National Development*, 108–126, Cincinnati: Harvest Press.

Tironi, E. (1984) *La Torre de Babel. Ensayos de Crítica y Renovación Política*, Santiago de Chile: Ediciones SUR.

Tironi, E. (1986) *El Liberalismo Real*, Santiago de Chile: Ediciones SUR.

Tokman, V. (1982) 'Desarrollo desigual y absorción del empleo. América Latina 1950–1980', *Serie de Trabajos Ocacionales*, no. 48, Santiago de Chile: PREALC.

Touraine, A. (1987) *Actores Sociales y Sistemas Políticos en América Latina*, Santiago de Chile: PREALC/OIT.

Urzua Valenzuela, G. (1986) *Historia Política Electoral de Chile*, Colección Documentos de Chile, Santiago de Chile: Fundación Friedrich Ebert.

Valenzuela, J. S. and Valenzuela, A. (1986) *Military Rule in Chile*, Baltimore: Johns Hopkins University Press.

Vega, H. and Ruiz-Tagle, J. (1982) *Informe Periódico Sobre la Situación Económica de los Trabajadores*, Programa de economía del Trabajo, Academia de Humanismo Cristiano, Santiago de Chile.

Vergara, P. (1982) 'Las transformaciones del estado Chileno bajo el régimen militar', *Revista Mexicana de Sociología*, XLIV(2), 413–52.

Vergara, P. (1984) *Auge y Caída del Neoliberalismo en Chile. Un Estudio Sobre la Evolución Ideológica del Régimen Militar*, Santiago de Chile, FLACSO.

Vergara, P. (1986) 'Changes in the economic functions of the Chilean state under the military regime', in J. S. Valenzuela and A. Valenzuela (eds.) (1986) *Military Rule in Chile*, 85–116, Baltimore: John Hopkins University Press.

Villamil, H. (1979) *Transnational Capitalism and National Development*, Cincinnati: Harvest Press.

Walker, I., *et al.* (1986) *Democracia en Chile. Doce Conferencias*, CIEPLAN, Santiago de Chile.

4

NEO-LIBERALISM AND THE DISMANTLING OF CORPORATISM IN AUSTRALIA

Ed Kaptein

INTRODUCTION

Under the successive Whitlam, Fraser and Hawke governments, Australia has been transformed from a corporatist and protected economy to an open economy in the neo-liberal mould. The transition has been a protracted process of trial and error which has not lacked political drama. Money capital (so central in the neo-liberal power bloc) in Australia as elsewhere has a very large foreign component. For this strongly transnational fraction of capital to gain ascendance on the domestic Australian scene it has therefore been necessary to construct a domestic support base for its 'neo-liberal' policies. That construction is not an easy task, nor is it without its internal contradictions. Neither has the transition been completed: present-day Australia is by no means a faithful copy of an ideal neo-liberal blueprint. But the main priorities of the country's current economic and social policies are in line with the ideological tenets of neo-liberalism and a new domestic power bloc has come to the fore to shape and carry out those policies. The replacement of Hawke by Keating (1991) signalled an intensification rather than a relaxation of these policies.

However, before we proceed to look at some of these developments in more detail, it is necessary to give some historical context. In the following section Australia's transition to neo-liberalism is therefore placed against the structural and institutional characteristics of the Australian economy and related to the worldwide trend from corporate liberalism to neo-liberalism.

An account of Australia's transition to neo-liberalism in the 1970s and 1980s is given in the third section. This includes a description of the construction of a domestic Australian support base for foreign money capital.

Finally, a brief epilogue attempts to determine the significance of the most recent developments in Australia, and particularly the replacement of Hawke by Keating.

STRUCTURAL CHARACTERISTICS OF THE AUSTRALIAN POLITICAL ECONOMY

For a more adequate understanding it is first desirable to place these developments against the background of the long- and medium-term structural processes shaping Australia's political and economic history in the twentieth century. In the capitalist era it is also necessary to place national political and economic processes in the context of the development of the capitalist 'world system' as a whole (Overbeek 1990: 11–34).

To provide such an integrated analysis of long-, medium- and short-term developments for Australia would be a substantial task which could not be attempted within the limited space of this Chapter. In this section we will therefore give only a brief account of the two most important longer-term factors which have affected Australia's transition to neo-liberalism, namely Australia's role as a primary exporter, and the particular relationship between capital and labour.

Australia's place in the international division of labour

The first of these factors is Australia's role as a supplier of agricultural and mineral resources to the world's more developed or more industrialized countries. The second factor is the class compromise between Australia's workers and capitalists in the domestic manufacturing industry which emerged in the first decade of Federation, i.e. in the early 1900s, and which can be seen as a device for redistributing part of the wealth generated by the 'leading' basic resource sector, which is strongly export-oriented, to Australia's capitalists and workers that produce predominantly for the domestic market.

The export of basic resources figures prominently on the credit side of Australia's balance of trade, whereas on the debit side the import of manufactured products prevails. The trading balance of many 'underdeveloped' countries shows a similar picture, but Australia has a much higher average income per head because the relationship between production (and export) of resources and population has, on the whole, been much more favourable than in the 'underdeveloped' countries. An important reason for this is that, at least until the beginning of the 1970s, steady – and often rapid – growth of the Australian population has been matched by successive growth waves in the export of resources.

After the initial establishment of a minimal infrastructure by convict labour, Australia took its place in the world market as a major supplier of wool.

A second major growth wave came with the discovery and exploitation of gold in the 1850s. In this decade Australia's population increased from 427,000 to 1.2 million people. This growth wave subsided at the end of the decade when the easily accessible alluvial gold was exhausted. Many of the 'diggers' went to the cities, whereas others became small farmers.

The next major development was a rapid increase in the export of wheat and meat. It was made possible by the clearing of large tracts of land for wheat farming, the availability of a railway transport network to carry the wheat to coastal cities for export and the development of refrigeration techniques. This wave of export growth started in the last quarter of the nineteenth century and continued until the First World War, with a temporary interruption by the agricultural and economic crisis of the 1890s which caused a sharp fall in the prices of agricultural (and mineral) resources and a slowdown of demand.

At the turn of the century Australia was one of the world's wealthiest countries in terms of average income per head, along with Argentina which had a very similar economy. During the depression of the inter-war years both exports and the growth of population slowed down, but in the post-war period rapid development occurred not only in the labour-intensive manufacturing and service industries but also in the capital-intensive basic resources sector. The favourable equation between population and production (and export) of resources was therefore maintained notwithstanding rapid population growth from 7 million in 1945 to 13 million in 1970.

Towards the end of the 1960s the growth in the export of resources developed into a major new growth wave or export boom which centred on the export of mineral resources, such as coal, iron ore and bauxite, to the fast-growing economies of the Pacific area and in particular to Japan. Rapid growth in the export of mineral resources was therefore accompanied by a shift in the geographical destination of Australia's mineral exports away from the traditional export markets of Europe – and in particular the UK – towards the countries of the

Pacific area. A similar shift also occurred in the export of agricultural resources and would be reinforced later on by Britain's joining of the EEC.

During the 1970s and 1980s the growth of Australia's resource export slowed down, whereas its manufacturing industries became more and more exposed to foreign competition, not in the least from the newly industrializing countries in the Pacific Basin. As population growth continued, the balance between resource production and export on the one hand and population on the other deteriorated and this contributed to a less favourable balance of trade. Australia was relegated to a lower ranking in the league table of the world's most affluent countries.

After the second oil shock of 1979, the Fraser government hoped that a major growth wave in the export of energy resources and energy-intensive products, such as aluminium, would reverse the emerging trend. The predicted energy export boom, however, failed to materialize, whereas the revenue from the existing export of resources went into decline because of lower world market prices for a number of important resources exported by Australia.

Australia's basic class compromise

The second structural factor which is important for an understanding of Australia's evolution during the 1970s and 1980s is the class compromise between capitalists in the domestic manufacturing industry and the industrial workers. This class compromise emerged in the first decade of Federation, i.e. in the first decade of the 1900s. To put it in perspective we briefly review Australia's economic evolution in the period from 1860 to 1900, i.e. from the end of the gold rushes to the formation of the Commonwealth of Australia as a Federation of six separate British colonies.

The gold rushes caused a considerable increase in Australia's population. Many of the 'diggers' eventually found their way into the coastal cities. The years from 1860 to 1890 were an economic boom period in Australia, during which these cities expanded to cater for returned miners, natural population growth and continuing immigration. A basic industrial structure was established, railways were laid to open up new agricultural areas and to provide urban transport.

During the 1880s there was a speculative urban land and building boom, stimulated by a large inflow of foreign capital, mostly of British origin. The boom collapsed at the end of the decade and the 1890s then became a decade of economic depression and stagnation with low activity in the building and construction industry and a sharp fall of the prices of agricultural products and minerals. A number of major confrontations between capital and labour took place, of which the most important ones were the shearers' strike in the pastoral industry and the dockers' strike in the maritime industry.

The period of economic and political turbulence of the 1890s and the steady improvements in the means of communications were important factors leading up to the federation of the six separate Australian States into the Commonwealth of Australia in 1901 and to the formation of national parties. In the first decade of the Commonwealth a national compromise between domestic capital and organized labour was then achieved. The institutions to support this class compromise remained substantially in place until the advent of the Hawke government in the 1980s.

The class compromise rested in the first instance on a trade-off between workers in the manufacturing industries and domestic manufacturing capital, in which the latter agreed to maintain a high standard of living for industrial workers, whereas the workers supported tariff protection for 'infant' manufacturing industry.

In giving shape to this compromise the workers were represented at the political level by the Australian Labor Party, which was formed in 1901 as a federation of the Labor parties of the individual States. The political representation of the domestic manufacturing class was through the Liberal Protectionists, one of the two initial national bourgeois parties.

The first federal governments rested on a coalition consisting of the ALP and the Liberal Protectionists. It was this coalition which institutionalized the class compromise between domestic manufacturers and workers in the manufacturing industry and extended its benefits to the working class as a whole through the acceptance of the notion of a 'minimum wage' to which all workers would be entitled. A legalistic system of compulsory conciliation and arbitration was established to determine periodically the minimum wage and to settle labour disputes.

The coalition between Labor and the Liberal Protectionists did not survive the first decade of Federation. It was succeeded by a first all-Labor government in 1910 which faced a united bourgeois opposition formed by the fusion of the Liberal Protectionists with the other bourgeois party, the Liberal Free Traders. The principles and institutions of the earlier class compromise, however, remained in place.

This specifically Australian class compromise can be seen as corporatist, in the sense that it is basically a compromise between two economic groups, i.e. industrial workers and manufacturing capital, which have opposite class interests. It is different in a number of important respects from the post-war 'corporate liberal' class compromise which has been the basis of the 'Keynesian era' in a number of key Atlantic Western countries and which has been analysed by van der Pijl (1984).

The corporate liberal class compromise has its basis at the industry level and relies on increases in industrial productivity (increase in 'relative surplus value') from which workers benefit directly through increased real wages and increased availability of cheap consumer goods produced with 'Fordist' methods and indirectly through social and other benefits dispensed by a Keynesian welfare state. The early Australian class compromise, on the other hand, rested on a direct political 'deal' at the national level between workers and capitalists in the domestic manufacturing industries.

From this first basic difference a number of important subsidiary differences follow. A necessary condition for the continued success of the Fordist class compromise is a high – and preferably growing – level of industrial productivity, especially in the mass consumer goods industries, so as to be able to increase (or at least maintain) real wages and other benefits to a degree sufficient to maintain social peace, while not jeopardizing the profits accruing to capitalists.

For the Australian-type of class compromise to work, on the other hand, it is necessary that the productivity and growth of the leading resource export sector is sufficient to allow real wages and other benefits to all workers, and not only those in the resource sector, to increase or at least stabilize at a high level. In Australia this condition was fulfilled during the post-war boom period. Australia experienced a healthy growth of the export of resources until the beginning of the 1970s. During the 1960s it became an important supplier of minerals and energy (such as coal and iron ore) to Japan and to other Pacific countries. There was also a strong expansion of Australia's protected domestic manufacturing industry. Although the methods of industrial organization and production used were, on the whole, relatively inefficient, some Fordist methods and practices were introduced, for example in the rather fragmented motor vehicle industry. The industrial expansion provided employment for a rapidly growing population and also provided subsidiary advantages in improving the 'economies of scale' in Australia's small – and geographically often segmented – industries and markets. During the post-war boom Australians were therefore able to partake in an increasingly 'Fordist' mode of consumption, without, however, sharing the social and economic conditions of the major Atlantic Fordist countries in all respects.

The first difference concerned the economic and political organization of the working class. Throughout the post-war boom the ALP remained a relatively 'old fashioned' and 'unreformed' social-democratic party. It had a strong traditionalist wing with important strongholds in craft-type unions, a militant left wing, and it lacked the major infusion of the 'new class' of highly educated workers and professionals which formed the social basis for the modernization of the Labor parties in the more 'advanced' Atlantic economies.

Gough Whitlam, who took over the leadership of the ALP in the late 1960s from his traditionalist predecessor Arthur Calwell, can be seen as a representative of this 'new class'. He attempted to reform the traditionalist and left stronghold of the Victorian branch of the ALP prior to the election of 1969, but was only partially successful.

A second difference between Australia and the more advanced Keynesian countries during the post-war 'boom' period was that it had a relatively underdeveloped – as well as highly fragmented and relatively poorly coordinated – Keynesian state. In a climate of rising expectations the relative backwardness of the welfare system and of certain public services, such as the lack of adequate sewerage in some of the rapidly expanding suburbs of Australia's major cities, was an important factor in the demise of the ruling conservative coalition and its succession by the Whitlam Labor government.

Having sketched some of the long term factors providing the context for Australian politics in the 1970s and 1980s, we can now move on to a more detailed account of those decades.

THE RISE OF NEO-LIBERALISM IN THE 1970s

The Whitlam experiment

Whitlam came to power in December 1972 after twenty-three years of uninterrupted conservative rule, at an unfortunate time. Having gained a mandate from the electorate for a programme of belated Keynesian reforms and nationalistic resource policies, he tried to implement this programme in a period when international capitalism was changing its priorities and the first attempts were made to reverse some of the achievements and policies of the post-war Keynesian welfare states. This period also saw the start of an anti-NIEO offensive by the major capitalist powers which has been highlighted in this volume by Fernández (Chapter 3) and Van der Pijl (Chapter 2). In these circumstances the nationalistic resource policies of the Whitlam government and in particular the attempt by its Minister Rex Connor to establish a direct financial link between (members of) the OPEC cartel and Australia, were bound to run into strong international opposition.

The Labor party, on coming to power, was still a relatively 'traditionalist' social-democratic party with a strong left wing. This increased the problems faced by the Whitlam government, because it led to policy differences between individual ministers which were skilfully exploited by the opposition.

The new government proposed a wide-ranging programme of reforms. Some of these reforms, such as a general non-contributory health insurance scheme, had a Keynesian flavour. Others were designed to increase Australia's share in the ownership of its mineral resources and to control the export prices of those resources, thus in effect allying the country to the progressive regimes in the Third World calling for a New International Economic Order (NIEO).

In the sphere of foreign relations, the new Prime Minister took pains verbally to reassure the US that his government would continue to be committed to the American alliance and would honour existing treaty relationships in ANZUS, but in effect he followed a far more independent line towards the US than his conservative predecessors. On coming to power in 1972 the Whitlam government withdrew Australia's forces from Vietnam and recognized the People's Republic of China. Labor also showed itself more inquisitive with respect to the operation of a number of important US bases in Australia than post-war conservative governments. The main tasks of these bases are in the field of communications and electronic surveillance, including support of US nuclear forces in case of war. Although they are nominally under joint control, the Australians have in effect very little say in their operation. The Australian-based activities of a number of US security agencies, including the CIA, also came under closer scrutiny. This caused great concern in Washington, culminating, according to one well-informed chronicler, into a full-scale 'security crisis' during the last few weeks of the Whitlam government (Kelly 1976: Chapter 5).

The Whitlam government introduced its economic reforms in a climate of rapidly rising inflation, which had domestic as well as external origins. The Whitlam Government fuelled the inflationary fires with big increases in public spending in order to finance its reformist programme and to honour its election promises. Generous wage and salary increases, originating in the public sector, spread very rapidly through the entire economy via Australia's institutionalized system of salary and wage fixing.

The Labor government ran into strong conservative opposition as soon as the outline of its reformist programme became clear. In due course the conservatives escalated their opposition into a full-scale and well-orchestrated campaign, built around a number of 'scandals' that were given extensive exposure in the highly monopolized and conservative media. The Murdoch press, though initially a supporter of the Whitlam government, was by then often in the lead. The effect of these 'scandals' was to destroy the credibility of a number of left-wing ministers and to reduce the electoral standing of the Labor government.

Prime Minister Whitlam reacted to these pressures with a number of policy reversals and minor and major cabinet reshuffles. In time most leading left-wing ministers were either dismissed or demoted and replaced by representatives of the right and centre factions of the Labor party. A brief account of two 'scandals' that were largely instrumental in sealing the fate of the Whitlam governnment is given below.[1]

In 1974–5 Treasurer and Deputy Prime Minister Dr Jim Cairns, an economist of Keynesian persuasion and leader of the Labor Party's left wing, proposed to combat rising unemployment and rising inflation with the standard Keynesian tools of an increase in public spending combined with price and income controls. The Australian Treasury, which has a strong free market orientation (its leading officials were early converts to monetarism), adopted an obstructionist posture to the proposals of their minister and all but refused to frame a budget along the lines favoured by Dr Cairns. When Cairns nevertheless persisted with his neo-Keynesian remedies for the economy, he was faced with a growing innuendo concerning his relations with a female staff member. Prime Minister Whitlam reacted by moving Cairns from the Treasury to the junior Environment Ministry. Within one month Cairns was dismissed from this new post after further 'revelations' in the media concerning 'improprieties' by Dr Cairns in his loan-raising activities during his period as Treasurer.

Real or imaginary improprieties concerning the raising of overseas' loans also led to the resignation, on 14 October 1975, of Labor's left-wing minister for Minerals and Energy, Rex Connor. Connor, the main architect of Labor's nationalistic resource policies, had an impressive grasp of his portfolio. He formulated a number of far-reaching reforms for the minerals and energy sector. But in carrying out these reforms he encountered strong opposition from mineral and energy interests and from the parliamentary opposition. Connor tried to speed up progress towards his goals – such as the construction of a government-owned intercontinental gas pipeline – by attempting to raise loans from OPEC sources. However, he failed to keep the Prime Minister and the Treasury fully informed of his negotiations, and acted through what used to be an unreliable London-based intermediary.

The conservatives were quick to capitalize on these mistakes. In October 1975 the intermediary, Mr Khemlani, was flown out to Australia by unknown sponsors – who used the good offices of the conservative Premier of the State of Queensland, Bjelke Petersen – and taken under the wings of a number of prominent Federal conservative politicians. The 'revelations' by Khemlani concerning Connor's loan-raising activities were given extensive media exposure and Prime Minister Whitlam dropped Connor from the Ministry. The opposition parties now used the 'Khemlani Affair' as a pretext for blocking the passage of the government's budget through the Senate.[2]

Ironically, the budget blocked by the opposition was in fact the 'responsible' budget which Bill Hayden, the new Treasurer and future Labor leader, had proceeded to construct along the monetarist lines favoured by the Treasury after Dr Cairns' removal from the Treasury post. Faced with a similar blockage of the budget in 1974 Whitlam had conceded to the opposition's demand for an early election, but this time, with the opinion polls showing a sharp drop in Labor's electoral support, he refused to do so and decided upon a test of strength with the opposition.

However, the Governor General Sir John Kerr, a former right-wing industrial Labor lawyer and Whitlam appointee, privately shared the opposition's objections. After nearly four weeks of mounting tension Kerr broke the deadlock by presenting the unsuspecting Gough Whitlam with a letter of dismissal, while simultaneously appointing Malcolm Fraser, the leader of the opposition, caretaker Prime Minister. After this event, known in Australia as the 'Kerr coup', the conservatives immediately allowed the passage of the blocked Labor budget through the Senate, thereby restoring the supply of funds to the government. In the general election held soon afterwards, the Fraser government was confirmed in office with a large majority.

Fraser's monetarism: a return to orthodoxy

During the Fraser period, from 1975 to 1983, the institutions of the Australian class compromise between domestic workers and manufacturers remained in place, but the economic conditions were no longer conducive to their use as an effective means of protecting the living standard of Australia's workers. The compromise became progressively undermined from two sides. Firstly, the wealth generated by the resource export sector and available for redistribution to the domestic sector was reduced, through a slowdown in the world economy and secondly, the protective tariff, the main mechanism for redistributing the mineral wealth, could no longer be relied upon to redistribute this wealth. The decline of the manufacturing sector brought about by increased foreign competition was reinforced by the restrictive 'monetarist' economic policies of the Fraser government. In fact, the Fraser government, guided by the Australian Treasury, proceeded to extend and deepen the monetarist policy initiated by Labor's Treasurer Bill Hayden. Monetary stability was given preference over 'Keynesian' goals such as full employment. Inflation, which had reached 17 per cent per annum under the Whitlam government, was attacked with the slogan 'fight inflation first'. The main policy tools used were restrictive budgetary policies and a reduction of real wages through less than full indexation. The value of the Australian dollar, which was fixed ('pegged') to a 'basket' of major currencies, was kept high. This made competition from imported products more effective, reduced Australia's exports and contributed to a rapid rise in unemployment.

Prime Minister Fraser indulged in strong anti-union rhetoric, in line with traditional conservative attitudes in Australia. He backed up his rhetoric with a number of legal and institutional measures, such as the establishment of an 'Industrial Relations Bureau', designed to outlaw certain types of union action such as secondary boycotts. Australia's powerful and well-organized trade union movement, however, suffered far more from the decline in employment and real wages brought about by the Fraser government's economic policies, than from Fraser's anti-union legislation. Not only the unions in the consumer goods industries (such as textiles, footwear and clothing), but also others such as the Australian Metal Workers' union (the union of skilled metal workers and key 'left' union), saw a weakening of their bargaining position during the Fraser governments as a result of Australia's industrial decline. This decline was not only due to Fraser's restrictive economic policies, but also to the structural changes in Australia's overseas' trade.

When Britain was Australia's major export market a large surplus in the trade with Britain was balanced by substantial 'invisible items' in the form of returns on British investments in Australia and shipping and insurance services rendered by Britain. In the post-war period Australia became more and more dependent, for the growth of its resource export, on the industrialized and industrializing countries of the Pacific area. But this required a quid pro quo in the form of improved access to Australian markets for the manufactured products of these countries. Large-scale export of basic resources was no longer compatible with the maintenance of high protective tariffs for Australia's domestic manufacturing industry. In the 1970s and 1980s Australia's light consumer goods industry in particular became more and more exposed to competition from the Newly Industrializing Countries (NICS) and went into progressive decline. This caused rapidly rising unemployment and its effects on the living standard of Australia's working class were reinforced by changes to the 'Keynesian' welfare measures introduced by the Whitlam government. For example, Whitlam's health insurance scheme was changed into a far less equitable one.

In the crucial resource sector the Fraser government removed, or weakened, the controls on the export prices of mineral and energy resources which had been brought in by the Labor government, and abolished a number of government authorities, such as the National Pipeline Authority, which could be seen as the beginning of a nationalized resource sector. The Fraser government also relaxed the restrictions on foreign ownership of enterprises in the basic resource sector and in the manufacturing industry introduced by the Whitlam government (Camilleri 1980: Chapter 3).

The foreign policies of the Fraser government extended the above pattern of a return to orthodoxy. Before the Whitlam era the attitude of conservative Australian governments towards its major US ally had often verged on the sycophantic as epitomized by Prime Minister Harold Holt's public declaration that he was 'All the way with LBJ', made during a visit to Washington in the late 1960s. After the Whitlam intermezzo, Fraser steered Australia's foreign policy back into charted waters by frequently emphasizing the value of the American alliance and the ANZUS relationship as an insurance against the Soviet threat which, in Fraser's view, was mounting because of a perceived build-up of Soviet naval power in the Indian ocean (ibid.: 37–8).

The critics of the Fraser government came from the right as well as from the left of the political spectrum. On the right ideology-conscious neo-liberals were the most vocal. They accused the Fraser government of failing to develop a comprehensive 'strategic' concept for its policies. The neo-liberal critique was formulated most clearly by – or on behalf of – a number of powerful foreign companies, which can be seen as testimony to the weakness of domestic Australian capital and its growing comprador status. Companies in the minerals and energy sectors were prominent amongst the corporate critics. They were supported by a number of large Australian mining firms such as BHP and one or two major banks.

For one, the Shell Company of Australia, a member of the Royal Dutch/Shell group and Australia's leading oil marketer,[3] expressed its concern about Fraser's policies in the form of a study of the Australian economy and its prospects by a number of neo-liberal academics which it sponsored (Kasper *et al.* 1980). A number of Shell Australia's top executives contributed actively to the work and discussions of the neo-liberal academics. In their study, dedicated posthumously to Adam Smith, the authors concluded that Fraser's economic policies lacked a clear strategic concept. They identified a number of road-blocks which would need to be removed if Australia was to have a more efficient market economy. These road-blocks included an inefficient manufacturing industry (which is rather broadly-based, but continued to be highly dependent on tariffs and other forms of protection), an institutionalized system of wage and salary fixing (which makes Australia highly inflation prone), and an over-regulated financial system including a 'pegged' exchange rate.

The Australian economy and its institutions were also critically examined in a study by the American 'futurologist', and director of the Hudson Institute in Tokyo, Herman Kahn (Kahn and Pepper, 1980). The large foreign and Australian resource companies, which were prominent amongst the financiers of Kahn's study, included Shell Australia and Conzinc Riotinto of Australia, the Australian subsidiary of the UK mining giant Rio Tinto Zinc. In their study Kahn and Pepper focused on Australia's economic role in the Pacific Basin. They arrived at the conclusion that Australia should specialize in the supply of basic resources to the highly industrialized and industrializing countries of the region, i.e. to Japan and the NICs (South Korea, Singapore, Hong Kong, Taiwan). This would in turn require that the traditional Australian aim of maintaining a strong and broadly based manufacturing industry be abandoned. Such a broadly-based industry could only be maintained behind high protective barriers which is not acceptable to Australia's trading partners in the Pacific region that are anxious to secure improved access to Australia's markets. Australia should therefore supplement the export of mineral and agricultural resources with the export of selected high technology products. A logical choice, in Kahn's view, because of Australia's relatively high labour cost and good educational infrastructure. Together with a burgeoning basic resources sector and an expanded domestic service industry, such a 'high tech' strategy would, in Kahn's opinion, be able to ensure a high level of employment and wealth in Australia. For this strategy to work, according to Kahn, it is a *sine qua non* that Australians abandon their hedonistic 'post-industrial' lifestyle and return to the work ethic. In Kahn's study the ethical conservatism which is such an important ingredient of the neo-liberal ideology, takes the form of a critique of the 'lazy Australian'.

On the left of the political spectrum the ALP remained shell-shocked for a considerable period of time after the 'Kerr coup' and the defeat of the Whitlam government. The most effective opposition to the Fraser government from the left came from non-parliamentary forces. A strong movement against the mining and export of uranium developed; it staged large demonstrations and was supported by Australia's well-organized environmental movement. In time the movement broadened out into opposition against any application of nuclear technology, including military, and against the US bases on Australian soil which would play a vital role in any future nuclear war. The opposition against uranium mining caused the Fraser government to have more regard for the safe operation of the uranium industry and for protection of the fragile environment in which the most important uranium mines are situated, than would have been the case otherwise. As a result of considerable pressure from its rank and file the Labor party included a ban on the production and export of uranium in its 'platform'. In the higher echelons of the party firm support for the ban was however largely restricted to the left wing.

While the Fraser government was digesting the neo-liberal critique of its policies, the price of oil doubled in the wake of the Iranian revolution of 1979. To Fraser and his government this raised the spectre of a new wave of economic growth caused by the export of energy resources and energy-intensive products such as aluminium. The timing of such an 'energy boom' would be very opportune for the Fraser government as its restrictive economic policies were causing growing unemployment, a decline in the standards of living the working class and consequently a decline in the government's electoral stocks.

The forthcoming election in 1980 provided Fraser with the incentive to publish exaggerated estimates of the economic effects of the 'energy boom'. The current economic problems facing the country would soon be over and Australia would be 'The Lucky Country' once again. In an atmosphere of growing euphoria a number of academic economists perceived only one potential problem with respect to the boom: how to cope with the large surpluses on the balance of payments and the resulting upward pressure on the Australian dollar.

Fraser successfully rode the wave of the predicted energy boom to his third electoral victory, but there was a heavy price to pay. Because the government itself had endorsed the extremely optimistic estimates of the employment effects of the energy boom, it became impossible to keep the lid on wage increases, and the inflation rate hit double figures early in 1983. With the global economy sliding into a recession and oil prices falling, it became clear that the predicted energy boom would fail to materialize or, in any case, would be of much more modest proportions than predicted earlier.

Prime Minister Fraser had therefore every reason to be concerned again about his election prospects. This time the concern was about the forthcoming 1983 elections. Fraser's reaction was to abandon budgetary restraint and to attack inflation with a twelve-months' wage freeze. But thereby he jettisoned his monetarist policy concept in an attempt to save his political skin. The result was a severe loss of credibility. Neo-liberal critics considered that their earlier judgement – that the Fraser government lacked a consistent economic strategy – was confirmed by the government's opportunistic actions.

Against the background of Australia's history it is understandable that Prime Minister Fraser pinned his hope for Australia's economic revival on a new growth wave in the export of resources. But Fraser and his advisers made a serious error of judgement by failing to recognize that the conditions in the world economy were no longer conducive to rapid growth in the basic resource sector. Neither side of politics in Australia had a consistent economic strategy at this stage, but Fraser's error of judgement did provide an opportunity for Labor to re-assume centre stage in Australian politics.

Bob Hawke takes over and mortgages Australia

The obverse side of the Fraser government's mounting economic and political problems was a mood of growing optimism in the Labor party. This optimistic mood was enhanced by Australia's leading newspapers as they began seriously to discuss Labor's chances of winning the forthcoming elections.

Within the Labor party, the dramatic dismissal of the Whitlam government initiated a long process of self-examination, as a result of which the party moved steadily further towards the right. Gough

Whitlam continued as stop-gap leader until the 1977 election and then handed over to Bill Hayden, the architect of the 'monetarist' budget of the latter days of the Whitlam government. Hayden adopted the cautious but unimaginative strategy of projecting a 'responsible image' towards the electorate (fiscal and otherwise) in the hope of thereby eradicating the memories of the 'scandals', 'extravagance' and 'incompetence' of the Whitlam government. This hope proved to be vain and in 1980 Labor lost the third election in succession.

At the end of the 1970s and beginning of the 1980s Federal Labor politics was dominated by the leadership contest between Bill Hayden and Bob Hawke. Hawke wielded a great deal of personal power as president of the ACTU, the Australian Council of Trade Unions, a position he had occupied since 1969.

The move into the parliamentary arena therefore represented a considerable risk to Hawke, as he had much to lose in case of failure. He finally made his long contemplated move during the 1980 Federal election and then served his parliamentary apprenticeship during the third Fraser government in the role of Shadow Minister for Industrial Relations. In that period he also increasingly spoke out on national issues. The themes emphasized by Hawke were the need for all Australians to work together (the 'consensus theme') and the need to modernize the industrial and government structures. In Australia the division of powers between the States and the Federation is heavily weighted towards the former and this was seen by Hawke as detrimental to the development of strong and consistent national policies.

In his shadow portfolio of Industrial Relations Hawke worked with the staff of the ACTU on the development of an 'Accord' which was negotiated and agreed between the industrial and political wings of the Labor movement (the ACTU and the ALP respectively). The intention was that, with Labor in office, the Accord would be broadened into a tripartite understanding between government, trade unions and employers.

Labor's revival was initiated by a series of wins in State elections from the late 1970s onwards. This brought a new generation of well educated Labor leaders to power to replace the old guard Labor politicians and increased Labor's self-confidence. In the run-up to the 1983 election the Federal ALP then moved further to the right by dropping the socialization of strategic sectors of the economy from its platform. The party also decided to honour existing uranium export contracts and to allow a limited expansion of the uranium industry.

With these contentious elements removed from its platform, a number of leading newspapers, including Rupert Murdoch's *The Australian*, started to argue that Labor could look forward with confidence to the coming elections provided it replaced the incumbent Federal leader Bill Hayden by Bob Hawke. Opinion polls were published to show that Bob Hawke was a great deal more popular with the electorate than his rival Hayden. Hawke was in fact trusted by the ruling class because of his emphasis on the consensus theme and he could be expected to have a much firmer grip on Australia's trade unions than his rival Hayden. The replacement of Hayden by Hawke therefore put the finishing touch on the ALP's grooming for office prior to the 1983 election.

Under the influence of this media campaign a sufficient number of Labor parliamentarians switched their support from Hayden to Hawke for the latter to fight and win the 1983 election for Labor. Eight years after the Whitlam defeat a nervous Labor party was back in office under a popular – and populist – leader, but a leader with a sharply different political agenda.

One of Hawke's first measures was to tighten cabinet decision-making in order to prevent the dangerous ministerial solo performances which had played havoc with the Whitlam government. The Treasury, which had proved to be a high risk area in the Whitlam days, was entrusted to Paul Keating, a young man in his thirties and leader of the party's right wing with a reputation of being one of the party's most astute politicians. Keating did not have formal training in economics but was very quick to adopt the language – and many of the ideas – of his leading Treasury officials. During the Fraser period these officials had based their advice on monetarist and neo-liberal doctrines. They now continued this practice under the Hawke government.

The Hawke government took early steps to review and liberalize Australia's financial system which continued to be fairly tightly regulated. A blueprint for its liberalization was provided by the Campbell report (Australia 1982), which had been commissioned by the Fraser government. Keating accepted many of the report's recommendations, and a number of foreign banks were given licences to operate in the domestic market as part of an extensive reform package. One effect of the liberalization was to increase the pressure on the Hawke government to float the Australian dollar. In December 1983, Treasurer Keating eventually yielded to the pressure.

The main problem faced by the successive Hawke governments in the economic policy area was an enormous growth in Australia's foreign debt. Australia's foreign debt increased from a very modest amount at the end of the 1970s to a level of Aus$108 billion in 1988–9, making Australia one of the world's most heavily indebted countries. This could not have occurred without the liberalization of Australia's financial system, but the reasons for the growth of the national debt are complex. The most important factors were:

1   the aborted 'energy boom' of the Fraser government, the investments for which had been obtained from overseas sources in the form of loan capital. In consequence, Australia's foreign indebtedness increased substantially, without a commensurate increase in the ability to service this debt through an increase in exports;

2   the depreciation of the Australian dollar with respect to the currencies of its major trading partners. Initially the value of the Australian dollar held up quite well, but in 1985–6 there was a series of sharp falls of the dollar amounting to a net depreciation of 30 per cent. Since most of Australia's foreign debt was in foreign denominations, the net effect of the depreciation was a substantial increase in the Australian dollar equivalent of Australia's debt servicing commitments;

3   the decline of Australia's terms of trade over the period 1983–6 of around 20 per cent (Indecs Economics: 124), contributing to a further increase of the payments deficit;

4   de-industrialization, which occurred as a result of the Fraser policies and which the Hawke governments had not done enough to reverse, led to a lack of domestic supply of consumer and capital goods, and thus to a still more rapid deterioration of the current account and a further impetus to the growth of the foreign debt.

The 1980s were not the first episode of a large-scale inflow of loan capital into Australia. During the late 1960s and early 1970s too, many Australians were concerned about the rapidly growing foreign control of their mining and manufacturing industry. Foreign control in the mineral sector increased from 36.8 per cent in 1963 to 58.1 per cent in 1968 (Camilleri 1980: 16). However, if we compare foreign capital investment in Australia in the 1960s with that of the 1980s, then important differences can be perceived.

In the 1960s and early 1970s a large proportion of foreign capital came in the form of equity capital. This increased foreign control, but there was also a substantial increase in Australia's productive capacity in the mineral as well as manufacturing industries. Australia's balance of payments improved substantially during the 1960s and this was due, in no small measure, to the export-enhancing and import-replacing effects of foreign investment. By the end of the 1960s the current account was showing a substantial and growing surplus.

However, during the 1980s, a large proportion of the foreign loans was used for speculative and asset rearranging purposes rather than for productive investments. The net effect of the loans, while they helped to finance Australia's large current account deficits, was to worsen Australia's balance of payments position in the longer term, because the growing burden of debt service was not offset by a commensurate increase in Australia's capacity to service the debt.

Foreign capital has been borrowed by large and small capitalists and by governments and instrumentalities of the six Australian States, but the operations of a number of flamboyant entrepreneurs such as Alan Bond, Christopher Skase and Robert Holmes a'Court have attracted most of the limelight. These entrepreneurs have used enormous amounts of foreign money to build their conglomerates. They have done so largely through the takeover of existing firms rather than through investment in new production capacity. As a testimony to the economic and political importance of the media in Australia a number of these entrepreneurs have also acquired substantial interests in Australia's commercial media and especially in TV channels.

By the turn of the decade, a number of the conglomerates were facing serious financial difficulties, while some, such as Robert Holmes a'Court and Alan Bond, had already succumbed to financial problems. In their fall, the lenders also endanger the Australian and foreign banks which provided the loans without adequate security. The most serious problems so far have arisen in the State of Victoria, where the government-owned State Bank has engaged in a risky lending policy stimulated by the liberal availability of foreign loan capital, lack of adequate banking controls, and a desire to keep up with other banks in their frantic lending operations. The total potential exposure of the State Bank to losses because of bad debts is estimated to be of the order of Aus$1.1 billion, whereas the potential losses to the banking sector in Australia as a whole are estimated to be more than ten times this amount (*The Age* 19 February 1990). The losses to the banks as a result of problems faced by the Bond Corporation alone could be as high as Aus$880 million. There are a number of borrowers which account for even larger potential losses to the banking system. *The Age* concluded as follows:

The new entrants into corporate lending – the new foreign banks, the banks which evolved from building societies and the state

banks – tended to take the biggest risks. Under financial deregulation, with instant and unrestricted access to overseas funds, the
banks effectively had unlimited deposits. They competed to lend
to over-borrowed, cashflow-deficient companies, without adequate security. (*The Age*, 19 February 1990)

The foreign equity investments of the 1960s had a stabilizing
mechanism built into them in the sense that declining export revenue,
e.g. because of a slump in world commodity markets, would be compensated, at least in part, by reduced profit remittances to foreign capitalists. Such a stabilizing mechanism was entirely absent from the
foreign borrowings of the 1980s which had to be serviced regardless of
the profitability of the enterprises which they helped to finance. It
appears that the losses because of bad debts will largely be absorbed by
the Australian banking system, including Australian subsidiaries of
foreign banks, and that they will not reduce Australia's growing foreign
debt to a significant extent.

In summary, we conclude that the investment of loan capital of the
1980s appears to be a more effective means of withdrawing an economic surplus from Australia than the equity investment of the 1960s:
by 1988–9 Australia's debt service ratio had reached 17.6 per cent and
was nearing Latin American proportions.

Hawke's Accord with the trade unions: formulating a neo-liberal accumulation strategy

As in Latin America and elsewhere, dealing with an increasing debt
implies dealing with organized labour: this deal was to be found in the
'Accord'.

Australia's trade union movement is powerful, in terms of a high
degree of union membership, but the movement is highly fragmented as
it consists of a large number of individual unions, many of which are
organized on a 'craft' principle. This form of organization gives rise to a
fair number of disputes between unions over the demarcation of jobs of
their members. It is one of the roles of the ACTU, the Australian
Council of Trade Unions, to mediate between individual unions in
disputes of this type.

A second role of the ACTU is to co-ordinate the unions' responses
to the macroeconomic policies of the government of the day. Before the
advent of the Accord between the government and the trade unions this
included the defence of general nationwide wage claims in hearings of

Australia's wage setting body, the Federal Conciliation and Arbitration Commission.

During a Labor government the problem of co-ordination of the policies of individual unions *vis-à-vis* the government is complicated by the fact that most trade unions are not only members of the ACTU, but also 'members' of the ALP. Up to 60 per cent of the votes cast at the ALP's policy-making congresses are union block votes. The size of the block vote of an individual union depends on the size of its membership. The structure of the labour movement in Australia thus closely resembles that in Britain (cf. Overbeek 1990, *passim*).

During the Whitlam government, the trade unions, led by Hawke in his capacity of President of the ACTU, had insisted on their independence and defended the real wages of their members while the government's priorities were shifting in the direction of wage 'moderation' in order to control the rapidly rising rate of inflation. This experience was probably relevant for the initial conception of the Accord. During the Hawke government the Accord developed, in close liaison with the leadership of the ACTU, into an effective tool for 'disciplining' the trade union movement and for making its policies subservient to the macroeconomic policy objectives of the Labor government.

Maintenance of real wages and wage increases in case of increased productivity were central to the initial concept of the Accord as agreed between the ACTU and the ALP before the elections of 1983, and explain why the majority of Australia's trade unions endorsed the Accord. Planning agreements along the lines first developed by the British Labour left during the Callaghan government were a second important element. Sections of the trade union movement such as the influential Australian Metalworkers Union saw in the planning agreements a means of reinvigorating Australia's industry and combating employment. They would be negotiated between unions and management at the plant or industry level. The initial Accord also had a section on the 'social wage', i.e. improved welfare benefits for employed and unemployed members of the working class. Under certain conditions the unions would consider a trade-off between the social wage and the money wages of their members. It will be clear from the foregoing that in its initial form the Accord, to which the ALP would be committed on coming to office, was based on a Keynesian rather than a monetarist or 'neo-liberal' policy concept.

Shortly after coming to office, in July 1983, Prime Minister Hawke organized a tripartite 'Economic Summit' to obtain the consent of

Australia's employer organizations for the Accord. But although the employers were happy to endorse Hawke's consensus principle, implying that disputes between labour and capital should preferably be settled by means of negotiations and not by strikes or other forms of conflict, they did not endorse the principle of real wage maintenance, i.e. the full indexation of wages for rises in prices.

A first test for the Accord came when the Hawke government began to tackle the rate of inflation of 11.5 per cent. To bring this down the ACTU agreed to forgo wage rises related to productivity increases during the first two years of operation of the Accord and to drop wage claims following from the price increases during the last year of the Fraser government (1982). A further 2.5 per cent reduction of the present wage claim was achieved by a redefinition of the consumer price index, while future claims would be reduced by an agreement that consumer price-related wage rises would be granted every six months instead of every quarter. The net effect of this 're-interpretation' of the Accord was not only a reduction in the rate of inflation from 11.5 per cent in 1982–3 to 5.1 per cent by the end of 1984, but also a substantial increase in the share of profits in Australia's national income at the expense of wage and salary earners.

A further redistribution of national income in favour of profits occurred as a result of the devaluation of the Australian dollar by 30 per cent in 1985–6 which, the government stipulated, was not to be followed by wage rises to compensate for the rise in domestic prices by 4 per cent which would result from the devaluation. The Accord was modified accordingly and came to be known as Accord Mark II.

We have seen that in its original form the Accord included the negotiation of planning agreements between unions and employers at the plant or industry level to improve the viability and productivity of Australia's industries. In this form the planning agreements were not very successful, but Accord Mark III, agreed between the government and the unions in March 1987, proposed an alternative consisting of what was termed 'award restructuring'. This amounted to a redefinition of the conditions of labour in individual industries or plants which would be carried out under the aegis of Australia's Conciliation and Arbitration Commission, which was renamed the Industrial Relations Commission to reflect this new task.

Mathews (1989) described the process of award restructuring and the rationale behind it as a tool for achieving a more flexible labour market, in line with the policies being advocated by the OECD. But whereas the British and US models of labour market restructuring depend on a bifurcation of the labour force of an enterprise into a core of skilled staff and a flexible pool of semi-permanent or contract staff, the award restructuring approach is in Mathews' view inspired by Japanese and Swedish models in which an attempt is made to achieve the goal of greater 'flexibility' of labour markets within the context of existing forms of unionization by training and retraining of the present work-force. Unions would retain control over their members – and would be able to protect them – as the restructuring proceeded.[4]

In line with this new approach it was agreed that wage rises would in future be granted in two parts or 'tiers'. The first would be a general wage increase, based on the principle of partial rather than full indexation. Initially the first tier wage rise would be 4 per cent as compared with a rate of inflation of 9 per cent. Second tier rises would depend on increases in productivity in individual sectors of the economy, with the understanding that the government would be entitled to place a 'cap' on total wage rises.

The Accord in its third incarnation combined centralized control of national wage claims with flexibility to allow for a different evolution of wages in different labour markets. It can be seen as an important first step in the direction of the neo-liberal model of flexible labour markets. The particular approach chosen can also be considered as a concession to trade unions. While the unions, through their endorsement of the Accord Mark III, accepted the need for retraining and redefinition of job demarcation to make labour markets more 'flexible', they retained a large measure of control over their current members. If the proposed award restructuring is successful it seems almost inevitable that in time the boundaries between unions will be reviewed. It is likely that a reform of the existing fragmented structure of Australia's trade union movement will then be the next item on the agenda, much as it has been in Thatcherite Britain (Overbeek 1990: 187–93, 211–13).

The Hawke government has indeed used the Accord not only as a tool to further its macroeconomic policy objectives, but also as a means of imposing a degree of 'discipline' and coherence on Australia's fragmented trade union movement. That this was indeed seen as a function of the Accord became clear from the vigorous actions taken by Federal and State Labor governments against unions that pursued wage claims or policies outside the context of the Accord.

One 'maverick' union of this type was the Builders' Laborers Federation (BLF), the Australia-wide union of unskilled building workers with its militant tradition. The BLF showed itself openly critical of the Accord and was 'deregistered', which meant that its members could now be 'poached' by a more 'moderate' union in the building industry (the BWIU) which was prepared to toe the line of the ACTU. When members of the deregistered BLF who did not join the BWIU continued to show up at building sites in the State of Victoria, they were forcibly removed by State police, acting on the instructions of the State Labor government. At the same time Norman Gallagher, the union's militant national secretary, was jailed because of an alleged impropriety in his financial dealings.

In a more recent case of a lengthy strike of the pilots of Australia's two major domestic airlines, the Federal Labor government actively organized strike-breaking measures (such as the use of military aircraft) and also supported the issue of writs by one of the airlines against individual pilots for loss and damage suffered.

These government actions to enforce the discipline of the Accord appear to have had the full support of the ACTU and of the majority of its affiliates. A few dissenting voices could, however, be heard in the Labor movement, and one of these belonged to Gordon Bryant, a former Federal Minister in the Whitlam government in whose opinion

> The Accord ... has now become a bludgeon to keep dissenters in line. What is no more than a vehicle for a restriction of the workers' share of the profits from their work has become an article of faith, a piece of monetarist mysticism and Messrs Hawke and Kelty (the secretary of the ACTU, E.K.) in particular denounce the backsliders with all the vehemence and self-righteousness with which a medieval cardinal sent heretics to the stake.

> (Bryant 1989)

In summary, the general drift of the economic programme on which Labor came to office in 1983, including the initial version of the Accord, was Keynesian rather than monetarist in inspiration and in that sense an anachronism. This became apparent very quickly when Labor was faced with the responsibilities and pressures of office and the advice of a monetarist-leaning bureaucracy. In time the underlying Keynesian concepts of Labor's programme were replaced by the wholesale and rather indiscriminate adoption of neo-liberal ideology and policy prescriptions.

What Labor was doing in fact was to remove all defensive barriers to the large-scale penetration of foreign money capital, while the Accord functioned as a device for gaining the acquiescence of the organized working class for this policy.

There can be little doubt that the present fragmented structure of Australia's trade union movement is not conducive to industrial efficiency. Having admitted this, however, one should question whether neo-liberal methods of restructuring Australia's labour markets will be sufficient to achieve the desired goals of industrial revival and of propelling the manufacturing industry into the 'high tech' age. Australia's industrial structure has only limited depth, especially with respect to the production of capital goods. An interventionist industrial policy would seem to be required, at least in the early stages of industrial modernization. This policy should include selective planning to avoid fragmentation and to channel efforts in the direction where success is most likely. Without such interventionist measures the most important net effect of 'award restructuring' may well be a substantial further weakening of the trade union movement with little effect to show for it in terms of rejuvenation of Australia's industrial structure.

The formation of a neo-liberal power bloc

The Hawke government's approach to industry policy only confirmed that it had been brought under the spell of the neo-liberal market ideology. We have already seen that, through far-reaching liberalization of Australia's financial system and removal of adequate controls on lending by the banking system, the Hawke government and Treasurer Keating assisted actively in shackling Australia to a crippling debt burden. Financial and industry policy (or the absence of the latter) are two aspects of the Hawke government's economic strategy which have mutually reinforced each other with respect to their effect on the burgeoning overseas debt.

After the debt crisis of 1982 international money capital was looking for alternative and safer havens. The 'paper empires' and conglomerates, of which the Bond corporation is the most notorious example, can, however, be seen as more than convenient receptacles for foreign money capital. As a form of investment they are perfectly compatible with an economic strategy emphasizing the role of resource producer, because they fail to contribute to broadly-based industrial development.

After the short and aborted Keynesian experiment of the Whitlam government, international money capital faced the problem of how to construct a domestic Australian basis for its neo-liberal policies. The Fraser government failed to develop and pursue a consistent neo-liberal strategy, but from the account given above it can be seen that the policies and attitudes developed by the Hawke government fitted the requirements of foreign money capital almost perfectly. Which groupings and class fractions in Australia made up the emergent class coalition that supported and promoted the Hawke government's neo-liberal policies, and thereby facilitated the massive penetration of foreign money capital?

The first and perhaps most important element in this 'coalition' are the state employees and urban professionals, who tend to have a technocratic attitude to policy-making and are strongly influenced by ideologies of the day as part of their socialization into professional groups. Most of the ALP's leading parliamentarians, ministers and staff members belong to this 'new class' as does a substantial proportion of Australia's top trade union leaders, including staff members of the ACTU. Members of the 'new class' are also well represented in the leading layers of the State and Federal bureaucracies.

The second element of the support base of foreign money capital consists of Australian entrepreneurs and conglomerate builders that have taken advantage of the liberal availability of foreign capital to build and expand their empires and to promote their ventures, which were largely of a speculative or 'asset-rearranging' type.

A third element of the coalition which has supported the Hawke government's neo-liberal policies are the leading foreign and domestic corporations in the mineral sector. These corporations have, in the main, given strong support to – and some have even tried to accelerate – the de-industrialization policies of the Fraser government which the Hawke government failed to reverse. Integration of Australia within the economy of the Pacific Basin is the main theme and objective of these companies. This has been supported, perhaps as a concession to national pride, with an objective of developing those 'high-tech' and high labour cost industrial activitites for which Australia is deemed to have a 'comparative advantage'. Some of the country's service industries, such as the tourist industry, can also be regarded as part of the coalition which has supported the policies of the Hawke government. Active support for national and international tourism has been a feature of the policies of State and Federal Labor governments throughout the 1980s.

The domestic Australian banking sector, while generally supportive of neo-liberal concepts, was not in the forefront of the moves towards financial liberalization. This is understandable as liberalization meant a substantial increase in foreign competition. Most domestic banks and financial institutions had engaged in imprudent lending operations –

and had joined the scramble for foreign funds – in order to retain their share of a banking sector which was no longer subject to any effective form of regulation or government supervision. A number of Australian banks and financial institutions are now paying the price for these policies in the form of severe financial difficulties. The worst problems appeared in Victoria where a subsidiary of the State Savings bank, Tricon, faced bankruptcy. The State Bank of Victoria, the major shareholder in Tricon, suffered large losses, not only because of its interest in Tricon, but also because of bad debts in its own lending operations (*The Age*, 19 February 1990). Traditionally, i.e. before the advent of financial deregulation, the State Bank had been the main bank for Victoria's small savers. The State Premier of Victoria, John Cain, expressed his intention to protect these small savers by supplying the State bank with additional government funds, i.e. by socializing part of its losses.

In the construction of a domestic support base for its policies and priorities foreign money capital has received substantial ideological support from Australia's economic and financial bureaucracies. This has already been highlighted in the foregoing with respect to the Federal Treasury, but important supportive roles have also been played by State bureaucracies, for instance by the economic bureaucracy of the State of Victoria. The specific role of these bureaucracies has been to devise specific neo-liberal policies for their political masters and to elaborate the 'free market' ideologies in terms of which these policies, such as the expanded 'free enterprise' role of the State Bank, have been justified.

The above account of the construction of a domestic Australian support base for foreign money capital would not be complete without highlighting the extraordinarily important role of the media in the political process. We have seen that the media played a critical role at two important junctures: in 1975 by providing extensive exposure of the 'scandals' pertaining to key government ministers, which helped to undermine the Whitlam government, and in 1982 by organizing a 'popularity contest' between the two contending leaders of the ALP, based on opinion polls from which Hawke emerged as the clear winner.

In this context it is also important to note that a number of the leading conglomerate builders, whose enterprises have functioned as receptacles for foreign money capital, acquired an important stake in Australia's media. These conglomerate builders showed a keen appreciation of the fact that Australia's highly monopolized media chains are not only important concentrations of economic power, but that they also yield considerable political influence.

The drawbacks of the unconditional surrender to neo-liberalism and the international class forces which support it are now becoming increasingly apparent. Serious difficulties in Australia's banking system due to reckless lending policies have eroded much of the electoral support for the Labor party.

Prime Minister Hawke and his government were therefore extremely lucky to have narrowly survived the March 1990 Federal election. A full analysis of the result could well confirm that crucial preferences directed to Labor by the environmental movement have saved the day for Bob Hawke. These preferences have been given not as an endorsement of Labor's policies, but as a means of extracting concessions, such as protection of forests, that are generally made very reluctantly. However, although Hawke was, for the time being, saved from the parliamentary opposition, within his own party he did not succeed to stifle Treasurer Paul Keating's open and continued challenge for the leadership, and towards the end of 1991 he was forced to give in. Keating stepped in to pursue an even stricter neo-liberal line.

EPILOGUE: FROM SOCIAL-DEMOCRACY TO NEO-LIBERALISM

As capitalism celebrates its 'victory' over socialism, marred somewhat by worries about possible ecological disasters, Australia adds up the balance of its achievements in the 1980s.

Not everyone is happy with the result. A traditional conservative, ex-Premier Malcolm Fraser, recently deplored the abdication of Government from its protective and sheltering role towards the under-privileged and towards indigenous business, such as farming and agriculture, at the expense of a 'milk bar, froth and bubble economy' (Fraser 1991). The monuments created by this froth and bubble economy – which are also monuments to neo-liberalism – can be seen in all Australia's State capitals in the form of large and towering office blocks, with an as yet rather low rate of occupancy. Less visible are the financial disasters, bankruptcies and bank crashes, the result of an overextended and badly managed financial sector, that are being sorted out at present.

Nevertheless, the Labor government claims, there are achievements. These include a more open economy, more open to foreign investors but also to financial speculators, including currency speculators, and to industrial goods from cheap labour countries that have undermined large sectors of Australia's indigenous consumer goods industries such as textiles, clothing and footwear.

There is also a giant overseas debt of Aus$170 billion, but to be set against that Australia's political and economic leaders can rightfully claim to have beaten inflation, which is at a historically low level of around 3 per cent, and the economy is also said to be more competitive internationally.

The structural problems, however, are there and in large measure they are a result of the policies of the 1980s. Australia's current sharp recession is not only due to a depressed world economy and low commodity prices, but is also a reflection of the tight money policies of Paul Keating, the former Treasurer. In the absence of re-regulation, Keating's tight money policies were the only instrument available to reign in imports and the growing gap in the balance of payments. The medicine, however, is proving hard to take for Labor's traditional followers and at present Keating is trying to recover some lost electoral ground by engaging in some mild and largely cosmetic pump priming.

It is doubtful whether his Aus$2 billion spending package will do much to reduce unemployment which has risen steeply to an official level of around 10 per cent, but which is in reality closer to 20 per cent. To counter this, Australia's policymakers would like to see a growing export of 'high tech' manufactured products, such as computer software and biotechnology. But Australian realities are stubborn: Japanese industrial interests, through their ministry of planning (MITI), have offered a partnership to produce and market these products on a large scale in a 'multifunction polis' in Australia, designed after Japanese examples, but also given an Australian flavour and serving the tourist industry, one of the few industries in Australia which is doing really well. The project, however, quickly became a cherished prize, to be fought over by different States, and the Japanese have politely withdrawn from the venture (Kaptein and Thomas 1991).

The official line is that Australia's future is in and with Asia.[5] However, Australia is not an Asian country and British colonial remnants remain strong. They include not only the British Queen, who is also the Queen of Australia when she spends time there, but also a fragmented and insufficient form of (three-tiered) government; a colonial legacy in a country which has been pieced together from six separate colonies not so long ago.

Almost obsessed by its own problems, not in the least through the efforts of the media, which are not only highly monopolized but also tend to be inward-looking and preoccupied with the appearance of political problems rather than their substance, Australia finds it difficult to take an objective look at itself; a precondition for orienting itself in a rapidly changing and increasingly turbulent world. Where does Australia's future lie and what does it do best?

There is little doubt that the neo-liberals and economic 'rationalists' who continue to dominate Australia's policy-making are likely to argue that the search for such an identity is fairly peripheral. If their policies are given a chance to work, then the 'market' will assign Australia's rightful place in the world.

NOTES

1   For further particulars concerning this episode reference is made to Kelly (1976).
2   They thereby flouted the convention that the Senate should not hold up money bills. To block the budget the opposition used its one-seat majority in the Senate which they had obtained as a result of the appointment of a non-Labor member to the Senate in a seat previously held by Labor. The Premier of Queensland, Bjelke Petersen, who was responsible for this appointment, thereby flouted another convention, i.e. that a 'casual vacancy' in the Senate, arising from the death or resignation of a sitting Senator, should be filled by an appointee of the same political colour. The conservatives tried to legitimize these controversial steps by pointing to the extraordinary and 'reprehensible' circumstances created by the Labor government, i.e. their incompetence and mismanagement as epitomized by the Khemlani affair.
3   Shell Australia had acquired substantial interests in non-oil energy resources (such as coal) and in minerals. These investments were made as part of a global diversification strategy and received an added boost in the wake of the 'second oil shock' of 1979 (cf. Spierenburg 1981, and Aarts and Meijer 1981).
4   For a good discussion of different forms of labour market organization, see the work of Robert Cox (1987).
5   See the 'Garnaut Report' (Garnaut 1989), and the discussion of its merits in Richardson 1991.

REFERENCES

Aarts, P. and Meijer, P. (1981) 'Over oliekoncerns en Haagse jaknikkers: de herstrukturering van de Nederlandse energiesektor', in F. Crone and H. Overbeek (eds) (1981) *Nederlands Kapitaal over de Grenzen. Verplaatsing van Produktie en Gevolgen voor de Nationale Ekonomie*, 187–213, Amsterdam: SUA.

Australia (1982) *Australia. Report of the Committee of Inquiry into the Australian Financial System* (the 'Campbell Report') Canberra: Australian Government Publishing Service.

Bryant, G. (1989) 'The air pilots' dispute', *Socialist Labor*, 1 (9), September.

Camilleri, J.A. (1980) *Australian–American Relations: The Web of Dependence*, South Melbourne: Macmillan.

Cox, R.W. (1987) *Production, Power, and World Order. Social Forces in the Making of History*, New York: Columbia University Press.

Crone, F. and Overbeek, H. (eds) (1981) *Nederlands Kapitaal over de Grenzen. Verplaatsing van Produktie en Gevolgen voor de Nationale Ekonomie*, Amsterdam: SUA.

Fraser, M. (1991) 'Ideology out as parties embrace the law of the jungle', *The Sunday Age*, 25 August.

Garnaut, R. (1989) *Australia and the Northeast Asia Ascendancy*, report to the Australian Government, Canberra: Australian Government Publishing Service.

Indecs Economics (1988) *State of Play 5*, North Sydney: Allen and Unwin.

Kahn, H. and Pepper, T. (1980) *Will She Be Right? The Future of Australia*, St. Lucia: University of Queensland Press.

Kaptein, E. and Thomas, K. D. (1991) 'The MFP and industrial policy in Australia', *The Australian Quarterly*, 63 (1), Winter.

Kasper, W., *et al.* (1980) *Australia at the Crossroads*, Melbourne: Harcourt Brace Jovanovich.

Kelly, P. (1976) *The Unmaking of Gough*, Melbourne: Angus & Robertson.

Mathews, J. (1989) 'Theoretical perspectives on restructuring in Australia', paper delivered to the After the Crisis Seminar, University of Amsterdam, Department of International Relations.

Overbeek, H. (1990) *Global Capitalism and National Decline: The Thatcher Decade in Perspective*, London: Unwin Hyman.

Pijl, K. van der (1984) *The Making of an Atlantic Ruling Class*, London: Verso.

Richardson, J. L. (ed.) (1991) *Northeast Asian Challenge: Debating the Garnaut Report*, Canberra: Australian National University.

Spierenburg, R. J. (1981) 'Een profiel van het SHELL-concern', in F. Crone and H. Overbeek (eds.) (1981) *Nederlands Kapitaal over de Grenzen. Verplatsing van Produktie en Gevolgen voor de nationale Ekonomie*, 175–86, Amsterdam: SUA.

5

ATLANTICISM AND EUROPEANISM IN BRITISH FOREIGN POLICY

Henk Overbeek

INTRODUCTION

In November 1990, the eleven-year reign of Margaret Thatcher, the longest serving British Prime Minister this century, came to an end. The turmoil which precipitated her resignation concerned both electoral tactics and political strategy.

On the one hand, the weak showings of the Tory Party in the opinion polls all through 1990, exacerbated by the ideologically moti-vated imposition of the immensely unpopular poll tax (or community charge as Thatcher euphemistically dubbed it), ignited a panic reaction among Tory backbenchers which forced Thatcher to step down.

But the more fundamental political conflict which led to Thatcher's demise was the division over Britain's European stance. The two sides in the debate have been labelled 'Atlanticist' and 'Euro-peanist', and the divide between the two is crucial to an understanding of British (foreign) policy in the 1980s. This view was borne out by the enduring prominence of the European question in British politics. The final political demise of the politician who had become the personific-ation of neo-liberalism in Britain (and to some extent in Eastern Europe) had been preceded late in 1989 by the resignation of the Chan-cellor of the Exchequer, Nigel Lawson, and the placing of the Prime Minister under the virtual guardianship of the triumvirate consisting of Foreign Secretary Douglas Hurd, Chancellor John Major, and Vice-Premier Sir Geoffrey Howe, who himself resigned in October 1990. Earlier still, in January 1986, the Thatcher government had already lost two of its most senior members: the Secretary of State for Defence, Michael Heseltine, resigned in protest of the way in which Prime Minister Thatcher handled the crisis over the Westland Affair, and the Minister for Trade and Industry, Leon Brittan, was forced to resign a

110

little later for his (mis)conduct in this affair. In all instances, these crises in the Conservative government were ignited by the European issue.

This contribution will analyse the factors which have made the divide between 'Atlanticists' and 'Europeanists' such a central one in Britain. More precisely, it will be shown that the 'Atlanticist' position of the Thatcher government represented a neo-liberal attack on the 'Europeanist' consensus (in ruling government circles) of the 1970s. After the signing of the Single European Act of 1986, it fused into the transnational neo-liberal offensive aiming to redefine the Europe 1992 Project in neo-liberal terms, ridding it of its corporatist and protectionist overtones with which EC President Jacques Delors had become identified.

In order to be able to evaluate the radical changes produced by the Thatcher government, it is first necessary to recount briefly the development of Britain's European and Atlantic position in the years between World War II and the advent of Thatcherism. In particular, it must be clarified how the strong Churchillian consensus of the 1940s and early 1950s was gradually transformed into a 'Europeanist' consensus during the mid-1970s.[1]

POST-WAR BRITISH FOREIGN POLICY REGARDING ATLANTIC RELATIONS

During the early post-war years there were three distinctive positions in Western Europe with regard to Euro-American relations. First, the Europeanist view advocated a position of European equality *vis-à-vis* both the United States and the Soviet Union, striving to eliminate or modify the bipolarity of East–West relations. Second, the Atlanticists saw the place of a united Western Europe at the side of the United States, as an equal partner in a strong Atlantic alliance, in opposition to the Soviet Union and her allies. Both these views had advocates in most West-European countries, with Atlanticists dominant in West Germany and the Netherlands (and usually in Italy), and Europeanists particularly strong in France. Third, in Great Britain, there were the Churchillians who aspired to a relatively independent role for Great Britain in world politics, which in the post-war reality could only be realized by cherishing the 'special relationship' with the United States.

From Empire to Europe

During the 1940s and early 1950s, this Churchillian view of Britain's place in the world clearly dominated British foreign policy making, under Labour (Bevin) as much as under the Conservatives (Eden).

In defence matters, European co-operation in British eyes should be dependent on and framed in by the Euro-American alliance. After taking office in 1951, Eden emphasized that successful long-term resistance to Soviet pressures depended on continental West European defence co-operation within the context of the Atlantic Alliance. The pacification of Western Europe along these lines was eventually achieved through the West European Union (WEU).

The British government was much less inclined to become involved in projects for West European economic co-operation. When the French minister Schuman on 9 May 1950 announced his plan for pooling the European coal and steel industries, British reactions were generally negative (Anouil 1960: 56–64). As Bevin remarked to a group of American advocates of West European integration: 'Great Britain was not part of Europe; she was not simply a Luxemburg' (quoted by Reynolds 1991: 198). In 1955 Britain declined to participate in the Messina conference which laid the foundations for the European Economic Community. As Blank concluded, it was the government's commitment to maintain Britain's international position (and the position of the City as a centre of international finance), which led to 'domestic economic stagnation and a failure to develop new techniques and institutions to cope with the structural problems of the economy' (Blank 1978: 131).

Blank's identification of the structural power of the City of London as a major obstacle to a more effective economic strategy touches on the essence of Britain's power structure. The historic bloc in Britain, the particular hegemonic coalition of social forces, had been dominated since the 1680s by what we might call the financial aristocracy. Two brief interludes of a relative weakening of the hegemony of this historic bloc (in the mid-nineteenth century and in the 1930s and early 1940s) had been followed by the reconstruction of the hegemony of the financial aristocracy, albeit adapted to the changes which had taken place in the global context in the meantime (cf. Overbeek 1990: 35–93).

The dominant concept of control of the financial aristocracy was that of liberal internationalism. During the years of the Great Depression of the 1930s, the rise of the relative power of heavy industry led to the temporary strength of the state-monopolist tendency. After 1945, the financial aristocracy succeeded in recouping its central power position by assuming a specialized role in the construction of an integrated Atlantic economy under American leadership, thus providing the 'special relationship' (primarily a political and military concept) with a firm economic foundation.

Ironically, it was this newly integrated Atlantic economic space which led to the growth of a new generation in the international bourgeoisie, the corporate liberals with their power base in the new Fordist industries (cf. Overbeek 1990: 29–34). In Britain, this gradual rise of corporate liberal interests was reflected in the changes in the balance of power within the Conservative Party. With the rise of Harold Macmillan, and in the aftermath of the Suez débâcle, the balance gradually tipped in favour of the corporate liberals. Around 1960, these changes also resulted in the FBI (Federation of British Industries) changing its position on Europe: in July 1961 the FBI came out in favour of British membership (Pfaltzgraff 1964: 269–71).

In the same year (1961) Britain indeed finally applied for membership of the EEC. But the position of Macmillan was such that his government could only do that after first concluding the far-reaching Nassau agreements on nuclear co-operation with the Americans, providing de Gaulle with the excuse to block Britain's application. Thus once again it was the unwillingness (or inability) of the British government to give up the Churchillian notion of Britain as a world power which blocked the road to European integration and economic modernization (Blank 1978: 132; Reynolds 1991: 221).

Within the Foreign Office Suez had set in motion a process of fundamental re-appraisal of the place of Britain in the world, resulting by the mid-1960s in the conviction that Britain could only hope to maintain at least second-rate power status if it would join the EEC (cf. Jessop 1980: 70–4). But it was only in the years after the French veto of 1963 that the forces opposing the move towards Europe weakened so decisively that their position became untenable.

First, the economic situation continued to deteriorate, convincing an ever larger share of public opinion that EEC membership was inevitable and necessary. A growing number of Britain's multinational firms, most notably ICI, were already investing heavily in Europe, recognizing that the European market provided the dynamics and the opportunities for expansion so dearly missed in the domestic economy (Schneider 1968: 102–3; Boyd 1975: 68).

Second, there was the change in the position of the City-Treasury axis, resulting from this changing position of Britain in the world economy. The 1960s showed an enormous increase in the size of the Eurodollar market, which even accelerated when the USA began exporting their inflation in order to finance the Vietnam war.

Consequently, the role of the City in world finance changed radically, making it less dependent on maintaining the value of Sterling (Ferris 1970: 172–3; Ingham 1984: 286n).

Third, there was a shift in the international reactions to Britain's wish to join the Common Market. Kennedy's ideas of Atlantic Partnership were an important factor in propelling Britain forward towards Europe. Also, the political changes taking place in France after 1968 diminished French resistance: in 1969 de Gaulle was succeeded by Pompidou, and, more important, the Atlanticist Liberal Giscard d'Estaing as Minister of Finance came to dominate French economic policy (van der Pijl 1984: 190, 223–5).

Thus, when the most Europeanist of British politicians, the corporate liberal Edward Heath, became Prime Minister in 1970, important conditions had been fulfilled for a new attempt to join the EEC. The 1971 application by Britain was indeed successful, and on 1 January 1973, Britain became a member of the European Community.

From Heath to Thatcher

Although Heath lost the 1974 election over a domestic issue (his handling of the trade union question), the European issue had also been important. The Labour Party, and particularly its Left wing, had been strongly opposed to Britain's EEC membership, and the new government was pledged to 'renegotiations', the results of which had to be put to the British people in a referendum. Because of this resurgence of anti-EEC sentiments, and because of the Labour Party's (though not its leadership's) commitment to Britain's 'sovereignty', Heath's defeat marked 'the end of the one distinctly 'European' phase in post-war British foreign policy' (Reynolds 1991: 247). This did not mean, however, that Britain returned to a 'Churchillian' posture.

While the Labour Party struggled with itself to come to terms with Europe, the mid-1970s saw the international rise of the policies promoted by the Trilateral Commission (TC), an initiative by liberal internationalist forces against the threat represented by Nixon's narrow sphere-of-interest policies after 1971. In the elections of 1975 the victory of Jimmy Carter brought scores of Trilateral Commissioners into the new US Administration (Gill 1990: 166–7), thus confirming the shift towards Trilateralism.

In Great Britain, the Trilateral line was supported by the right wing of the Labour Party. Fairly soon after the second Labour victory (in October 1974), the balance of forces within the Labour government shifted to the right. The decisive outcome of the European Referendum (2 to 1 in favour of the renegotiated terms of entry, cf. Butler and Kitzinger 1976) gave the right the leverage to demote Tony Benn, the left's most influential Cabinet Minister.

Harold Wilson's sudden resignation in March 1976, and James Callaghan's succession, confirmed the shift to the right. Callaghan and his Chancellor, Denis Healey, were strongly connected to the Trilateral Commission, and joined the TC after leaving office in 1979 (Gill 1990: 100).

Labour was not the only social-democratic party to support the TC. Others, particularly the German SPD, did so too, and the activities of the Socialist International, rejuvenated under the leadership of Willy Brandt, reinforced this Trilateral orientation.

When the Carter administration had been in office for about two years, the political tide in the US began to flow against the original corporate-liberal Trilateral policies (Scheer 1982). With the election of Ronald Reagan this new tide was strengthened. The TC now gradually moved to a neo-liberal orientation. In Europe, there was little open opposition to Reagan's policies: in general the enormous expansion of defence expenditure had a favourable effect on the European economies, although the aggressiveness of Reagan's policies towards the Soviet Union and the Third World worried many European leaders and the wider public. The coming to power in 1979 of the Conservative Party, led by the right-wing MP Margaret Thatcher, thus in a sense reflected and reinforced a more global phenomenon.

THE EVOLUTION OF BRITISH FOREIGN POLICY UNDER THATCHER

Since Suez, British foreign policy had moved in the direction of what President Kennedy labelled Atlantic Partnership: a strong alliance between the United States and a united Western Europe, of which Britain had striven to become a member since 1961. Decolonization of the British Empire met with little domestic opposition, and by the end of the 1970s only a few spots of British presence remained (Rhodesia, Hong Kong, Falklands), while of course South Africa was still an unresolved problem.

The Thatcher government broke with this consensus and attempted a fundamental reorientation of Britain's foreign policy in response to the crisis in the post-war international order and the changes taking place in American foreign policy from 1978–9. American foreign policy under President Reagan was, certainly during his first term in office, 'unilateralist': its main traits were a very aggressive policy towards the Soviet Union (the Empire of Evil) and towards signs of independence in the Third World, and a relative indifference towards Europe, in line with the shift of America's economic interests from the Atlantic to the Pacific Ocean.

The strategic choice of the Thatcher government was to follow America's lead. Not that there were no instances of conflict or disagreement between the USA and Britain during the Thatcher years: one has only to think of the American economic embargo on the Soviet Union after the invasion of Afghanistan or of the US invasion in Grenada to realize that (cf. Smith 1988). In terms, however, of the general view of what the world should look like, Thatcher and Reagan were in agreement. In fact, Britain was the first developed capitalist country (even before Reagan came to power in January 1981) to take an active role in shaping a new neo-liberal international order. This new order was characterized by Western aggressiveness towards the Soviet Union and its allies, the 'roll-back' of the 'statification' of international relations which had been essential to the NIEO episode, and the forceful promotion of free trade and free markets.

Within this global context, the new Thatcherite foreign policy (reminiscent in many of its aspects of Churchill's) was characterized by three constants.

First, Thatcher's view of Britain's role in the world was that of (junior) partner of the USA in the global order, with responsibilities of its own. 'Churchillianism', when taken to its ultimate consequence, meant opposition to any European defence co-operation scheme, in which the United States was not directly involved.

Second, Thatcher's foreign policy posture was in overall accordance with the interests of the hegemonic class coalition (the financial aristocracy and transnational capital) with its internationalist orientation.

Third, this liberal internationalist orientation also entailed a bias against interventionist industrial policy (considered to be 'dirigiste', corporatist, and inefficient). Equally important, it implied a bias against strong, redistributive, social policies.

In what follows we will take a closer look at two distinct but clearly related issues which have dominated Britain's foreign policy debate in the years since 1979: defence policy and European policy.

Defence policy

For the greater part of the 1980s, the Churchillian view dominated British defence policies. This orientation meant that priority was accorded to relations with the United States and the Commonwealth, and that Europe was relegated to second rank. Of course, over time, the relative importance of the Commonwealth diminished in relation to the weight accorded to the 'special relationship', especially after Suez, when recognition gradually became more widespread that Britain was no longer a great power in its own right.

The voices raised against the strong identification with the USA were few and politically weak. Only the extreme right and the far left sometimes voiced isolationist views, calling for a looser relationship with the USA (and on the left complemented by calls for unilateral nuclear disarmament). On the right, Britain's own Gaullist, Enoch Powell, has said that 'successive British governments down the last 30 years have Finlandized the United Kingdom in relation to the USA'. (Powell 1983).

In the 1970s, critical views were temporarily stronger, both in the Labour Party and in the form of the Europeanist Heath government. But Thatcher, as said, revived the 'special relationship', and the Falklands War strongly reinforced the strategic alliance with the USA (Sharp 1991: 399–403). In a very down-to-earth way, the new relationship was confirmed by small quid pro quo's: '... according to one diplomat, Britain's support for the bombing of Libya in 1986 resulted in the removal from a trade bill of clauses harmful to certain British interests' (Sharp 1991: 405).

That there were ideological contradictions over defence policy in Thatcher's Cabinet first came to light in the upheaval over the Westland Affair. This affair played a pivotal role in the struggle over both defence policy and over European policy, thus revealing the very deep strategic division within the Conservative Party over these issues (cf. Linklater and Leigh 1986, Freedman 1987; also see Overbeek 1986).

On the surface, the affair was much ado about very little. Thus, it has been interpreted as a matter of personal rivalry between two strong characters, i.e. Thatcher and Heseltine (cf. Young 1989: 427–63), while it can also be looked at from the constitutional angle, which Heseltine explicitly referred to upon resigning his Cabinet post (cf. Hennessy 1986, and Oliver and Austin 1987). These two interpretations, important though they may be, could explain only minor political disturbances. However, the affair led to a semi-permanent rift within the Cabinet which continued long after Thatcher lost two of her most prominent Ministers in the aftermath of the affair. Secretary of State for Defence, Michael Heseltine, resigned his post in the Ministry of Defence (MoD) on Thursday 9 January, after a long drawn-out conflict with the Prime Minister and most of his other colleagues concerning the attitude to be taken by the government towards the financial difficulties of Britain's only independent helicopter manufacturer, Westland plc. On Friday 24 January, the Secretary for Trade and Industry and loyal Thatcherite, Leon Brittan, resigned because his position became untenable after it was established that he had been responsible for the leaking of a letter by the acting Attorney-General Sir Patrick Mayhew to Heseltine, an action intended to be harmful to Heseltine's position (House of Commons Report HC 519 1986: p. lxix; also see Linklater and Leigh 1986: 133–4).

In hindsight, there were three more important dimensions to the affair:

1   it was a debate over industrial policy (market-oriented or interventionist) and over defence-industrial policy: does Britain need an independent defence-industrial base? (cf. Hartley *et al.* 1987);
2   another way of looking at the affair is to interpret it in the context of military procurement policies and the role of European co-operation in this area (e.g. Freedman 1987);
3   finally, it was a foreign policy debate, clearly bringing to the fore the major strategic divisions, and tied in with the wider European debate (as argued in Overbeek 1986).

What all this made clear was the relevance of understanding political struggles such as these in terms of competing comprehensive concepts of control. Indeed, Thatcher's monetarist free-market hyperliberalism was challenged by Heseltine's supply-side interventionist state capitalist project, and this division would dominate political life in Britain until Thatcher's eventual resignation in November 1990, and beyond.

Defence-industrial policy

The application of liberal economic doctrines by the Thatcher government after it came to power in 1979 led to large-scale de-industrialization, and to unprecedented numbers of bankruptcies. Important sections of manufacturing industry found themselves in desperate need of a programme which would take the restoration of industrial production in Britain as its central aim. In addition, the rapid demise of the industrial base of the British economy during the last decade has given rise to a debate on the necessity of maintaining productive capacity and know-how in industries that cannot compete on the world markets but are deemed to be indispensible to an advanced industrial nation, and that are therefore considered as strategic (for an exposé of these arguments, see Hartley *et al.* 1987). Roughly the same arguments that were used concerning Westland (and later Nimrod) were exchanged over foreign (usually American) involvement in British firms without a military dimension, such as the attempt by Ford to take over the passenger car division of British Leyland (that is Austin-Rover) (*The Economist*, 8 February 1986).

British military-industrial policy was an issue over which there had been a broad bipartisan consensus during most of the 1950s, 1960s and 1970s (cf. Jones 1987; also Davidson 1986). The military aspect of industrial policy in Britain is crucial. Military expenditure as a proportion of the national income in Britain is the highest of all West European countries at 5.4 per cent in 1985 (*SIPRI Yearbook*, 1986), and has increased over the years 1979–85 by 23 per cent in real terms (Linklater and Leigh 1986: 19). Military research and development spending is higher in Britain than in any other Western country except the United States, and causes a chronic shortage of skilled experts in civilian high-technology sectors such as electronics (Kaldor *et al.* 1986: 31–49). In 1987, the British government has announced, however, that it aimed to reduce military R&D spending (totalling £2.3 billion) in order to 'keep the MoD from sopping up so much of the country's research manpower' (*The Economist*, 9 May 1987). Decisions made over military procurement, it is clear, have a vital impact on the British industrial structure, as well as on British foreign policy. The Westland affair thus in fact concerned the basis of Britain's military-industrial policy, and the strategic choice between European defence co-operation or reliance on the 'American connection' (Freedman 1987: 18). As the House of Commons Defence Committee concluded, 'It would be no exaggeration to say that British policy on helicopter collaboration had become a touchstone of British policy on defence collaboration.' (HC 519 1986: para. 42).

In the Westland affair, the case for European co-operation rested on the Independent European Planning Group (IEPG), a group of all European NATO countries formed in 1976, which had been reactivated by Michael Heseltine and the Dutch State Secretary for Defence Jan van Houwelingen in 1983. In fact, the IEPG, in the area of defence co-operation, came to perform the role of rallying Trilateralist forces in the face of increasing unilateralist pressures from the United States. Michael Heseltine played a prominent role in the attempts to rationalize the European defence industries in order to make them into more attractive partners for American arms manufacturers:

> ... Alliance equipment procurement cannot be based on US domi-nation of the high technology end of the market. There has to be a genuine two-way street across the spectrum of defence equipment or the Europeans will have no choice but to rationalise amongst themselves and buy from each other. I do not underestimate the difficulties in evolving an effective transatlantic partnership; but the prize is worth the effort.
>
> (Heseltine 1984: 3; see also Heseltine 1987: 255–74)

However, Heseltine had trouble convincing his government that Euro-pean defence co-operation was desirable, and eventually he lost. The unilateralist line pursued by the Thatcher government was reconfirmed, and Heseltine's attempt to further the case of West European co-oper-ation in arms procurement received a serious, albeit temporary, setback (Freedman 1987: 18).[2]

The Westland Affair was, we may safely conclude, one important moment in the reorientation of Britain's foreign economic and defence policies. The new policies were aimed at strengthening the competitive position of Britain's military-industrial complex, through introducing competition in the defence procurement business by abolishing the prac-tice of cost-plus contracts, by discouraging mergers and acquisitions, and by opening up the markets to international competition, instead of turning towards European co-operation (Walker and Gummett 1989: 422–4).

The enormous expansion of military expenditure in the United States provided a favourable climate for this new orientation. Indeed, after the elections of 1987, the Tories renewed their commitment to purchase the new American Trident nuclear weapons system, with estimated outlays during the 1990s ranging from £9 billion to £12 billion or more. Trident will consume a major proportion of the MoD's procurement budget when it is brought into service (Laird and Robertson 1987: 196).

Great Britain was also the first European power to participate without significant restrictions in the American Strategic Defense Initia-tive, despite initial political reservations (Taylor 1986: 217–19). It was 'apparently on the personal insistence of the PM' that Great Britain eventually agreed to participate in SDI on 6 December 1985 (ibid.: 219). During the negotiations over the final agreement, Heseltine had demanded that it would contain a guarantee for $1.5 billion worth of orders for British companies. The demand was rejected, but continued to play a role in the public discussion, and many of the companies in the British military-industrial complex actively sought to win orders from the Pentagon (*Financial Times*, 26 February 1986). However, the great expectations were not rewarded: by March 1987, the orders for British companies in the context of the SDI programme amounted to only $34 million (out of a total of $7 billion) (*Financial Times*, 25 March 1987). Due to the continuing *détente* between Reagan and Gorbachev after 1986, the SDI programme subsequently lost most of its dynamism, and the expected bonanza never materialized.

Meanwhile, in December 1986 there was a much bigger example of the British government sacrificing the interests of a British company in favour of an American deal: the case of Nimrod, the airborne radar system developed for the MoD by General Electric Company, but abandoned in favour of Boeing's Advanced Warning Airborne Control (AWACs) system. Although there was broad agreement among commentators that the Nimrod-project failed to meet the quality standards that might be required of it (vehemently denied by GEC's James Prior), the government refused to publicize the test results on which it based its appraisal. GEC Avionics was projected to lose 1,500 staff because of the cancellation of Nimrod; most of these engineers would find work, it was expected, in the other electronics companies which Boeing could involve in its 'compensation orders' (*Financial Times*, 20 December 1986), or which have lucrative export orders. It is worth while emphasizing that deals such as the enormous 'Al Yamamah' contract with Saudi Arabia made the United Kingdom the second largest arms exporter in the world in 1986, with overall sales amounting to $5.8 billion. Deals negotiated in 1987 (a.o. 3 frigates to Pakistan, Sea-Harriers for India and Italy), and the success of British Aerospace's Rapier short range anti-aircraft missiles, led to the expectation that this position might be continued in the following years (*The Economist*, 4 July 1987: 31).

From 1988 onward, there was a progressive shift in the orientation of Britain's defence-industrial policy, brought about by a number of external developments. The development of the relations between the superpowers (summit meetings between Reagan and Gorbachev, arms limitation agreements, reductions in the strength of American forces in Europe), the consequent unrest in Europe – particularly French unease over a possible revival of the 'German Question', and the changing competitive relations in the electronics sector (the rise of Japanese competition, the shadows of the coming of the internal market in 1992), all these factors made for a 'shift towards Europe' in the last years of the 1980s (cf. Walker and Gummett 1989: 425–9).

Underlying this shift, and reinforcing it at the same time, was the process towards concentration and centralization in the European defence industry. Geographically, the defence industry is concentrated more and more in just three countries (Germany, France and Britain); the sectoral concentration is particularly strong in electronics and in aerospace; and finally, centralization leads to the formation of huge monopolistic conglomerates (ibid.: 432–4).

In Britain, General Electric Company has played an absolutely central role in these processes. This enormous conglomerate, formed in 1968, went through a deep crisis in 1986, with the Nimrod fiasco and the failed bid to take over Plessey (*Financial Times*, 13 January 1986). But its fortunes started to turn after 1988. After a long battle, involving averting a counter-attack led by Lazards for Plessey, and involving a positive ruling by the Monopolies and Mergers Commission, GEC succeeded in its second bid to acquire a controlling stake in its biggest competitor Plessey (*Sunday Telegraph*, 3 September 1989). The combined sales in defence electronics of the new combination amounted to $4.8 billion (1987 figures). British Aerospace followed with annual sales in this tranche of $1.15 billion; Ferranti had a turnover of just under a billion dollars in the same year (*The Economist*, 19 September 1989). Three months later, GEC beat the combination of Thomson CSF and British Aerospace' in the race to acquire Ferranti (*Observer*, 21 January 1990). The deal was eventually clinched thanks to intervention behind the scene by the Ministry of Defence, which strove to prevent the contract for radar for the European Fighter Aircraft (a £2 billion contract) to fall into the hands of Thomson (*The Economist*, 27 January 1990; *Sunday Telegraph*, 28 January 1990). Thus, the demise of Ferranti turned out to be yet another stage in the creation of one huge 'national champion' in British defence electronics. And that creative process has probably not reached its final stage yet. There has already been speculation that Westland (!) may fall prey to GEC (*Financial Times*, 3 September 1991), and that GEC cannot stand idly by if British Aerospace's most recent problems would lead to foreign bids for its defence-related operations (*The Economist*, 22 February 1992).

This short history of GEC over the past few years illustrates perfectly, that the process of concentration mentioned above has a remarkably dual character. Governments in Europe aim to create 'national champions': their 'own' defence producers will only be able to compete internationally if governments allow monopolization at the national level. But at the same time it is recognized that participation in forms of international co-operation is necessary with an eye to technological development and to the enormous scale which profitable production requires. The resulting pattern shows national concentration (such as the amalgamation of Daimler-Benz, Messerschmidt Bolkow Blohm (MBB), and AEG in Germany), paired to internationalization through tolerating the acquisition of second-rate producers by foreign firms (e.g. Westland) or the formation of international alliances (such as between British Aerospace and the French firm Thomson CSF, or between Siemens and GEC) (cf. Walker and Gummett 1989: 435; also Hayward 1989).

And so we come to the second issue, that of the very recent past and immediate future of Britain's relation to European integration, with defence taking on an increasingly central role as the Soviet Union has disintegrated and ceased to be a credible threat and effective counterforce.

Thatcher and Europe: the twelve-year guerrilla

The European question has been of central importance not only in the foreign policy debate, but in British politics in general in the 1970s and 1980s. Both when Mrs Thatcher became Tory Party leader (in 1975) and when she became Prime Minister (1979), domestic issues (primarily the 'trade union issue') dominated the political scene. But 1975 was also the year in which the Labour Government organized its Referendum on the renegotiated terms for British membership of the EC (resulting in a 2 to 1 vote in favour of membership). And, right from the start of her first term in office, Mrs Thatcher made a major issue out of Britain's contribution to the EC budget (cf. Grahl and Teague 1990: 293–7). She got off to such a vehemently anti-European start, in fact, that the Foreign Secretary, Lord Carrington, backed by six other Cabinet ministers, had to intervene and restrain her in 1980 (Reynolds 1991: 265). For four and a half years, Mrs Thatcher haunted the EC with her demands for a 'rebate'. The budget discussion was intimately linked to the Common Agricultural Policy (CAP), which absorbs almost two-thirds of the EC budget. On historical grounds Britain traded less with her EC partners, and more with countries outside the EC, than the other European countries, and thus paid more into the Community's 'own resources' than other European partners. Further, Britain (with its very efficient agricultural sector) was unhappy to subsidize the less efficient farmers of France and Germany.

Thatcher eventually triumphed at the Fontainebleau Summit of June 1984: Britain would get a rebate of £850 million on average for three years. However, the fundamental problem of the CAP, which ius a fundamental problem for the whole Community and not just for Britain, is still there. Britain's strategy of making progress in other areas (such as technology policy) dependent upon a restructuration of the agricultural policies proved counterproductive for several years by blocking progress in all areas of co-operation (see Riddell 1983, 211–15). And finally, the CAP also put a great strain on EC–US relations, culminating in the 1990 breakdown of the GATT negotiations on the 'Uruguay Round'.

Economic and monetary integration

A further crucial debate has been the one over membership of the European Monetary System (EMS) (see Grahl and Teague 1990: 297–302). Joining would partially stabilize the fluctuations in the exchange rate, and would thus facilitate lower interest rates (see Keegan 1986). For these reasons the Confederation of British Industries (CBI), as the mouthpiece of British industrial capital producing for the domestic market and for export, has long been in favour of Britain's joining the EMS. Such big British multinationals with extensive interests in Europe as British Aerospace, British–American Tobacco, and Imperial Chemical Industries joined the British Association for Monetary Union in Europe, along with amongst others, Barclays Bank, Citibank, Midland Montagu, Ernst & Young, Goldman Sachs, Salomon International, Shearson Bros., and S.G. Warburg, all City firms (some American) fearful that London might lose its central role in European finance to Frankfurt if Britain were to stay out of the coming monetary union (Frieden 1991: 447–8). For three years the Thatcher government held off, although internal dissension was noticeable all along.

Britain's position on EMU made her the mouthpiece of globally operating capital: finance, oil, certain high-tech sectors, and such 'global' conglomerates as Shell and Unilever. This view of Europe as essentially a free-trade area and little more, freed from any obstacles obstructing the free movement across the globe of capital and goods (though not labour) can rightly be characterized as hyperliberal. This tendency is described by Cox as a

return to nineteenth-century economic liberalism and the rejection of the [corporate-liberal] attempt to adapt economic liberalism to the socio-political reactions that classical liberalism produced. ... The overall impact of the hyperliberal tendency on the social formation is thus toward a polarization of labor .... [It] requires a new basis in legitimacy, ... sought in a nonhegemonic, populist appeal to the sanctity of traditional values. ... The appeal to traditional values is strengthened by the strong military stance of the hyperliberal state.

(Cox 1987: 286–9).

The EC Commission, under the leadership of Jacques Delors, has in contrast become the mouthpiece of 'European' capital. Basically, this means the 'Fordist' core of car manufacturers, consumer electronics and computer manufacturers, etc.: capital highly internationalized at the European level, engaged in fearsome competition with American but especially Japanese capital, and in desperate need of strong Europe-wide state backing in order to be able to withstand the Japanese onslaught on its home markets. The European Roundtable of Businessmen led by the top people of such firms as Philips and Volvo was supported in their 'closed', interventionist, '1992' project by finance capital in the late industrializing countries of Southern Europe, particularly Spain, whose Prime Minister Gonzalez was one of Delors' closest allies in his confrontations with Margaret Thatcher (cf. Holman 1989; also see his contribution to this volume, Chapter 7). The 1992 project, at least in Delors' version of it, can be characterized as state capitalist.

The state-capitalist approach is grounded in an acceptance of the world market as the ultimate determinant of development. ... The broad lines of this policy consist of, in the first place, development of the leading sectors of national production so as to give them a competitive edge in world markets, and in the second place, protection of the principal social groups so that their welfare can be perceived as linked to the success of the national productive effort.

(Cox 1987: 290)

As Cox points out (p. 293), the attempt inherent in a state-capitalist project to reconstitute social hegemony through (new forms of) corporatism faces great obstacles, as can be surmised from the recent crisis in the state-capitalist formation *par excellence*, Japan. How much greater will be the obstacles to be overcome in the case of a European Union consisting of twelve (and soon maybe eighteen, or twenty-four) countries!

The inherent 'latent contradiction to democratic legitimacy' (Cox 1987: 297) in this case is indeed enormous.

Having elaborated on the wider context of the debate over Britain's membership in EMS, let me now return to the more tangible issue of the concrete struggle over this issue within the Thatcher Cabinet. In June 1989, in the wake of the disastrous elections for the European Parliament (with Labour scoring 40 per cent of the vote against the Tories' 35 per cent), the Foreign Secretary, Sir Geoffrey Howe, and the Chancellor of the Exchequer Nigel Lawson forced Thatcher to spell out, at the European Summit in Madrid, the specific conditions under which Britain would be prepared to join at least the Exchange Rate Mechanism (ERM) of the EMS.

Margaret Thatcher would not have acted in character if she had not taken revenge for this humiliation. Later in the summer, in the annual cabinet shuffle, she maltreated Howe in a very public manner and appointed him to the newly created but almost totally ceremonial position of Deputy Prime Minister. John Major, second man in the Treasury, was promoted to Howe's job, although he had absolutely no experience with foreign affairs. Observers at the time concluded that Major was being groomed by Thatcher to succeed her once her time came.

In October, a long-simmering conflict between Lawson and Thatcher's personal adviser in economic affairs, Sir Alan Walters, exploded into a public row. Lawson, the architect of Thatcher's economic policy since 1983, demanded that Thatcher would publicly support him and would fire Walters. When she refused, Lawson could draw only one conclusion, and he resigned. He was the second senior Cabinet Minister (after Heseltine) to resign after a serious dispute with the Prime Minister, and in both cases the European issue had triggered the conflict. Major was moved to the Foreign Office, which confirmed his position as the heir apparent to Thatcher's throne.

The Madrid conditions were to haunt Thatcher for more than a year. Public pressure to join the ERM mounted continuously: individual firms such as Imperial Chemical Industries, the CBI, and even the National Federation of Self-Employed and Small Businesses (which could be considered a 'natural' supporter of Thatcher) came out in favour of British membership. The Franco–German agreement of December 1989, reached in Strasbourg, provided extra ammunition for the pro-ERM lobby: the danger that London might lose its central position to Frankfurt loomed large for the financial services industry, which accounts for 10 per cent of British GNP and provides 1.2 million jobs.

When entry into the ERM was finally announced in October 1990, it was done so largely for internal political reasons with a view to the annual Conservative Party Conference in November. A second objective of the move clearly was to create a positive atmosphere for the European Summit to be held later that month in Rome. In Rome, however, Thatcher ruined any positive atmosphere that might have been created by a vehement speech against any further steps to be taken towards Economic and Monetary Union (EMU). On this occasion when a definite timetable for EMU was agreed upon, Thatcher's point of view was summed up brilliantly in her statement that sterling is 'the most powerful expression of sovereignty you can have' (quoted in Reynolds 1991: 288). This in fact was the speech that was to cost Thatcher her job.

Her position was already shaky due to overwhelming domestic opposition to the Poll Tax. When Sir Geoffrey Howe surprised everyone by resigning in protest against Thatcher's performance in Rome and subsequently in the House of Commons, and on top of that delivered a devastating statement in Parliament, the struggle for the leadership of the Party and the Government could no longer be subdued. Heseltine's bluff was called and he was forced to step forward and challenge Thatcher.

Although the Thatcher camp maintained that the issue was essentially of a personal nature and that there were no serious policy differences, Thatcher herself underlined the deep divisions over Europe by writing a lengthy ('hyperliberal') statement for the *Financial Times* outlining 'My vision of Europe: open and free' (19 November 1990). Her view of the future as outlined there was of

> ... a Community which is based on competition, enterprise, choice, and free trade; and a Community in which the basic political rights of the people of this country can continue to be exercised through Parliament rather than made over to a body beyond their control. A Community whose member countries freely co-operate more closely with one another, but clearly retain their national identity and accountability.

Mrs Thatcher did not survive the political battle, and was eventually succeeded by the man she had wanted to succeed her for some time, John Major. Although he was generally expected to be less anti-European than his mentor, his government's policy has not departed from the premises which underlay Britain's posture all through the 1980s.

Rather, it was external circumstances which gradually led to changes in Britain's European policy. Looking back, those changes originated in the transformation of the European political landscape by the rise of Mikhail Gorbachev in the Soviet Union.

AFTER GORBACHEV AND THATCHER: TOWARDS A NEW EUROPEAN ORDER

The agreement in principle to remove middle range nuclear weapons from Europe, which Reagan and Gorbachev reached in Reykjavik in 1986, caused great confusion and unrest in ruling European circles. Thatcher was even forced to hurry to America 'to review with the President the central role of nuclear weapons in NATO's plans for the defense of Europe', as a British diplomat euphemistically put it later (Sharp 1991: 405–6). Rather suddenly, talk of European defence co-operation assumed quite a different quality than only a short while earlier, and most remarkably even the Thatcher government seemed to move into the direction of closer European co-operation and independence *vis-à-vis* the USA (Smith 1988: 17). The new entente between France and Britain and the joint positions taken with respect to Gorbachev's initiatives in 1987 seemed to confirm the new trend. Increased willingness to discuss West European defence co-operation also expressed itself in the enlargement of the West European Union in December 1988, when Spain and Portugal acceded.

For Mrs Thatcher, however, this was a road down which she could only go reluctantly, and no further than strictly necessary. She had made this quite explicit in her seminal speech of 20 September 1988 in the Europa College in Bruges.

In this speech she acknowledged that Britain's future was irrevocably tied in with that of the other EC countries. But she added two qualifications which had everything to do with her ambition for Britain to remain (or once more become) a power with global responsibilities. Thatcher pointed out that Europe extends beyond the boundaries of the EC of the twelve, and made it clear that Britain's European policy should also be concerned with Eastern Europe. Striking a familiar cord, Mrs Thatcher further expressed her conviction that the EC was still part of 'that Atlantic Community – that Europe on both sides of the Atlantic – which is our greatest inheritance and our greatest strength.' (quoted in *The Economist*, 24 September 1988). The Bruges Speech thus represented a strong reaffirmation of the basic orientation of Thatcherite foreign policy.

Reykjavik had hinted at one possible global development which might bring about a reappraisal of Britain's basic alliances: if the USA was willing, in exchange for a deal with the Soviet Union, to sacrifice the interests of her European allies, the British would have to redefine their relation with Western Europe, and especially with the second European nuclear power France, in matters of foreign policy and defence.

In the field of economic and monetary policy, Britain was in a marginalized position, not only because of Thatcher's policies in the past, but also because the Franco–German axis was very strong in this area. Motivated by continuing fears of a new German *Alleingang* the French have always allowed the Germans to take the lead in economic matters in return for the thorough encapsulation of Germany into the fabric of West European integration. From their side, the Germans have always looked upon European integration as the political frame for making their economic expansion acceptable to their allies. The EC provided the political legitimacy for the expansion of German capital which the Federal Republic was unable to provide given the Cold War realities and the effective Soviet veto. This compromise, struck in the early 1950s and consecrated by Adenauer and de Gaulle in the Franco–German Friendship Treaty, was severely shaken by the events of 1989 and 1990.

In December of 1989, when the East Germans were already putting their own personal German unification into practice by the tens of thousands, France and Germany were still of one mind and reached an agreement with regard to EMU. However, from September 1990 (i.e. after German monetary union), the Germans started to have second thoughts. German unity, and the collapse of the Soviet Union's countervailing power, have created a wholly new situation, in which the German need for legitimation from the European institutions has grown appreciably weaker, and in which the Germans will be looking towards the East for economic expansion. This slow realignment led some to voice fears of a new German expansionism. One of Thatcher's trusted friends and senior Cabinet Ministers, Nicholas Ridley, had to resign in July 1990 for remarking about Germany's new role in the EC that 'you might as well give it to Adolf Hitler, frankly' (quoted by Reynolds 1991: 286).

But of course, these sentiments quickly had to make way for a sobering touch of *Realpolitik*. German preoccupation with internal problems in fact forged a 'systemic' alliance between Germany and Britain, who now share an interest in keeping the Community open to possible enlargement towards the East (cf. Reynolds 1991: 287). This *rapprochement* has been visible from early in 1991 (cf. *The Economist*,

9 March 1991, reporting on 'Britain: Turning to Germany').

Some commentators have expressed their expectation that the globalization of German capital 'will prevent any substantially inward-looking mercantilism or economic nationalism' (Gill 1991: 306). The new German strategy might 'forge an alliance with the globalist perspective of the interests in the City of London and the largest UK transnationals, and indeed the UK government, [and could thus] obviate any Euromercantilist tendencies ... and prevent the emergence of a fortress Europe' (ibid.: 307).

It would seem, however, that such a view might take the importance of developments in the ideological and the geopolitical spheres too lightly. The rise of Neonazis in Germany has already prompted the government to shift considerably to the right in the area of immigration, which is certain to be one of the key issues in Europe in the coming decades. And the temptation to forge special relations with the Baltic states, the Ukraine, and Russia, may prove to be a strong stimulus for the Germans to pursue a continental rather than a global strategy (cf. *The Economist*, 12 October 1991).

We can see here the makings of another decade of ambiguity in British foreign policy. On the one hand, the 1990s started out with yet another round of Anglo–American partnership. The Gulf War, the establishment of Bush's New World Order, was fought basically by American and British forces. But more importantly, it had in fact been Thatcher who took the lead when right after the Iraqi invasion of Kuwait, Bush for a short while seemed uncertain about the right course of action: 'if British diplomats are to be believed, she repeated her leading role [i.e. after setting Reagan straight after Reykjavik, H.O.] after the Iraqi invasion of Kuwait' (Sharp 1991: 406). And the continued presence of American troops in Europe is in the eyes of the Tories of course the best guarantee against undesirable German expansionism.

On the other hand, a shift towards a more expansionist posture for Germany is likely to be a relative one, to be conducted within the framework provided by the European Union (cf. van der Pijl 1991). Therefore, if these potential tendencies towards a German *Alleingang* are to be held in check, it will indeed have to be done through the European structures, and Britain has no other option but to work through these.

Even after Maastricht (December 1991) the debate over the precise direction of the European Union is not over: and for that reason, neither is the debate within the British ruling class.

NOTES

1   The structural changes of the British economy (nationally and globally), although of crucial importance in understanding this transformation, will be touched upon only incidentally. The interested reader is referred for more detail to my earlier book which deals extensively with these questions (Overbeek 1990)

2   In Italy, the Westland Affair created a similar disturbance: FIAT's move in support of Sikorsky not only offended the Italian partner in the European consortium, Agusta, but also the Socialist-led government of Bettino Craxi, who strongly supported Heseltine's attempts to strengthen European co-operation in the areas of military production and defence procurement policies. (See Linklater and Leigh 1986: 194).

REFERENCES

Anouil, G. 'La Grande Bretagne et la Communauté Européenne du Charbon et de l'Acier', University of Bordeaux: PhD Thesis.

Blank, S. (1978) 'Britain: The politics of foreign economic policy, the domestic economy, and the problem of pluralistic stagnation', in P. J. Katzenstein (ed.) (1978) *Between Power and Plenty. Foreign Economic Policies of Advanced Industrial States*, 89–138, Madison: University of Wisconsin Press.

Boyd, L. V. (1975) *Britain's Search for a Role*, Farnborough: Saxon House.

Butler, D., and Kitzinger, U. (1976) *The 1975 Referendum* London: Macmillan.

Cox, R. W. (1987) *Production, Power, and World Order. Social Forces in the Making of History*, New York: Columbia University Press.

Davidson, I. (1986) 'The Westland Affair: policy issues', *The World Today*, 42(3), March: 37–8.

Ferris, P. (1970) *Men and Money. Financial Europe Today*, Harmondsworth: Penguin Books.

Freedman, L. (1987) 'The case of Westland and the bias to Europe', *International Affairs*, 1: 1–19.

Frieden, J. (1991) 'Invested interests: the politics of national economic policies in a world of global finance', *International Organization*, 45(4) Autumn: 425–53.

Gill, S. (1990) *American Hegemony and the Trilateral Commission*, Cambridge: Cambridge University Press.

Gill, S. (1991) 'Reflections on global order and sociohistorical time', *Alternatives*, 16: 275–314.

Grahl, J. and Teague, P. (1990) *1992 – The Big Market. The Future of the European Community*, London: Lawrence & Wishart.

Hartley, K. F., Hussain, F. and Smith, R. (1987) 'The UK Defence Industrial base', *Political Quarterly* 58(1): 62–72.

Hayward, K. (1989) 'European Cooperation in Aircraft Manufacturing', *The European Journal of International Affairs*, 6, Autumn: 129–49.

Hennessy, P. (1986) 'Michael Heseltine, Mottram's Law and the efficiency of

Cabinet', *Political Quarterly*, 77(2) April–June: 137–43.

Heseltine, M. (1984) 'The Atlantic Alliance: and Agenda for 1984', *NATO Review*, 32(1) March: 1–3.

Heseltine, M. (1987) *Where There's A Will*, London: Hutchinson.

Holman, O. (1989) 'In search of hegemony: socialist government and the internationalization of domestic politics in Spain', in K. van der Pijl (ed.) (1989) 'Transnational relations and class strategy', *International Journal of Political Economy*, 19(3): 76–101.

House of Commons Report HC 518 (1986) *The Defence Implications of the Future of Westland plc*, 3rd Report of the 1985–6 Session of the House of Commons, London: HMSO.

House of Commons Report HC 519 (1986) *Westland plc: the Government's Decision-Making*, 4th Report of the 1985–6 Session of the House of Commons, London: HMSO.

Ingham, G. (1984) *Capitalism Divided? The City and Industry in British Social Development*, London: Macmillan.

Jessop, B. (1980) 'The transformation of the state in post-war Britain', in R. Scase (ed.) (1980) *The State in Western Europe*, 23–93, London: Croom Helm.

Jones, P. M. (1987) 'British defence policy: the breakdown of inter-party consensus', *Review of International Studies*, 13(2) April: 111–32.

Kaldor, M., Sharp, M. and Walker, W. (1986) 'Industrial Competitiveness and Britain's Defence', *Lloyds Bank Review*, October: 31–49.

Katzenstein, P. J., (ed.) (1978) *Between Power and Plenty. Foreign Economic Policies of Advanced Industrial States*, Madison: University of Wisconsin Press.

Keegan, W., (1986) 'Towards a new Bretton Woods?', *The Royal Bank of Scotland Review*, 149, March: 3–10.

Laird, R. and Robertson, D. (1987) '"Grenades from the candy store": British defense policy in the 1990s?', *ORBIS*, Summer: 193–205.

Linklater, M. and Leigh, D. (1986) *Not with Honour: The Inside Story of the Westland Scandal*, London: Sphere Books.

Oliver, D. and Austin, R. (1987) 'Political and constitutional aspects of the Westland Affair', *Parliamentary Affairs*, 40(1) January: 20–40.

Overbeek, H. (1986) 'The Westland Affair: collision over the future of British capitalism', *Capital and Class*, Summer: 12–26.

Overbeek, H. (1990) *Global Capitalism and National Decline. The Thatcher Decade in Perspective*, London: Unwin Hyman.

Pfaltzgraff Jr., R. L. (1964) *Great Britain and the European Economic Community: a study of the development of British support for Common Market membership between 1956 and 1961*, Dissertation, University of Pennsylvania.

Pijl, K. van der (1984) *The Making of an Atlantic Ruling Class*, London: Verso.

Pijl, K. van der, (ed.) (1989) 'Transnational relations and class strategy', *International Journal of Political Economy*, 19(3) Fall.

Pijl, K. van der (1991) 'German reunification and world politics', *Sheffield Papers in International Studies*, 7, Sheffield: University of Sheffield.

Powell, E. (1983) 'Bad days for British foreign policy', *Guardian Weekly*, 25 September.

Reynolds, D. (1991) *Britannia Overruled. British Policy and World Power in the 20th Century*, London: Longman.

Riddell, P. (1983) *The Thatcher Government*, Oxford: Martin Robertson.

Scase, R. (ed.) (1980) *The State in Western Europe*, London: Croom Helm.

Scheer, R. (1982) *With Enough Shovels. Reagan, Bush and Nuclear War*, New York: Random House.

Schneider, H. (1968) *Großbritanniens Weg nach Europa*, Freiburg: Rombach Verlag.

Sharp, P. (1991) 'Thatcher's wholly British foreign policy', *ORBIS*, Summer: 395–410.

Smith, M. (1988) 'Britain and the United States: Beyond the "Special Relationship"?', in P. Byrd, (ed.) *British Foreign Policy Under Thatcher*, 8–34, Oxford: Philip Allen.

Taylor, T. (1986) 'Britain's response to the strategic defense initiative', *International Affairs*, 2: 217–30.

Walker, W. and Gummett, P. (1989) 'Britain and the European armaments market', *International Affairs*, 65(3), Summer: 419–42.

Young, H. (1989) *One of Us. A Biography of Margaret Thatcher*, London: Macmillan.

6

TRANSNATIONALISM IN SPAIN

The paradoxes of socialist rule in the 1980s

Otto Holman

INTRODUCTION

In this chapter, the theoretical notion of comprehensive concepts of control will be used to analyse the intrinsic and complex relationship between economics and politics in advanced class societies, and place it in an international, or global, perspective. In fact, two important features of the development of the contemporary international system (and more specifically the Western, Atlantic world) in the 1970s and 1980s have made it mandatory to rethink this relationship:

1   the introduction of universal suffrage and the subsequent consolidation of national political systems which are ordinarily designated as parliamentary democracies;
2   the long-term process of the internationalization of capital and the emergence of a transnational bourgeoisie, the characteristics of which have no historical precedent.

After World War II both features have become increasingly intertwined, thus decisively altering discussions and theoretical insights about the economic basis of political decision-making. In this context the notion of concepts of control has been developed to combine theoretically the relation between economics and politics with the relation between internal and external factors within the Atlantic world.

This raises an important question: to what extent can or must the theoretical notion of concepts of control be applied to such diverse countries as Japan, the Soviet Union, Chile or Spain, countries which to a greater or lesser extent do not share the same characteristics as the highly industrialized, parliamentary democracies in the Atlantic area? That is, to what extent do different political systems and different levels of economic development determine the impact of concepts of control in the political articulation of economic interests?

In this chapter we will offer a partial answer to these questions by examining the economic and socio-political developments in Spain in the twentieth century, in the light of its growing orientation towards the Atlantic world and, more especially, Western Europe. Necessarily, the answer will be partial because an analysis of Spain does not offer us a blueprint, applicable to all those countries which show some historical deviation from the 'democratic route to modern society' (Barrington Moore 1981). It does give us, however, a greater knowledge about both the abstract theoretical and the concrete historical significance of the notion of comprehensive concepts of control in explaining socio-political and economic modernization and integration under specific conditions. Or to put it in other words, this chapter will examine the validity of extrapolating from the ideal-typical to the atypical, using Spain as a case-study.

THE PECULIARITIES OF THE SPANISH CASE

The Spanish adoption of Western economic and socio-political structures, the so-called 'Westernization' of Spain, occurred at a moment in which the international political and economic system had changed in a substantial way with respect to the nineteenth and early twentieth century (and even with respect to the immediate post World War II period). In this sense it is necessary to stress the importance of what some have called 'world time'. By this Anthony Giddens (following W. Eberhard) means that 'an apparently similar sequence of events, or formally similar social processes, may have quite dissimilar implications or consequences in different phases of world development' (Giddens 1981: 167). In the Spanish case this notion of world time may be applied, for instance, to the shift from an Estate system to a genuine class-society in the course of the twentieth century, or to the transition from the authoritarian Franquist state to the liberal capitalist state in the 1970s. Both long-term developments were, at least partially, determined by the specific moment in world history at which they took place.

The same may be said with regard to the increasing emancipation of Spanish civil society in the 1960s and 1970s, leading on the one hand to a fundamental shift in the relation between state and civil society and on the other to the coming into existence of comprehensive concepts of control in order to regulate the smooth transition to and consolidation of capitalist democracy. To understand this, let us first consider four points of a general nature about the conjunction between state-civil society relations and the notion of concepts of control.

First, a distinction must be made between those authoritarian political regimes in which the formal subordination of civil society to the state is arranged either by administrative and legal or by repressive means, and liberal democratic regimes in which state-civil society relations are characterized by a cyclical pattern, depending on the rhythm of the business cycle (and the articulation of national and international cycles) without reaching a permanent institutionalized level. This implies that a formal transition from dictatorship to democracy may coincide with a cyclical decrease in the role of the state and a subsequent increase in the autonomy of civil society, yet it may not.

Second, the alternation of global concepts of control within particular nation-states is strongly related to the formal 'insulation' of private economic power and public political and military power, to the succesful implementation of some kind of bourgeois revolution, to the predominance of industrial over agrarian class-structures, to societal integration within the context of nation-state building, and to the effectuation and consolidation of capitalist democracies.

Third, concepts of control, ideal-typically related to the fractionation of capital into money capital and productive capital within the framework of the capitalist mode of production, are continuously reproduced and transformed in the course of concrete historical development. Both economic liberalism and the state monopoly tendency are therefore, as ideal-typical concepts of control, quite dissimilar in present times from their original formulation.

Fourth, as concepts of control originate in civil society, and as the post-World War II process of internationalization has generated a transnationalization of civil society in the Atlantic area, it may occur that the rise of concepts of control in a particular country may precede the formal transition to democracy, thereby in itself creating the socio-political framework for change.

Weak and strong states: the case of Spain

Spanish history from the Restoration of the constitutional monarchy in 1875 to the death of Francisco Franco in 1975 and to the socialist victory in the 1982 elections can be summarized as a long-term shift from oligarchical and elitist rule to liberal democracy. While recognizing this long-term transition, many contemporary observers of modern Spain have attempted to subdivide this period into minor phases or stages of socio-political development (e.g. Payne 1987). In such cases an ideal-typical sequence of stages is used to explain political or economic modernization in individual countries. Periodization then becomes an analytical tool in itself, both in explaining long-term national development and in comparing different countries on the basis of ideal-typical patterns of sequential, progressive change.

Contrary to this view, this contribution argues that periodization always remains a process in thought, and has no analytical power in its own right. Theoretical and empirical analysis must precede periodization. Moreover, periodization is a way of ordering the past from the viewpoint of the present, reflecting our present knowledge of the past, helping to understand our present situation without offering us more than a tendential insight into future developments.

What concerns us here are the underlying developments in Spanish society which have broken the so-called 'vicious circle' (i.e. a weak state which foments individualism and particularism, leaving the field open for the so-called *poderes facticos* who tend to counterbalance any strengthening of the state), and gradually replaced it by a 'virtuous circle' (i.e. a strong state which foments a civil culture based on socio-political mass participation, strengthening interest groups who tend to counterbalance excessive state centralism and tend to insist upon a less hypertrophic state) (Tortosa 1985: 20–1). In this context a 'weak' state implies the virtual amalgamation of political and economic power within an oligarchical ruling class, a class-divided society separating this oligarchic or aristocratic class (or estate) from the dominated classes (or lowest estate), an all-embracing network of patron-client relations serving as a mechanism to contain popular uprisings at an individual level, the absence of nationalism and in general a lack of societal vertebration and incorporation, and finally the fusion of religious, military and political élites resulting in a predominant position of religion at the ideological level and a strong Praetorian tradition. In Spain such a 'weak' state existed from the onset of the Restoration of the Monarchy in 1875.

A 'strong' state, on the other hand, does not have to rely on direct or indirect military intervention in domestic politics in order to safeguard regime stability, making possible the effective subordination of the military apparatus to civil institutions. The same applies to religion at the ideological level, giving rise to the formal separation of the Church and the state. At the socio-political level, a strong state is characterized by a formal separation or insulation of economic and political power leading to the emergence of a political ruling class which obtains a relative autonomy *vis-à-vis* the social classes at the political level while at the same time safeguarding class-domination at the socio-economic level. Finally, a strong state is characterized by a high degree of societal incorporation making clientelistic, oligarchic or authoritarian modes of political domination not only increasingly unnecessary but more important, also highly undesirable and counter-productive. In the case of Spain, the formation of such a 'strong' state cannot simply be related to the transition from dictatorship to democracy after the death of Franco in 1975. Some characteristics developed long before this particular event, while others remain to be developed to their full extent. Still it could be argued that particularly the socialist project of socio-economic and political modernization as implemented after the victory of the PSOE in the 1982 elections must be analysed in the light of the historical formation of a 'strong' state in Spain, and must be seen as a project for further strengthening this very state.

One final point must be made with respect to the relative 'strength' of states. As Wallerstein has stated, 'a state is stronger than another state to the extent that it can maximize the conditions for profit-making by its enterprises (including state corporations) within the world economy' (Wallerstein 1984: 5). This definition includes the position of strength of a state *vis-à-vis* foreign capital operating or aspiring to operate within its territory. From this point of view, the Spanish state was fundamentally weak with regard to its dependence on foreign capital and technology in the early phase of industrialization from 1850 onwards. But what about the protectionist legislation in the 1880s and more generally the steady rise of economic nationalism after the turn of the century, eventually leading to the creation of state monopolies in such strategic areas as the distribution and commercialization of oil products in the 1920s (see for instance Shubert 1980)? And what about the gradual liberalization of Spanish legislation regarding direct foreign investments after the Stabilization Plan of 1959 (see Martinez Gonzalez-Tablas 1979), eventually leading to the famous agreement between the Spanish government and Ford Espana in 1972–3 (see Munoz *et al.* 1974; and Vellas 1979)? And, finally, how do we interpret the attempts of the successive democratic governments, in particular the socialist one, to enforce economic modernization and the subsequent internationalization of Spanish capital in the light of full entrance into the Common Market after 1992?

In the final analysis all these examples illustrate the importance of two related problems when talking about 'weak' and 'strong' states.

First, every analysis of the strength or weakness of a particular state *vis-à-vis* both national and foreign capital has to be a historical one in the sense that it ultimately must be based on an analysis of the historical development of the socio-political power structures within that state. The relative strength of a state is thus always inwardly a function of continuously reproduced and transformed inter- and intra-class structures. Second, any analysis of the relative strength of a particular state with regard to the outside world (may it be the world economy or the international state system) necessarily has to take into account the historical changes at the global level. That is, a position of strength at one particular moment in world history may be a position of fundamental weakness at another moment. The loss of control of the Spanish state over its colonies at the end of the nineteenth century was a sign of weakness; the entrance into the Common Market in the 1980s, and the subsequent loss of part of the sovereignty of the Spanish state over its territory, is a sign of strength inasmuch as it implies the maximalization of the conditions for profit-making by Spanish enterprises within the world economy.

This distinction between weak and strong states may be confusing in the context of the discussion on state-civil society relations in recent literature. Strong states are usually viewed as the counterpart of weak civil societies, and vice versa. This also applies to the distinction between the Hobbesian and Lockeian state. The problem with this way of defining 'strong' states is its predominantly quantitative character. As a comparative category, strong is measured in conjunction with the level of bureaucratization, repression and so on, i.e. with the overall presence of the state in society. As a matter of fact, this view may lead to an a-historical line of reasoning, inasmuch as it cannot explain why a so-called strong state in the course of events may lose its dominance over civil society. That is, the strength of a state is reflected in its relation to civil society, and therefore it seems difficult to explain how a state may lose its absolute dominance over civil society without losing its material, quantitative existence in a substantial way. Moreover, how do we measure the strength of a particular state in a situation where no civil society exists, as was the case in Spain at the end of the last century?

Rather, we should give a qualitative meaning to the strong/weak dichotomy, relating the strength of the capitalist state to the social, economic and political structure of which it is a reflection. Development and modernization (which in the twentieth century imply internationalization) are the processes which may in the long run lead to a strengthening of the state, and to the elaboration of comprehensive concepts of control for that matter. This argument can be resumed in the following scheme:

Civil society	State	Concepts of control
Weak	Weak	Absent
Strong	Strong	Operational

Applying this scheme to Spain, it may be stated that, on the eve of the Restoration, Spanish civil society and the Spanish state were extremely weak, and no concepts of control existed in the strict sense. Conversely, in the 1980s Spain developed a relatively strong civil society and a relatively strong state, while at the same time the alternation of different comprehensive concepts of control was institutionally assured by the new democratic political regime. The Franquist state (1939–76) must be seen as a developmental state: its Hobbesian character (which it definitely had) does not signify its inherent 'strength' but rather its transitional character.

Socio-political and economic modernization

When considering the structural processes underlying the historical shift from the vicious circle of the Spanish Estate system to the virtuous circle of the new parliamentary democracy, we can distinguish five major developments. In doing this, we have to keep in mind that we are dealing with developments that are inextricably interrelated. Moreover, they can be divided into two sub-periods and are layered in the sense that each first sub-period incorporates the characteristics of the next in a rudimentary way. As a matter of fact, contradictions in the first produce an 'erosion from within' and an evolutionary transition to the second sub-period, rather than leading to spectacular ruptures. Not even the Spanish Civil War (1936–9) represented a fundamental historical break with the preceeding period with regard to these five structural processes, although it did produce a rupture in other respects (for instance the virtual extermination of working class representation at the political level, which since then has never again reached its pre-Civil War dimension and content).

In all five cases it was the period of the Franquist regime which in one way or another represented the transition to modernization and Westernization. The following developments can now be distinguished:

1   A transition from a pre-capitalist agrarian economic structure to a predominantly national industrial structure, which became manifest in the first two decades of the Franquist regime; and subsequently, through the internationalization of capital in Spain after the economic liberalization of 1959, the transition from an inwardly oriented industrial structure towards full integration in the world market, resulting in an increasingly internationalized economic structure.

2   A shift in the power bloc from a coalition between big landowners, private financiers and the emerging big bourgeoisie in Catalonia and Basque country, to a coalition between bank capital and national industrial capital in the first period; and a shift from a coalition between Spanish bank capital and national private and public industrial capital to a coalition between Spanish and foreign finance capital in the second period.

3   A transition from an Estate system, in which society is divided into an oligarchical ruling class, characterized by a high degree of particularism and the 'primacy of authorisation over allocation' (Giddens 1979: 162), and the dominated classes, characterized by a low degree of organization, the gap between these 'estates' being imperfectly filled by the so-called traditional middle classes; to a polarized class society in which antagonistic class relations, increasingly caught in the setting of a predominantly capitalist mode of production, eventually reach an actual state of civil war. In the second period this polarized class society, under the banner of the authoritarian Franquist state, experienced a high degree of incorporation through the rise of the so-called new middle classes, and the gradual revival of civil society and its subsequent transnationalization.

4   A transition from a state which formally controlled the whole of the Spanish territory (for instance in its diplomatic contacts with the outside world) but was factually characterized by a lack of a real national unity, by enormous socio-economic and political regional disparities and by a total absence of any form of national integration (let alone any unifying, national ideology); to a highly centralized, hypertrophic nation-state, implemented and directed from above, using national Catholicism as a unifying national ideology and repressing regional autonomy (without however neutralizing the existent regional inequalities). In the second period the excessive degree of nationalism and centralism gradually levelled out, and after the death of Franco it was formally replaced

by a system of 'vertebrated regionalism', which is still controlled from above but gives constitutional space to some form of regional autonomy.

5   Finally, a transition from a system of interest mediation which is usually referred to as clientelism (the Spanish variant of which is known as the system of '*caciquismo*') to a system of state corporatism during the franquist era; and, in the second period, a shift from state corporatism to societal corporatism, which formally takes place after the collapse of the Franquist dictatorship but has its origins in the 1960s.

From state corporatism to societal corporatism: state strategies, civil society and concepts of control

The period of the Franquist dictatorship played a decisive role in changing directions and priorities. In a crude way it might be argued that in the decades preceding the Spanish Civil War politics was heavily dominated by the so-called social question, i.e. the increasing antagonism between the social classes. At the same time this period was characterized by an increasing inability at the political level to find a structural solution to this social question, something which became apparent during the Second Republic (1931–6). As Hugh Thomas stated,

> politicians are the expression of public moods which are the masses' collective dreams. The republic really fell for the same reasons that upset both the dictatorship and the restoration monarchy: the inability of the politicians then active to resolve the problems of the country within a frame generally acceptable, and, on the other, a willingness, supported by tradition, of some to put manners to the test of force.

> (Thomas 1977: 194)

On the eve of the civil war there was no longer a political strategy capable of harmonizing conflicting interests, no ideological discourse could even approximate the general interest. Eventually the Franquist regime came to power after a bloody class war. From that moment on the social question was 'resolved' by force and repression, establishing a framework of social peace (or was it a truce?) in which all issues of domestic and foreign policy could be subordinated to the objectives of economic development and modernization. In this sense the coming to power of the Franquist regime marked the shift from the primacy of socio-political issues to the primacy of economic issues in overall state policy.

This does not mean however, that the political ruling class of the Franquist regime was able to resolve the economic problems of Spain within a framework which was generally acceptable. The 'general interest' was imposed from above through the mechanisms of state corporatism.

Corporatism, as a system of interest mediation, includes both vertical and horizontal forms of political integration. In a dictatorship the vertical forms are imposed by the state in a repressive and coercive way and the horizontal forms are restricted to the *de facto* amalgamation of interests at the top of the corporations; in a parliamentary democracy horizontal co-operation comes into existence, whether or not in a formally institutionalized way, on a voluntary basis, while at the same time downward vertical political integration takes place within the corporations. Every manifestation of corporatism thus consists of both (downward) vertical and horizontal forms of political integration. In fact therefore, the concept of corporatism can be applied both to the system of interest mediation under Franquist rule and to the tripartite consultation between the democratic governments, the trade unions UGT and CCOO, and the employers' organization CEOE in the post-Franquist era.

Moreover, corporatist arrangements are always the result of an initiative from part of the state, and their implementation is the result of a state strategy for managing socio-political conflict, for containing and controlling the labour movement and conditioning the political practices of the working class, as Joe Foweraker puts it:

> Corporatism contributes to the construction of the institutional terrain where political struggle takes place and so contributes to the *conditioning of the development of the social forces in struggle*. It is not denied, of course, that there may be a material economic or social base for the interests held collectively by the 'interest associations' of the civil society; and precisely because of this such (corporatist arrangements) are seen to *condition* rather than *constitute* these social forces.
>
> (Foweraker 1987: 57–8)

From this theoretical point of view we may speak of the similarities between corporatist arrangements under and after Franco. This raises the question as to the differences.

Obviously, the main difference consists in the fact that under

Franquist rule corporatist arrangements were imposed from above in a repressive and coercive way through the Vertical Syndicate; that is, they were characterized by the primacy of vertical mechanisms of political integration. After Franco (neo-)corporatism evolved through a voluntary arrangement between the state, the trade unions and the employers' organization, as such stressing the primacy of horizontal mechanisms of political integration.

Taking the process of transition from dictatorship to democracy into account, we could interpret the eventual fall of the dictatorship as a mere formal act in a structural development from 'state corporatism' to 'societal corporatism', taking those as two sub-types of corporatism. We are concerned here with an institutional transition from a predominantly vertical to a predominantly horizontal system of interest mediation, inextricably bound up as ideal types with the transition from an economically backward and authoritarian state to an economically developed democratic welfare state.

> Societal corporatism appears to be the concomitant, if not ineluctable, component of the postliberal, advanced capitalist, organized democratic welfare state; state corporatism seems to be a defining element of, if not structural necessity for, the anti-liberal, delayed capitalist, authoritarian, neomercantilist state.
>
> (Schmitter 1974: 105)

The use of Schmitter's distinction, however, calls for caution.

First, as with the approach of 'comparative politics' in general, an ideal-typical sequence of stages is suggested, extrapolated from the experiences of highly developed nation-states and subsequently applied to countries in which transitions to democracy have taken place in recent years, as for instance in Southern Europe and Latin America (see O'Donnell and Schmitter 1986). Apart from not being able to explain the similarities (and differences) between individual countries as the result of the particular level of analysis used (see Holman 1987; and Holman and Fernández 1989), this approach focuses on the intrinsic characteristics of state and societal corporatism, conceived in isolation (see Foweraker 1987), without being able fully to explain the historical shift from one form to the other.

Second, the transition from state to societal corporatism cannot be explained exclusively by endogenous factors or developments, even if these developments are part of a global, ideal-typical (and thus generally applicable) process of modernization. The specific form of corporatism depends to an important degree on the position of the particular nation-state in the world economy. In this sense, the strategic initiative of the Franquist state to implement a system of state corporatism cannot be explained without referring, at the ideological level, to the international context in which it took place. Corporatist practices in fascist Italy, the predominance of corporatist ideologies within the Catholic Church at that time, and in general, the anti-liberal, anti-democratic and totalitarian spirit which swamped Europe in the inter-war years, all clearly influenced (and gave ideological direction to) the authoritarian, state corporatist project of the Franquist state. In the same sense, after World War II state corporatist practices in Spain were increasingly confronted with a fundamentally hostile environment, impeding the entrance of Spain into Western economic and politico-military alliances, while after the economic liberalization of 1959 and the subsequent internationalization of capital an increasingly trans-nationalized civil society became highly vulnerable to the logic of capitalist democracy.

Third, and finally, a static and a-historical distinction between state and societal corporatism may result in quite erroneous conclusions as to the transition from the former to the latter. That is, coming back to what we have referred to as world time, a shift from state to societal corporatism in the 1970s in Spain may have other implications than an apparently similar shift at previous moments or phases in world history produced in other states. The formal implementation of societal or neo-corporatist arrangements in the post-Franco years took place in the setting of global economic crisis, internationalization of austerity and the general advance of neo-liberalism in the Western world. In a decisive way this international context determined the margins and the ideological content of the successive state initiatives to reach tripartite agreements. In order to avoid a recurrence of the hegemonic crisis of the democratic regime during the Second Republic, the Spanish political ruling class had to resolve the problems related to the transition to democracy within a generally acceptable framework, in an international economic context of crisis, and without having the ultimate recourse to the use of force.

At this particular point in our argument we have to return to the notion of concepts of control. When we apply this notion to the Spanish case, two points stand out.

First, the productive-capital concept has not come into existence in reaction to the pre-existing dominance of the money-capital concept. If anything it is just the other way round: the plea for economic liberalization in the 1950s, led by the technocrats of Opus Dei and resulting in the opening of the Spanish economy in 1959, was directed against the excessive state monopolistic tendencies in the first decades of Franquist rule.

Second, the specific system of interest mediation in Franquist Spain played a decisive role in the way the two ideal-typical concepts of control were elaborated, reproduced and transformed in Spain. To explain this second point let us consider the notion of hegemony more closely.

Concepts of control are long-term strategies related to particular fractions of the bourgeoisie and presented as the general interest in order to become hegemonic. That is, a class or class fraction is hegemonic,

> not so much to the extent that it is able to impose a uniform conception of the world on the rest of society, but to the extent that it can articulate different visions of the world in such a way that their potential antagonism is neutralised.
>
> (Laclau 1977: 161)

In this sense there is an important difference between dominance and hegemony inasmuch as hegemony refers to the capacity of a class or class fraction to take into account the interests of other classes or class fractions in the formulation of its specific interest as the general one.

Robert Cox has made a second useful distinction, i.e. the one between institutionalization and the use of plain force being each other's counterpart inasmuch as the former tends to minimize the latter (Cox 1986: 219). Hegemony, then, refers to a certain degree of institutionalization and to the capacity of the dominant class to ideologically represent diverse interests without obstructing its own particular interests or material position within the prevailing power structure.

There is a further distinction to be made between hegemonic concepts of control and the concept of corporatism. Both notions have an institutional and an ideological component. Moreover, both notions stress the relationships between the capitalist state and civil society, descriptively in the sense of 'blurring the division between the two', but theoretically in the sense of 'contributing to construct it' (Foweraker 1987: 57). However, hegemonic concepts of control are political strategies, originating in civil society and using the state as a politiccal platform, whereas corporatism is a political strategy of the state. This particular point indicates the main difference between the two notions. Concepts of control are operative in a state-civil society configuration 'in which civil society has achieved a degree of autonomy and self-sustaining cohesion, relegating the state to a minimal, executive role for the hegemonic bourgeoisie' (van der Pijl 1988: 8), while corporatist arrangements are necessary in a state-civil society configuration in which no such self-sustaining cohesion of civil society is yet realized either because of a high degree of particularism or because of extreme class polarization. In this sense, the distinction between state and societal corporatism becomes useful for an additional reason, i.e. the latter being a transitory form of interest mediation from one particular state-civil society configuration to another, from domination to hegemony.

TRANSNATIONALIZATION OF SPANISH CIVIL SOCIETY AND THE 'INTERNATIONALIZATION OF DOMESTIC POLICY'

The capitalist state forms the objective framework within which the elaboration, reproduction, and transformation of specific, ideal-typical concepts of control can take place. Apart from this function as a political platform on which particular concepts can be articulated, the capitalist state has to organize and safeguard the interests and hegemony of the bourgeoisie as a whole. The state can accomplish this only when it can take a stand as an autonomous subject *vis-à-vis* the separate fractions of the bourgeoisie, if necessary.

In the case of post-Franco Spain, the terms on which democratic policy-making had to take place did not favour a mere platform function of the liberal capitalist state. The death of Franco produced a political impasse, in which, on the one hand, the staunchest supporters of continuation ('Franquism without Franco') opted for a mere cosmetic reform from within the old regime, while, on the other hand, the left-wing democratic opposition pleaded for a democratic break with the past ('ruptura democratica'). By far the largest part of the Spanish bourgeoisie objected to both alternatives (see for instance Pérez Díaz 1987). The left-wing option for a democratic break might generate, it was feared, additional pressures to 'break' with existing socio-economic power structures. This detested scenario had to be prevented at all costs. On the other hand, the alternative of the so-called Franquist 'bunker', a moderate reform from above without subverting the foundations of the Franquist state, was rejected for not being far-reaching enough. This last point can be explained by, among other things, one of the most important features of socio-political development and modernization after 1939: the coming into existence of one single 'national' upper class. Franquism 'finally created one single ruling class, and finally put an end to the traditional clashes between the different local interests of each sectorial or regional ruling class'. (Giner and Sevilla 1980: 209) However, we should not conclude from this the creation of a national ruling élite, whose common interests have a neutralizing effect on fractional differences, for that would neglect the modernizing impact of economic and socio-political nationalism on the previous, particularistic mentality of the several ruling classes (Catalan industrial bourgeoisie, Basque industrial and financial bourgeoisie, Andalusian landowners, Madrid financial bourgeoisie). Under Franco, different fractions of the bourgeoisie learned to translate their particular interests in comprehensive and national formulations, appealing to the general (national) interest. The Franquist era generated an increasing social and ideological cohesion of the Spanish bourgeoisie, which resulted not only in the articulation of different projects in such a way that their potential antagonism was neutralized, but also in an increasing preoccupation among the Spanish bourgeoisie with foreign policy.

In itself this fundamental feature of the Franquist era was not enough to induce the Spanish bourgeoisie to reject the cosmetic reform as proposed by the 'bunker' after the death of Franco. It did, however, create the objective basis on which 'the hegemonic classes ... would begin to try to extricate themselves from the (Franquist) regime and turn in search of a new political formula for their continued domination' (Giner and Sevilla 1980: 210–11) once they found the authoritarianism of the Franquist regime inadequate for their own situation under changed socio-economic and political conditions. The elaboration of comprehensive concepts of control, a 'new political formula', was, however, obstructed from the beginning because no self-evident social cohesion existed between separate classes, let alone any natural, historically developed willingness among the labour movement to co-operate with the Spanish bourgeoisie, a situation which was aggravated by the international economic crisis. In this context, in the immediate post-Franco years the Spanish bourgeoisie had to rely heavily on the capitalist state in order to achieve their two fundamental objectives: democratic transition and continued class domination. The centre-right UCD (Union de Centro Democratico), which gained an absolute majority in the first parliamentary elections after the death of Franco (in 1977), could fulfil this role. Recruiting its party leaders from the moderate cadres of the old regime (as for instance, among many others, prime minister Adolfo Suarez), this party could guarantee as no other both socio-economic continuity and political democratization. The method it used has become known as *ruptura pactada* (negotiated break), meaning the continued negotiation of the path to democratic consolidation with the left and centrist democratic opposition. To this end, several neo-corporatist, extra-parliamentary arrangements were made with the most important economic interests' organizations. This negotiated transition to democracy in conjunction with corporatist arrangements succeeded mainly because of the continuous fear for a coup by part of the army. The new liberal state could not, in this context, be relegated to a minimal, executive role and could not serve as a mere political platform for the articulation of hegemonic concepts of control. Instead, it had to take an active, initiating role in order not to repeat the same errors as in the Second Republic. In the words of Hugh Thomas, the ability of the UCD politicians (and especially Suarez) 'to resolve the problems of the country within a frame generally acceptable' determined the course of events in a decisive way. As a matter of fact, the political climate of the late 1970s and early 1980s was in several respects the opposite of that of the 1930s, as was illustrated by the frustrated coup of February 1981.

> Spanish society of the eighties was in no mood for military government. Spain had changed profoundly during the long years of Franco's authoritarian rule. Those who wished to turn the clock back were a nostalgic minority.
>
> (Graham 1984: 4).

Turning back to our theoretical point of departure, an additional remark has to be made: comprehensive concepts of control transcend the strict, national political framework, operating both within and across national frontiers, only insofar as, and because, class formation becomes transnational in character. In this respect the specific role of the capitalist state is not confined to its strict, national character as political platform, but forms the political framework in which the formulation of transnational concepts of control takes place in relation to the accumulation of capital both on the national and the international plane. The state in fact is the very medium through which national, hegemonic concepts of control transcend national frontiers.

The 'transnational bourgeoisie' is that internationally operating bourgeoisie whose global, transnational interests not only transcend but also tend to neutralize the specific and exclusive national orientation and articulation of its economic interests at the political level. The internationalization of capital during the second phase of Franquism (i.e. after the economic liberalization in 1959) did not 'transnationalize' the Spanish bourgeoisie. That is, internationalization was realized through the entrance of foreign capital into the Spanish market, without producing a substantial internationalization of Spanish bank or industrial capital itself. This particular feature has resulted in a close co-operation between foreign and national capital, based on mutual interests, but without changing the predominantly (not to say exclusively) national orientation of the Spanish national bourgeoisie. Of course, the increasing external dependence on trade with, especially, Western Europe did generate an outward looking mentality in the Spanish business community, but did not generate a cosmopolitan view on domestic politics. The internationalization of the Spanish economy remained confined to the national perspective. Indeed, only after the Spanish socialist party took power in 1982 did things start to change in a radical way, leading to the transnationalization of domestic policy to the benefit of some and the detriment of others. And as a matter of fact, this change took place in conjunction with a historical shift in the origin of direct foreign investments in Spain: from a predominance of American foreign investments to a predominance of West European and, more specifically, West German foreign investments. In this context, the growing importance of trade with Western Europe in the 1960s and 1970s did not yet imply a growing global, transnational perspective among the Spanish bourgeoisie. It did, however, form an indication for the direction and orientation of its future transnationalization.

In order to appreciate the historical significance of the hegemonic project of the PSOE we have to return to the period of the Franquist dictatorship. And we may borrow the simplified but useful distinction Benny Pollack made between 'a series of competing ideologies of modernization' during this period. Pollack separates a non-democratic–nationalist ideology, which can be identified with the first, autarkic phase of Franquism (1939–59); a non-democratic – internationalist ideology, which is related to the internationalization of the Spanish economy after 1959, inspired by Opus Dei, without calling into question the authoritarian political system; and a democratic–internationalist ideology, which was adopted by the main anti-regime opposition throughout most of the Franquist period (Pollack 1987: 131). Characteristic for this last ideology was its 'internationalization through democratization' stand. In order to achieve modernization and integration into the Common Market, a prior transition to a democratic political regime was necessary. This was also the position of the UCD government in the immediate post-Franco years, and, for that matter, the opinion of the Spanish bourgeoisie. The ideology of modernization of the PSOE can be summarized as 'democratization through internationalization', which is reflected by the internationalization of domestic politics after 1982, and, even more important, by the transnationalization of Spanish civil society. Both the socialist stand in favour of the continuance of the Spanish membership of NATO, and its efforts to integrate Spain into the EEC, must be interpreted in this manner. The Socialist Party was one of the first Spanish organizations which experienced a true process of transnationalization, long before it even came to power. The Socialist International, and more in particular the German SPD, have had a decisive influence with respect to the ideological formation of the party's leadership (Felipe Gonzalez being a case in point, not in the least because of his personal relationship with Willy Brandt), the spectacular deradicalization of the PSOE in the 1970s and the direction of the party's foreign policy objectives, and because of the financial support the PSOE received from its sister parties. The party's leadership developed a global (West European) perspective from which it interprets domestic politics and economics. The only way for Spain to become an internationally respected and politically and economically powerful nation, it is argued, is to think and act internationally.

THE HEGEMONIC PROJECT OF THE PSOE

Once in power after the 1982 elections, the PSOE was confronted with several objective constraints as to its ability to develop an alternative comprehensive project.

In the first place, the new socialist government was confronted with a context of international economic crisis and the so-called 'internationalization of austerity policy'. As a matter of fact, Spanish socialists learned from the experiences of the Mitterrand government in France and the PASOK government in Greece (both elected in 1981) with their policy of economic stimulation. Right from the start of its first term in office the PSOE began to implement a policy of adjustment characterized by the priority of deflation over employment. Initially this policy was supported by the socialist trade union UGT and institutionalized by regular tripartite consultation. However, in the course of events and especially after the second victory of the PSOE in the 1986 elections, the Spanish economic picture improved considerably. A boom in foreign investment, a substantial decrease in the rate of inflation, rising corporate profits and even an increase in employment were all factors which paradoxically resulted in increasing socio-political tensions between the socialist government and the trade unions, reaching its climax in the general strike of December 1989 and leading to the final break-up of the so-called 'concerted action' between PSOE and UGT. The increasing pressure of the trade unions for improving the conditions of the work-force, and more generally their plea for a *giro social* in the overall policy of the PSOE, was met by a reluctance on the part of the government to change the basic premises of its economic policy.

Secondly, when coming to power the new socialist government had to take into account the continued presence and influence of the so-called *poderes facticos*, the factual powers (the Spanish business community, and especially the large private banks, the army, and, to a lesser extent, the Catholic Church). In fact, the party leadership anticipated this socio-political reality even before the PSOE took office in 1982, which partly explains the gradual deradicalization of the party's political objectives at the end of the 1970s. Characteristic for the position of the PSOE in this respect was a statement by Felipe González on the eve of the 1982 elections:

> I am satisfied if we now implement a bourgeois-reform, through which democracy can be stabilized, and my children are able to realize a genuine socialist programme in the future.
>
> (cited in *Keesings Historisch Archief* 1982: 706)

Initially, the absolute majority of the PSOE in parliament was received with great reticence (and in some cases even with overt hostility) among a considerable part of the *poderes facticos*. In due course it became clear, however, that they had nothing to fear from Spanish socialism in the 1980s, and were even better off. As Pedro Toledo, the president of one of the largest Spanish private banks (Banco de Vizcaya), repeatedly stated, 'the right would have done things worse than the socialist government' (*Tiempo*, 21 March 1988).

Thirdly, in the field of foreign policy the socialist government was confronted in 1982 with a contradictory situation. On the one hand a nation-wide consensus existed as to the desirability of full entrance into the Common Market. From left to right, all social and political forces favoured the formal Europeanization of Spain, although major differences existed about the future direction the process of European integration would have to take, and the role Spain could play in it. At the same time a considerable reluctance prevailed from part of some member states (especially France) with regard to Spanish membership in the near future. On the other hand, a fierce resistance from a large part of the Spanish population existed as to the Spanish membership of NATO, while at the same time great eagerness was displayed by the governments of the United States and other NATO member states for the socialist government to remain in NATO. Finally, the remaining of Spain in NATO was approved in a national referendum, held in 1985, and the formal entrance of Spain into the EEC took place 1 January 1986, being the result of a succesful trade-off by the PSOE government between both memberships, neutralizing both opponents at home and abroad.

Finally, right from the start of its first term of office the party leadership of the PSOE was well aware of the uncertain future with respect to the maintenance of the party's absolute majority in parliament. A deficient party organization, a limited membership and militant support in relation to the electoral base of the party, and, more generally, a poor political performance of the PSOE in the interior, would make the socialist party highly vulnerable to the unpredictable behaviour of the Spanish electorate, or at least could not guarantee stable electoral support over time, as can be shown by the dramatic loss of votes by the centre-right UCD in the 1982 elections (see Caciagli 1986: 231; and Maravall 1982). In order to avoid such a situation and to increase the institutional and electoral stability of the PSOE, the party élite opted for a double strategy, containing both old and new methods. In the first place, the PSOE continued an old tradition, dating back at least to the Franquist state, inasmuch as it attempted to realize a socialization of the party by using the state apparatuses, a case in point of what Lyrintzis has called 'bureaucratic clientelism'.

> Bureaucratic clientelism ... consists of systematic infiltration of the state machine by party devotees and the allocation of favours through it. It is characterised by an organised expansion of existing posts and departments in the public sector and the addition of new ones in an attempt to secure power and maintain a party's electoral base. When the state has always played a central role in both economic and political development, it is very likely that the parties in government turn to the state as the only means for consolidating their power, and this further weakens their organisation and ideology.
>
> (Lyrintzis 1984: 103–4).

This strategy of bureaucratic clientelism was carried through by the so-called 'Guerristas' within the party élite, named after the former deputy prime minister Alfonso Guerra, who controlled the party executive almost completely. And it resulted in what some have called the enormous difference between the 'institutional power' of the PSOE and its 'social presence' (see Sotelo 1984: 48). In the second place, and in order to maintain their political hegemony, the party élite carefully elaborated the constituent elements of the 'catch-all' strategy on the basis of which PSOE had obtained an absolute majority in the 1982 elections. Once in power, an ideological offensive was carried through, aimed at presenting the comprehensive hegemonic project of the PSOE as the only possible one, the only way to realize what was seen as essential for the future of Spain: the country's modernization and Europeanization. Each part of the government's domestic, social and economic policy was presented and legitimized by referring to the necessity of adjusting Spanish socio-economic and political structures in the light of its future membership of the EEC, and, after 1986, by stressing the implications of the magic year 1992 (the end of the period of transition with regard to Spanish entrance into the Common Market, and the creation of the European Single Market).

Theoretically, in the course of the 1970s and early 1980s three alternative projects, to a large extent mutually exclusive, were available to the PSOE party élite, both with respect to the elaboration of its succesive electoral strategies and to the implementation of a comprehensive 'socialist' policy after 1982.

First, the PSOE could have opted for a policy of dissociation, implying the suspension of negotiations with the European Commission and the withdrawal from NATO. Needless to say, such a programme would probably have impeded the PSOE from obtaining an absolute majority, apart from the fact that the resulting political and economic isolation of Spain could only have been based on a vision of global relations which can be labelled as 'eurosclerosis' (*El Pais*, 20 November 1988), a vision totally contrary to the existing, nation-wide Europeanist mood at the time.

Second, the PSOE could have opted for socio-economic state intervention and a Keynesian expansionary policy at home (aiming at the social protection of man and nature), while accepting the conditions of free trade within a single West European market. As indicated above, the Spanish socialists did not implement such a policy of stimulation, partially because they anticipated its negative, macroeconomic effects (see Holman 1987–8: 29–35). Moreover, and this increasingly became the predominant legitimation of the pursued adjustment policy (as the entrance into the Common Market was realized in 1986 and a conjunctural upswing of the world economy took place in the course of the 1980s), reference was (and is) made to the necessary modernization of the Spanish economy from an archaic capitalist and protectionist system to a highly competitive one without frontiers. To this end a tight monetary policy was carried through, in combination with a reduction of public spending to curtail government deficits, and a so-called 'industrial conversion' aimed at restructuring or closing down inefficient or uncompetitive industries while developing new high tech industries. The mentors of this economic policy are known as the 'technocrats' of the PSOE, headed by superminister Carlos Solchaga (Finance and Economy), together with the above mentioned 'Guerristas' forming the most influential 'families' within the Spanish socialist party.

Third, the PSOE could have hypothetically chosen *laissez-faire* and economic liberalism at home, in combination with politico-military protection under the banner of American hegemony within the Western, Atlantic alliance. In fact, this project is the one which is best presented by the neo-conservative Partido Popular (the former Alianza Popular) embodying the neo-liberal and Atlanticist current in Spanish politics. It is interesting to take a look at the links this political party maintains with the so-called *derecha economica* (the economic right), especially if compared with those of the PSOE with other sectors of the Spanish business community. Partido Popular is predominantly tied to businessmen stemming from real estate companies, insurance companies and the finance sector (see *El Independiente*, 17 February 1989: 5). With respect to the seven largest banks, privileged relationships exist with the most reactionary entities, Banco Español de Crédito (Banesto), and to a lesser extent Banco Central and Banco de Santander.

Having said all this about the hypothetical options the PSOE had at its disposal when aspiring to power, we may now summarize the constituent elements of the hegemonic project of the PSOE, part of which only became clear and took definite shape during the ten years in office since 1982. This 'catch-all' political strategy consists of:

1 A 'socialization' of the party by using its power in state institutions to increase the institutional and electoral stability of the PSOE ('bureaucratic clientelism'), an effort organized and directed by the so-called 'Guerristas';

2 An 'internationalization of domestic and foreign politics', which

not only comprised an interpretation of national, economic problems from a global, transnational vantage point (global interdependence determining the specific content of the pursued crisis management), but also a global, non-particularistic vision on international politics, reflected, for instance, in the foreign policy of the PSOE towards Central and Latin America (and the Middle East) which is increasingly moulded in an European setting;

3   Full integration into the Common Market, trying to play a prominent role in the construction of 'Europe 1992', which was interpreted in the light of a transnational European counter-offensive against global neo-liberalism (Gonzalez and Delors versus Thatcher);

4   The remaining of Spain in NATO, albeit under special conditions, attempting to strengthen the European (Mediterranean) pillar in NATO from within;

5   An attempt to neutralize the excessive influence of the *poderes facticos* (army and Spanish bank capital) on domestic politics through a comprehensive project of transnationalizing (part of) Spanish civil society and some elementary state functions in the field of security policy. In this sense, NATO membership intended to shift the function of the Spanish army away from a repressive and predominantly national one (as was the case during the Franquist dictatorship), to an international security one (a case in point of the 'internationalization of security policy' in Spain). In addition, full membership of the EEC would change the attitude of the Spanish business community from a predominantly national one to a transnational, European one;

6   Finally, an attempt to neutralize excessive economic demands from part of the trade unions through enforcing continued tripartite negotiations over the general direction of (socialist) economic policy.

It is this hegemonic project, comprehensively interrelating such areas as labour relations, socio-economic policies, and the international socioeconomic and political order (which might be referred to as 'Felipismo'), which differed in a fundamental way from 'global neo-liberalism' (as can be shown by a comparison with, for instance, the Thatcherite project in Great Britain; see Overbeek 1990) as to its social origins and its socio-economic and political content and impact. When talking about the implementation of 'Felipismo' in Spain, we have to stress the elaboration of a synthetic, hegemonic project in this country, with social-democracy as its natural representative and the obvious counterpart of a nascent Spanish, transnational bourgeoisie on the political level. The constituent elements of this synthesis are corporatism and liberalism as state strategies, and modernization and Europeanization. In this respect, Spanish social-democracy forms the only reliable force with regard to the structural implantation of a hegemonic concept of control which may be denominated as a 'corporate liberal-internationalist' one, lowering the risk of a general systemic crisis or the generation of severe social conflict as much as possible, and thus safeguarding the interests of the bourgeoisie as a whole.

Finally, the 'corporate liberal-internationalist' concept of control of the PSOE was reflected in its ties with determinate segments of the Spanish business community. First, a large part of public enterprise was (and still is) controlled by affiliates or sympathizers of the socialist party, organized in the so-called 'Club de Empresarios'. This employer's club was founded after the PSOE came to power in 1982. Among its members were representatives of the major Spanish public or semi-public companies: Luis Solana, president of Telefónica; Narcís Andreu, president of Iberia and Aviaco; Julián García Valverde, president of Spanish railways Renfe; Carlos Payá, president of Repsol-Exploración and, in sum, directors and managing directors of all the major companies belonging to the public holding Instituto Nacional de Industria. One of the main currents within this 'Club de Empresarios' favoured a conception of (public or private) enterprise as an element of modern society, whose traditional objective of generating profits is conditioned, as regards the method used, by the 'consolidation of the values of modern democracy within the institutional channels' (*El Independiente*, 2 December 1988: 21–3).

Second, the socialist government was inextricably linked with the so-called 'beautiful people of the PSOE', a group of personal friends who occupied leading posts in the Administration and the private (financial) sector: Mariano Rubio, governor of the Bank of Spain; Claudio Boada, ex-president of Instituto Nacional de Industria and former president of Banco Hispano Americano; José Maria López de Letona, ex-minister of Industry under Franco and ex-managing director of BANESTO (imposed by the socialist government against the will of the Board of Directors of this private bank); Miguel Boyer, ex-super-minister in the first socialist government and during the late 1980s involved in a spectacular battle with Mario Conde, president of BANESTO, over the future leadership of this bank (an attempt which, at least in part, was arranged at the highest levels of the socialist party);

and Carlos Solchaga, at present superminister in the socialist government. This group of 'beautiful people' has had a decisive impact on the formulation of the government's economic policy. However, it is important to note that, in constructing the monetarist elements of the pursued ajustment policy, the productive capital vantage point was never out of sight. In fact, it may be argued that the socialist economic policy has essentially the same objectives, although it pursues them in a very different manner, as those of Keynesianism in the European core in the immediate post-war period: to establish a fairly balanced, mixed economic system, resting on the combination of free market mechanisms and moderate state interventionism. In order fully to understand this point, one has to remember the important but excessive role the Spanish state traditionally played in controlling the process of economic development in the course of the 1960s and 1970s, not only through political-economic intervention but also through state ownership of industrial capital. In order not to become a structural constraint on further capitalist development, state interventionism and public spending had to be rationalized and curtailed to moderate proportions, in the interest, first and foremost, of private national and foreign large-scale enterprises. In this respect, it is of interest to note that almost every member of the group of 'beautiful people' had a professional career with an industrial background, either in the public state holding (INI) or the Administration (Ministry of Industry).

Third, close relationships existed between the socialist government and two of the most enlightened private banks, Banco de Bilbao and Banco de Vizcaya, the Basque banks which in 1988 agreed to a merger. José Angel Sánchez Asiaín and the late Pedro Toledo, the respective presidents of these banks, were known to have close personal relationships with Felipe Gonzalez. They were even sometimes called the 'socialist' bankers, not so much for their genuine socialist ideas, as for their ideological and strategic proximity to the hegemonic project of the PSOE (see Rivases 1988). In this sense, it may be concluded that Spanish capital is clearly divided as to its preparedness to co-operate with the socialist government. In fact, when speaking of 'Spain's duel of the century' (*International Management*, March 1989), referring to the attempt of the socialist government to obtain control over Banesto, it must be remembered that we are dealing here with just the *laissez-faire* fraction of Spanish bank capital, and with just a part of industrial capital for that matter.

EPILOGUE

From the very beginning of the first socialist mandate, there were internal conflicts over the contents and general direction of the government's social, economic, and foreign policies, although they were rarely visible to the outside world. The 'neo-liberals' (who liked to call themselves 'social liberals') were initially much less assertive than the 'guerristas' who not only controlled the party apparatuses but also occupied the second most important seat in the government. The prevalence of the guerristas over the neo-liberals was clearly indicated by the forced resignation, in 1985, of the Minister of Economics and Finance Miguel Boyer after a long drawn-out confrontation with vice prime minister Alfonso Guerra.

But in the course of the second half of the 1980s things gradually changed in favour of the neo-liberals. First, the relaunch of the process of European integration through the 1992 project gave increasing legitimacy to the austerity measures of the Spanish 'technocrats'. Second, the economic upswing after 1984-5 effectively raised their popularity, both inside and outside the socialist party. Third, the collapse of the communist regimes in Eastern Europe in 1989 and in general the so-called 'defeat of the left' had an important impact on the power position of the guerristas within the party and the government. Fourth, a couple of private and political scandals further weakened the position of the guerristas (and thus indirectly strengthened the hand of the neo-liberals), and most importantly, forced Alfonso Guerra to resign in January 1991. Finally, the agreements during the European Council meeting in Maastricht in December 1991, and more particularly the conditions set for entering the third phase of European Monetary Union, again have had the unintentional effect of making the neo-liberals in the socialist government look like the objective champions of the 'Europeanization of Spain'.

These factors have turned the original, regenerative and dynamic, hegemonic project of the PSOE into a poor rehash and regressive internalization of the principles of global neo-liberalism.

REFERENCES

Caciagli, M., (1986) *Elecciones y Partidos en la Transición Española*, Madrid: Centro de Investigaciones Sociologicas.

Cox, R., (1986) 'Social forces, states and world orders: beyond international relations theory', in R. O. Keohane (ed.), *Neorealism and its Critics*, New York: Columbia University Press.

Foweraker, J. (1987) 'Corporatist strategies and the transition to democracy in Spain', in *Comparative Politics*, 20(1) October: 57–72.

Giddens, A. (1979) *Central Problems in Social Theory. Action, Structure and Contradictions in Social Analysis*, London: Macmillan.

Giddens, A. (1981) *A Contemporary Critique of Historical Materialism*, London: Macmillan.

Giner, S. and Sevilla Guzman, E. (1980) 'From despotism to parliamentarism: class domination and political order in the Spanish state', in R. Scase (ed.) *The State in Western Europe*, 197–229, London: Croom Helm.

Graham, R. (1984) *Spain. The Change of a Nation*, London: Michael Joseph.

Holman, O. (1987/1988) 'Semiperipheral Fordism in Southern Europe. The national and international context of socialist-led governments in Spain, Portugal and Greece in historical perspective', *International Journal of Political Economy* 17(4), Winter: 11–55.

Holman, O. and Fernández Jilberto, A. E. (1989) 'Clases sociales, crisis del regimen autoritario y transición democratica: los casos de Brasil y España en una perspectiva comparativa', *Afers Internacionals* 16: 5–22.

Laclau, E. (1977) *Politics and Ideology in Marxist Theory. Capitalism, Fascism, Populism*, London: Verso.

Lyrintzis, C. (1984) 'Political parties in post-junta Greece: a case of 'bureaucratic clientelism'?', in G. Pridham (ed.), *The New Mediterranean Democracies: Regime Transition in Spain, Greece and Portugal*, 99–118, London: Frank Cass.

Maravall, J., (1982) *The Transition to Democracy in Spain*, London: Croom Helm.

Martinez Gonzalez-Tablas, A. (1979) *Capitalismo Extranjero en España*, Madrid: Cupsa.

Moore, B. (1981 [1966]) *Social Origins of Dictatorship and Democracy*, Harmondsworth: Penguin.

Munoz, J. *et al.* (1974) *La Economia Española 1973*, Madrid: Cuadernos para el Dialogo.

O'Donnell, G. and Schmitter, P. (1986) *Transitions from Authoritarian Rule. Tentative Conclusions about Uncertain Democracies*, Baltimore/London: Johns Hopkins University Press.

Overbeek H. (1990) *Global Capitalism and National Decline. The Thatcher Decade in Perspective*, London: Unwin Hyman.

Payne, S. (1987) *El Régimen de Franco 1936–1975*, Madrid: Alianza.

Perez Díaz, V. (1987) *El Retorno de la Sociedad Civil. Respuestas Sociales a la Transición Política, la Crisis Económica y los Cambios Culturales de España 1975–1985*, Madrid: Instituto de Estudios Económicos.

Pollack, B. (1987) *The Paradox of Spanish Foreign Policy. Spain's International Relations from Franco to Democracy*, London: Pinter Publishers.

Pijl, K. van der (1988) 'Concepts of control in international relations', Department of International Relations, University of Amsterdam, unpublished manuscript.

Rivases, J. (1988) *Los Banqueros del PSOE*, Barcelona: Ediciones B.

Schmitter, P. (1974) 'Still the century of corporatism?', in F. B. Pike and T. Stritch (eds) *The New Corporatism. Social-Political Structures in The Iberian World*, 85–131, Notre Dame: University of Notre Dame Press.

Shubert, A. (1980) 'Oil companies and governments: international reaction to the nationalization of the petroleum industry in Spain: 1927–1930', in *Journal of Contemporary History*, 15, October: 701–20.

Sotelo, I. (1984) 'Poder institucional y hegemonía social', *Leviatán*, 16, verano 1984: 47–56.

Thomas, H. (1977 [1961]) *The Spanish Civil War*, London: Hamish Hamilton.

Tortosa, J. M. (1985) *El 'Cambio' y la Modernizacíon. OTAN, CEE y Nuevas Tecnologías*, Alicante: Instituto Juan Gil-Albert.

Vellas, F. (1979) 'Ford Fiesta Spain. A case study of international investment and trade', *Journal of World Trade Law*, 13(6), November–December: 481–94.

Wallerstein, I. (1984) *The Politics of the World Economy*, Cambridge: Cambridge University Press.

7

NEO-LIBERALISM IN GERMANY?

The 'Wende' in perspective[1]

Richard van der Wurff

INTRODUCTION

The political unification of Germany in 1990 constituted the major and most surprising political event at the beginning of the 1990s. At home, it temporarily diverted attention from more prosaic questions such as economic growth and unemployment, the environment, and social welfare, thereby contributing to the victory of the conservative-liberal coalition government of Chancellor Helmut Kohl in the 1991 elections. Abroad, it gave rise to an intense debate on the future position of a united Germany in world politics, kindled by (exaggerated) fears for a renewed German orientation towards Eastern Europe and/or a new German bid for supremacy and world power.

Since then, however, both the euphoria and the fears seem to have faded. Other urgent and important issues have claimed the political agenda: the Gulf War, the breaking up of the Soviet Union and Yugoslavia, the European Political and Monetary Unions, and, most recently, the traditional economic topics of inflation, interest rates and world recession. Contrary to some expectations and fears, the position of Germany in these issues has been much more an expression of continuity than of a German *Alleingang* or quest for supremacy and power, although undoubtedly a gradual shift to a more assertive and self-confident international stance can be observed.

The causes for this continuity in recent German politics are twofold. First, politics in the new Germany can to a large extent be interpreted as a continuation of West German politics. As a result of the skewed balance of power between the former East and West German states, unification takes the form of 'West-Germanization' of the former GDR, and not of a mutual adaptation. Consequently, (former) West German interests, class relations and concepts of control dominate the new German politics and will probably continue to dominate German politics in the (near) future.[2] The second cause for the continuity in German politics must be located in the political and economic structure of (West) Germany itself. In this chapter, these structural traits, as well as the dominant concept of control which underlies present German policies, will be analysed.

The dominant concept of control in Germany can superficially be seen as just another branch of the neo-liberal tree. The conservative-liberal coalition under the leadership of Chancellor Helmut Kohl, which came to power at the end of 1982, ended a period of thirteen years of liberal–social-democratic government.[3] In tune with the rise of neo-liberal and neo-conservative politics all over the Atlantic world at that time, the new West German government too preached a moral and economic revolution (*die Wende*). Cultural and ideological restoration and supply-side economics were the new catch-phrases. The Kohl government chose, at least verbally, the internationally flourishing neo-liberal camp.

This transfer of power from the social-democratic to the conservative camp – underwritten by the voters at the 1983 elections – seemed to represent a remarkable occurrence in post-war West German history. Only once before, at the end of the 1960s, had such a transfer of power occurred, then in the reverse direction.

Closer scrutiny, however, reveals a different story. It has been noted by various scholars that the policies of the Kohl government seem to differ much less from those of the previous social-democratic–liberal coalition than is suggested by neo-liberal rhetoric (cf. Alber 1986, Väth 1984, Dolata 1986, Grande 1987a). German neo-liberalism, when compared with the neo-liberal governments in the United States and in Great Britain, can be characterized as quite moderate (see Kastendiek and Kastendiek 1985: 381–2, 395–7; Kleinert 1986: 555).

In this contribution, the question of why neo-liberalism did not sweep away corporate liberalism in Germany as it did in most of the countries in the Atlantic area will be addressed. Why does neo-liberalism take such a different and moderate form in Germany? Can we speak at all of neo-liberalism in the German case? And how does the dominant concept of control structure the German response to the unification and the renewed integration of Eastern Europe and the former Soviet Union in the world economy?

I will argue that the answers to these questions must be located in specific structural traits of the West German political economy. In the first section, these traits will be presented, and the dominant West German capital fractions and concepts of control will be situated in that context. The second section is devoted to a brief analysis of the impact of the crisis of international Fordism on West Germany, providing the background for the rise of neo-liberalism. Thirdly, the development of the political debate in West Germany, particularly in the SPD and the CDU/CSU, will be analysed. Here, special reference will be made to the solutions these parties proposed for the socio-economic problems. Finally, the emergent new concept of control which will probably dominate most of the 1990s will be analysed, and the specific character of West German neo-liberalism will be assessed.

STRUCTURAL CHARACTERISTICS OF THE WEST GERMAN POLITICAL ECONOMY

Continuity in governmental policies and consensus between social-democrats and conservatives in fact characterize the whole of post-war West German politics (Katzenstein 1987). This relative continuity of German politics, in spite of such seemingly far-reaching changes as the transfer of power from the social-democratic to the conservative camp or political unification, reflects the absence of a power struggle between competing concepts of control, which in turn reflects the specific structure of the West German political economy.

In this section, the continuity in German politics will be shortly outlined. Subsequently, the structural traits of the West German political economy which can explain this continuity will be presented.

Stability in economic policies and class relations

The economic policy of the post-war West German governments has always been directed towards a synthesis of a market economy and a welfare state: the *soziale Marktwirtschaft* (the social market economy). This 'third way between unrestrained liberalism and totalitarian socialism' fits in with historical traditions and forms a reaction to the experiences of the 1920s and of National Socialism. It essentially means a combination of a free market economy (seen also as guarantee for political liberty) and a redistributive fiscal policy (Meißner and Markl 1988: 28). The most important elements in this economic strategy are price stability, the creation of favourable conditions for production, a system of social security, and international free trade (Katzenstein 1987: 83–107; Meißner and Markl 1988: 27–32;

164

Lampert 1988; see also Hellema 1980).

It is remarkable that the regulatory role of the state in this approach was and still is by and large restricted to securing general conditions. Until 1967 (the year of the first serious recession after the war) this regulation was restricted to monetary and fiscal policy. In the following years, the coalition government of CDU and SPD introduced certain elements of Keynesianism, but to a lesser extent than in many other countries, including the USA and Japan (Katzenstein 1987: 91, 93). And in the early 1980s these Keynesian measures were partially turned back.

Technology policy formed the only area where through the years the role of the state has steadily grown. In the 1950s, the state was only responsible for the provision of the educational infrastructure. Later on, state responsibility increased when in the 1960s financial support for innovating industries became a new policy objective. This tendency towards greater state responsibility continued in the 1970s and 1980s, when the strategic support for spearhead technologies and the support for small and medium firms became part of the governmental technology policy as well (Bruder and Hofelich 1982; Väth 1984).

A second remarkable feature of West German economic policies is that almost all political and economic actors supported the relatively moderate changes that economic policies underwent since 1945. The change to a more Keynesian style economic policy at the end of the 1960s was introduced by the Grand Coalition of CDU/CSU and SPD, and was supported by the independent and powerful Deutsche Bundesbank (the German central bank) and the influential Council of Economic Advisers. Also, the partial reverse of these changes and the turn to more neo-liberal policies in the early 1980s by the conservative government was already foreshadowed in the policies pursued by the social–liberal coalition of the 1970s (cf. Katzenstein 1987; Esser 1986; Dolata 1986; Väth 1984; Alber 1986).

The consensus on economic policies is paralleled by the relative consensus between capital and labour. In West Germany, a specific system governing the regulation of labour relations has been developed, in which conflicts between capital and labour are depoliticized and resolved in a technical manner. This system is maintained by the reformism of the trade unions, the sharing of the workers in economic growth, and the need for employers to secure the supply of highly skilled (and therefore expensive and demanding) workers (Katzenstein 1987: 126–7, 136–44).

Free trade, price stability, limited state intervention, relatively high

RICHARD VAN DER WURFF

wages and high taxes, and corporatist traditions and institutions, thus seem to be the main ingredients of the concept of control which have dominated West German politics since World War II. This concept closely resembles the corporate liberal concept of control which came to dominate in much of the rest of Western Europe on the basis of the active intervention of corporate liberal forces from the United States. The dominance of corporate liberalism in West Germany however, cannot solely be reduced to this general trend. It reflects important long term developments and characteristics of the German industrial structure itself as well. Only if we take these internal forces into account, can we explain the lasting strength of corporate liberal ideas even in the 'era of neo-liberalism' in Germany, which clearly distinguishes the German case from developments in the rest of Western Europe and the United States.

Historical roots of the West German political economy

In comparison with other West European countries, and particularly with Great Britain, the process of industrialization in Germany only occurred late in the day (from around 1860 onward). This had major consequences for the German industrial and economic structure.

Germany industrialized in a period in which the world economy was more integrated and the methods of production were more highly developed. It was also a period in which the sector producing means of production had surpassed the sector producing consumer goods as the most important industrial sector. As a first consequence, industrialization in Germany was concentrated in the means of production sector. Since German industrialists were able to build up their industries on the basis of the newest technologies, this German capital goods industry was from the start very advanced and internationally competitive.

Second, because of the increased international interdependence and world trade, the strong competitive position of the German capital goods sector on this growing world market, thanks to its modernity, and because of the lagging demand on the German domestic market, the German capital goods sector was from the very start an export-oriented sector as well.

Third, because only the banks could provide the high initial capital investments and advanced management methods that were needed, these banks played a prominent part in the industrialization process and acquired a pivotal position in the German economy (Francke and Hudson 1984: 2, 4–7). Fourth, the need for large-scale production provided the foundation for inter-firm co-operation and cartellization.

And finally, these developments partly determined the introduction of class co-operation in Germany, which can be considered as a fifth characteristic of the German industrial structure (cf. Katzenstein 1987: 127–31; Armingeon 1988). Employers – due to the nature of the production process – accorded a high priority to a stable, loyal and well-trained layer of the industrial working class. Moreover, the state pacified the working class through the early introduction of social security. From the start, therefore, workers shared in the growth of the economy. Consequently, there was fertile soil for the growth of class co-operation between (the reformist sections of) the trade union movement and the socialist party (*Bernstein*), and the representatives of the industrial bourgeoisie.

These five characteristics of Germany's pre-war industrial structure (concentration on a strong and export-oriented investment goods sector, cartellization, the central and industry-oriented role of the banks, and the system of class co-operation) anticipated the dominance of corporate liberalism after World War II. They were all, in one way or another, confirmed or strengthened by the events in the first half of the twentieth century. After World War II, i.e. after the loss of the agrarian regions in the east and the decline therewith of the aristocratic landowning class of the *Junkers*, they started to determine not only the industrial structure of the new West Germany, but the whole economic structure in the wider sense of the word (cf. Junne 1980; Spohn and Bodemann 1989). They thus structured the post-war balance of power which underlay the dominance of corporate liberalism in West Germany.

As noted above, the German banks in the nineteenth century were hardly integrated into the international circuits of money capital. Instead, they were strongly linked to German industrial capital (van der Pijl 1984: 44–5). Consequently, they were directly dependent on the fortunes of the industrial firms in which their capital was invested. In contrast to, for instance, the British and Dutch banks, they were much less dependent on the profits they earned from their operations on the international capital markets and in financing international trade.

The integration of large sections of German money capital with the advanced and export-oriented sections of productive capital within one country (i.e. the classic form of finance capital), which contrasts particularly with the British case, prevented the emergence of a powerful money capital concept in Germany. The interests of large sectors of German money capital were much more reflected in a progressive and internationally-oriented productive capital concept, which in its turn reflected the interests of the advanced electrical and chemical industries.

In addition to this 'proto-corporate liberalist' camp, two other capitalist fractions could be distinguished in pre-war Germany: an internationalist, pure money-capital fraction based on the 'comprador financiers' which were heavily dependent upon Atlantic money-capital (van der Pijl 1984: 74); and a conservative nationalist fraction based upon the backward part of heavy industry and landed interests, with a reactionary productive capital outlook. Between World War I and II, political struggles between these three fractions and concepts dominated the German political scene (van der Pijl 1984: *passim*).

Concepts of control and fractions of capital in West Germany

Just as in other European countries, Fordist production methods were introduced on a large scale in the Federal Republic in the 1950s. Underlying this modernization process was a corporate liberal synthesis between the interests of money capital and of productive capital. In most European countries the dominancy of corporate liberalism was dependent on the active intervention by corporate liberal forces from the United States, where this synthesis had materialized during the 1930s in the New Deal (van der Pijl 1984). In these countries, the tension between the classical liberal leanings of the money capital interests (and the associated colonial interests) and the protectionist leanings of industrial capital were subdued, but not transcended.

In the Federal Republic however, developments took a different turn. Here, the pre-war protagonists of the pure money and reactionary productive capital concepts had lost their autonomous power base. Therefore, corporate liberalism arose not so much as an (unstable) compromise between money and industrial capital but, on the basis of American intervention, as an adaptation of the existing finance capital concept to the growing international competitiveness of the German industry.

After World War II, three fractions of productive capital could be distinguished in the FRG:

1   The old heavy industry (mining, iron and steel);
2   The modern export-oriented capital goods sector (engineering, electrical engineering, chemical industry and car industry), which develops more and more into the direction of so-called high tech sectors;

3   The consumer goods industry and other manufacturing primarily producing for the domestic market (firms in this sector are in many cases heavily dependent on American firms).

In the first post-war decade, the old heavy industry lost most of its prominence (Hellema 1980: 10–11). The industrial equipment sector on the other hand, was and remained the strongest and most successful branch of West German industry.

The German banks are closely related to the capital goods sector. They therefore tend to associate themselves with the interests of the capital goods sector. Through their links with the heavy industry, the banks moreover integrate the heavy industry into this powerful coalition as well.

The economic climate and economic policy in the FRG were thus determined by (the struggle between) the US-oriented consumer goods industry, and the equipment sector's preference for European collaboration and state intervention. Atlanticism was predominant in the periods of active US intervention during the Marshall and Kennedy offensives, the Europeanist tendency grew stronger during the episodes of US isolationism and sphere-of-interest policies (during the Eisenhower and Nixon years) (cf. van der Pijl 1984). However, this struggle was one between two competing strategies for internationalization within corporate liberalism, and not between an international money and a national/continental industrial option. Furthermore, during the 1970s, the Europeanist and the Atlanticist strategies converged more and more into one internationalization strategy as a consequence of the ever increasing integration of the Atlantic economy, the enduring division of Europe, and the strengthening international competitiveness of the German industry.

Thus, the predominance of the modern export-oriented manufacturing industry after 1945, and the historically determined industry-oriented role of the banks, constituted the power structure behind the continuing hegemony of corporate liberalism in the FRG. Competing concepts like a money-capital concept or a nationalist productive capital concept simply lack a power base. This explains the political continuity in West German politics.

The West German 'Ostpolitik'

As is the case with any successful concept of control, German corporate liberalism also determined the conditions for the FRG's foreign policy.

The *Ostpolitik* illustrates this.

Central Europe used to be the traditional zone of expansion for German capital. After 1945 however, (West) German capital lost its access to most of the Central and Eastern European countries. It was only after 1970, when the era of *détente* between the West and the East arrived, that a normalization of the FRG's relations with the East could be effected.

At that time, East–West trade increased rapidly. In Eastern Europe and the Soviet Union, there was a huge demand for high technology products and modern equipment for the manufacturing industry. East–West *détente*, and Soviet oil exports and Western bank credits made the exports of these products to these countries possible.

This conjuncture of international politics provided a perfect fit with the market needs of West Germany's leading industrial conglomerates. The SPD's *Ostpolitik* provided the perfect expression of this conjuncture of domestic German and international developments. West German banks became the largest lenders to the East European countries and the Soviet Union. And West German exports to the East increased. Consequently, when the CDU came back to power in 1982, it had no other option but to continue basically the same foreign policy, notwithstanding the fact that while in opposition it had always opposed it (cf. de Beurs *et al.*, 1989). This is reflected in the fact that Genscher, foreign minister in the social-democratic coalition, remained in this position in the new Kohl government.

Presently, traditional links of Germany with Eastern Europe and the successor states of the Soviet Union, as well as the large outstanding claims of (West) German banks on these countries and their market potentialities, seem to influence German policy towards Eastern Europe. German companies as well as companies from many other countries try to get their share of the new markets.

Fears for a renewed exclusive orientation on Eastern Europe and a related loosening of West European ties seem however largely exaggerated. These fears tend to overlook the major importance of the EC market for the German industry and the growing intertwining of German capital with other European and American capitals. Until now, the German *Ostpolitik* has been largely formulated within a European or even Atlanticist framework (cf. Gill 1991: 306–7).

THE CRISIS OF FORDISM

The West German economy enjoyed a long period of sustained growth after 1945. It was only in 1967 that the first post-war recession occurred: West German GNP fell by 0.2 per cent. This recession in Germany was the first sign of the structural crisis which would engulf the whole capitalist world during the 1970s.

During the 1950s and 1960s, Germany could restructure its economy while at the same time full employment could be maintained, thanks to high economic growth. In the 1970s, this was no longer possible. On the contrary, 'the dynamic of growth itself, because of the predominance of rationalizing investments, deepened the crisis' (Väth 1984: 84). From 1971 onward, the growth industries could no longer absorb the labour expelled by other sectors, and unemployment grew rapidly. In 1974-5, the second full-blown recession meant the end of the era of Fordist growth. 'Since the mid-seventies the fall of the rate of profit in the FRG has become a reality, the long wave of Fordism has eventuated in its structural crisis' (Esser and Hirsch 1984: 56).

In this restructuring crisis which lasted until the early 1980s, large parts of the 'old industries' (coal mining, iron and steel, shipbuilding) were drastically reduced, reorganized and rationalized. New centres of economic growth developed in the high tech sector (microelectronics, new materials) which is widely expected to form the engine of growth for a new long wave of capitalist development. These new technologies therefore became the focus of an international restructuring race, in which national governments played their part by stimulating and partly financing R&D (Roobeek 1990). However, a new long wave of growth presupposes a new social structure of accumulation, and a new concept of control successfully presenting the interests of these new sectors as coinciding with the general interest. What are some of the central moments of crisis for which such a new concept will have to present a 'solution'?

Four aspects of the crisis of Fordism

The crisis of Fordism was first of all a structural economic crisis. The post-war Fordist mode of growth, based on mass production and mass consumption, was no longer able to generate further stable growth. This crisis must ultimately be explained by reference to the capitalist mode of production's inherent tendency towards overproduction (or underconsumption), or disjunction between production and consumption. This implies that a new mode of growth must provide not only a new mode of organization of production, but at the same time a new social organization of consumption. The emphasis on the role of new technologies tends to push this second aspect of the mode of growth unduly into the background.

A second aspect of the crisis of Fordism is the crisis in the Taylorist organization of the labour process, which has reached the limits of its ability to contribute to raising labour productivity. 'Increasing intensification of labour, dequalification, monotony, and alienation give rise to different forms of resistance' and create inadequately skilled and demotivated workers, making impossible the necessary product innovation and specialization. 'The newly created dequalified "mass worker" now [seems] himself to become the main obstacle to the validation of capital' (Hirsch 1985: 169). Flexibilization and new technology are to bring the solution to these problems.[4]

The crisis of the 'corporatist' welfare state is the third element of the crisis of Fordism. The social security system proved to become too expensive in a period of recession, and the co-operation between the state, unions and employers at the national level hindered the adaptation to changing competitive conditions (flexibilization etc.).[5] Corporatism – which was based on the integration of the masses into the state through an elaborate system of material concessions and compensations (Hirsch 1985: 171) – was unable to produce the constant adaptations to changing world market conditions necessary for successful competition by German capital. The increasing number of social casualties of this restructuring process ultimately undermined the legitimacy of the state and the political system – a fact which was reflected in the erosion of electoral support for the established parties (Feist and Krieger 1987: 33; Alber 1985: 212), and which led to the demise of the social-democratic hegemony of the 1970s (Esser 1986: 203).

The environmental crisis is the fourth aspect of the crisis of Fordism. The new environmental awareness has put an end to the idea of unlimited availability of cheap raw materials, energy sources and possibilities for disposal of industrial waste. Although the first impulse was to develop a new source of energy (nuclear), the awareness gradually grew that new technologies and production processes which would reduce the input of raw materials and energy were necessary. Environmental arguments were thus often (if not always rightly so) used to propagate the introduction of new technology.

For West German medium-sized industry the environmental crisis represents an extra cost factor, but many of the large enterprises have discovered that 'green' production can be profitable: the market for environmental technology has become a matter of billions of DM, and the FRG has become 'undisputedly no. 1 with respect to development, production and export of modern, future-oriented and "intelligent" environment-protection technology' (Meckel 1988: 595), with environmental legislation playing an important stimulating role.

The changing balance of power between capital fractions

The crisis of Fordism was accompanied by important changes in the international and (at least in most countries) national balance of forces between different fractions of capital. Internationally, the crisis of Fordism led to the resurgence of rentier capital and the renewed dominance of money capital in the course of the 1970s (cf. Fennema and van der Pijl 1986). In the Federal Republic, however, the crisis primarily led to the reinforcement of the position of the capital goods sector.

Apparently, the restructuring of the economy entails the demise of the iron and steel industry and the rise of a multitude of small innovating 'high tech' firms, often supported by state subsidies. However, the capital goods industry controls these new firms both directly and through the banks associated with them. This sector is therefore able to appropriate most of the profits, new products and innovative ideas developed by the small- and medium-sized firms (SMF) (Esser and Hirsch 1984: 58; Schirmeister et al. 1988: 77). Consequently, the rising innovative SMF are no threat to the dominant position of the large engineering firms. They are rather incorporated into the dominant sector. A side-effect of this development has been that the engineering sector has come to accept government support and government involvement in industry (cf. Esser 1986: 206–7). These changes underlie the growing governmental support for R&D, as noted earlier.

Unlike other Western countries, restructuration in the FRG does not seem to entail the rise to dominance of the financial sector. Self-financing is still the norm (Bundesbank 1984: 12–14; 1986: 43, 45; 1988: 53–7), and the banks seem to consider offering services to companies rather than speculation in their shares as their new market (Schirmeister et al. 1988: 96; Der Spiegel, 13 March 1989; Bundesbank 1989: 14; Arbeitsgemeinschaft 1988: 20–5). The rather restrained developments on the German stock exchanges, especially when compared to developments on Wall Street, reflect the continued marginal position of speculative money capital in Germany. The most important reason for this state of affairs is that the German engineering sector, traditionally strong in the application of new technologies and with highly skilled and highly paid labour, was well placed to adapt quickly to the demands of the international restructuring race. On the basis of its international success this fraction of German capital has been able to maintain and extend its hegemony over other capital fractions, and this in turn gave macroeconomic policy in Germany its extraordinary continuity.

Cultural changes in the FRG

The economic changes and the crisis of Fordism as an economic system are accompanied by an important shift in the value system of the German people. The central element in this shift is the rise of the idea of individual self-fulfilment, which complemented and here and there even replaced the traditional sense of duty and the old labour ethos (Schmid 1986: 10; cf. Roth 1988: 35). This shift is sometimes called the rise of post-materialism, and can be understood as resistance against the 'colonisation of the sphere of living (Lebenswelt)' to borrow a phrase from Habermas; as resistance against the all encompassing process of rationalization.

This resistance is shaped through a number of ideologies: there is the progressive, anti-capitalist variant which is expressed in the rise of the new social movements and the *Grünen*, and the nationalist and conservative variant, expressed in the rise of the *Republikaner*. It is also embraced by the protagonists of the new technologies, who proclaim to offer a solution to the environmental crisis and to humanize the labour process.

The rise of post-materialism is closely related, but cannot simply be reduced, to the crisis of Fordism. Rather, it must be understood as a phase in the rationalization process inherent to capitalism, in which the rationalization of life, resistance to rationalization, and the incorporation of elements of resistance into a new wave of rationalization follow each other. The economic and environmental crisis set unmistakable limits to the rationalization process, causing the rise of independent movements on the basis of anti-rationalization tendencies. Any successful new concept of control facilitating a new phase of capitalist growth and expansion will have to incorporate elements of this critique in order to overcome it.

POLITICAL REACTIONS TO THE CRISIS OF FORDISM

In the previous section it has been shown that the crisis of Fordism, which reached the FRG in the 1970s, in fact strengthened the dominant position of German heavy engineering *vis-à-vis* the financial sector. In this section we will take a closer look at the debates regarding the resolution of the crisis which were held in the two largest political groupings of the country, the Christian-Democratic/Liberal CDU/CSU/FDP coalition and the Social Democratic SPD. At the centre of these debates were two politicians, who since then have receded into the background. One of them is Oskar Lafontaine, the SPD's candidate for the Chancellorship in the 1991 elections, and for a long time considered to be the coming man in the SPD (Lafontaine 1986, 1988, 1989a, 1989b, 1989c). However, because of his unpopular position with regard to unification – which seems to have been fairly realistic in the light of recent economic problems – he lost the elections for the SPD and returned to Saarland, his home *Land* where he is prime minister. The other politician is Lothar Späth, the former prime minister of Baden Württemberg, Germany's 'high tech' *Land* (Späth 1985, 1987a, 1987b, 1989a, 1989b, 1989c). Mr. Späth was for a long time Chancellor Kohl's main rival for the party leadership. A bribe scandal in 1991 made Mr. Späth disappear from the German political stage. But the ideas of Mr. Späth and Mr. Lafontaine, which in my view reflect the new dominant concept of control in Germany and continue to occupy a central place in German strategic political debates.

The discussion within the SPD

After the fall of the Schmidt cabinet in 1982, which forced the SPD back into opposition after sixteen years, and after the worst election results since 1961, the SPD went through a process of political reorientation. The social-democratic model of the 1970s (economic growth, full employment, redistribution of income, social security) proved to have been overtaken by the structural economic crisis, technological developments, environmental problems, and the rise of post-materialist values (Padgett 1987: 335; cf. also SPD (*s.a.*): 3). A special commission, chaired by Mr. Lafontaine, analysed the *Godesberger Programm* (1959) in the light of the new developments and suggested that a new programme was necessary. This new *Grundsatzprogramm der SPD* was presented in December 1989.

The main issues in the discussions regarding this new programme were: security policy, the relation between economy and ecology, the economic role of the state, the significance of post-materialism, and the attitude the socialists should adopt towards the *Grünen* and the green electorate.

There were three major factions in the SPD. First, there was the right-wing faction oriented towards the traditional labour movement, which still (though with growing doubts) puts economic growth before the environment and is unwilling to give up the protection of the Keynesian state. The other two factions recognize the priority of the environment over growth, and also support other non-economic demands (women's rights, Third World aid). They differ over the methods to be used in pursuit of these goals. The most radical faction wants the state to enforce these goals through legislation, and tries to enlist the support of the traditional wing in order to get these demands for state control into the party programme. The third faction hopes to achieve its objectives basically through the market, and through fiscal means.

This last faction was led by the prime minister of Saarland, Oskar Lafontaine. It is his view that the only way for the SPD to come to power again and to realize its progressive goals is through linking the environmental issue to a market-oriented economic policy, a redefinition of (the right to) work, and a sound budget policy. In defence of his line, Lafontaine can point to the fact that both the FDP and parts of the CDU would be interested in co-operation with an SPD taking this general line.

The discussion within the CDU/CSU/FDP-coalition

The Kohl government first of all aims to restore the operation of the free market and to strengthen the international competitive position of the FRG. The power of the unions must be reduced, the flexibility of capital and labour increased, and the role of the state restructured. Deregulation, tax reduction, support for new and innovating enterprises, and political and ideological support for those employers who, in pursuit of these ideals, come into conflict with their work-force, are the instruments with which these goals are to be achieved (Esser 1986: 203–9). Characteristic for the moderation shown by West German neo-liberalism, however, is that neither government nor capital want to exclude the trade unions. Nor do they strive to abolish the present regime for the regulation of labour relations. Instead, they attempt to achieve flexibilization and a shift in power in favour of capital within the existing structures (Kastendiek and Kastendiek 1985, 391–7; Esser 1986: 208–11).

The Kohl government seems to have abandoned the old perception of the state as a centralized corporatist state, dominated by social interest groups and earning legitimacy through its redistributive income policies. In its place, the traits of a new view of the state can be perceived. The present coalition tries to create a state which is as independent as possible from societal interests and is considered to be no longer responsible for the well-being of its citizens. Such a state can thus free money, which it can use for an active and directive industrial policy. The independence from societal interests groups allows the state to pursue its industrial policy as efficiently as possible (Esser 1986: 207; Esser and Hirsch 1984: 59–60). The role of the political parties in this view is to address directly the individual citizen in order to 'discursively and ideologically homogenise' the 'deeply divided society, characterised by its segmented corporatist structures, in the context of decreasing possibilities for material concessions' (Hirsch 1985: 179).

Although this analysis seems to imply that the Kohl government follows a purposive strategy, 'the "muddling through" which is characteristic for "Kohlism"' (Grande 1987a: 319) suggests a different view. According to various authors, the CDU is an instable coalition of different political currents.

Edgar Grande has analysed the ideological heterogeneity in the ranks of the West German conservatives (Grande 1987a, 1987b). He distinguishes five competing currents with regard to economic policy:

1 'Neo-liberals', who argue for the withdrawal of the state from the economy, the reduction of the welfare state, and the restoration of the market;
2 Traditional conservatives, who accord absolute priority to a balanced budget and a reduction of government debt;
3 Pragmatics, who accept the primacy of the market in principle but are willing, on electoral grounds, to violate these principles (and maintain farm subsidies, for instance);
4 Social reformers, who still argue that the state must play a role in the alleviation of social inequality;
5 A neo-technocratic wing which argues that the state must help the market in the process of economic restructuration.

Also, four moral-cultural tendencies in the conservative camp can be distinguished (Grande 1987a: 307–8; Steil 1987):

1   Authoritarian conservatism, which wants to strengthen industrial–capitalist growth but repress ideological changes or divergent morals;

2   Value Conservatism (*Wertkonservatismus*), wary of industrial and technological progress;

3   Neo-conservatism, which is close to authoritarian conservatism, but which, in the fact of the individualizing tendencies of modern capitalism, tries to maintain social cohesion less by repression, but rather by reinforcing and re-emphasizing the mormal importance of the family, the nation, and 'national history';

4   Modern conservatism, which tries to create not a moral, but an 'instrumental' cohesion in society.

According to Grande, West German neo-liberalism must be seen as a compromise between these different tendencies and fractions. The strongest tendencies are the 'economic' neo-liberals and neo-technocrats in the economic sphere, the neo-conservatives and modern conservatives in the ideological and moral sphere.

The ideological heterogeneity in the conservative camp seems to explain the ambiguous policies of the Kohl government with its neo-liberal restoration of the market, its neo-technocratic industrial policy, and its neo-conservative ideological homogenization of society. But, are we dealing here with an uneasy and unstable compromise, or have these diverse elements become integrated into a new comprehensive concept of control which adequately expresses the interests of the dominant capital fractions in Germany in the new world market conditions of the 1980s, as the account of Esser and Hirsch seems to suggest? This last view is supported by the fact that German business supports both the neo-liberal and the technocratic elements in Kohl's policies (Esser 1986: 206–7; Dolata 1986: 431–4), and by the fact that this new strategy was explicitly formulated as a possible foundation for policy formation within the CDU by Lothar Späth. The following facts speak against this interpretation:

1   The constant struggle between the neo-liberals in the Ministry of Economic Affairs and the neo-technocrats in the Ministry of Research and Technology;

2   The uncertain stance and *ad hoc* policy formation of the present government;

3   The refusal of the government to publicly adopt Späth's 'positive compromise' as the basis for its macroeconomic strategy.

These contradictions might be resolved by pointing out that Kohl came to power in an international political conjuncture of rising neo-liberalism. In such circumstances, neo-liberal rhetoric was inevitable, even though the real situation in Germany rather required strong technocratic industrial policies. Partly because of Kohl's weak performance, this deviation from neo-liberalism was never reformulated into positive terms. Government policy remained dependent on the outcome of a struggle between different currents and tendencies, and was constantly influenced by electoral considerations (e.g. *Der Spiegel*, 24 April 1989).

This struggle did not, however, form the expression of a confrontation between two competing concepts of control, or between two powerful fractions of capital with diverging interests. On the contrary, the hegemony of finance capital with its basis in the capital goods sector was if anything strengthened by the course of events in the 1980s, resulting in the specific combination of neo-liberal and neo-technocratic elements. This combination was formulated in positive strategic terms not by the government, but by such politicians as Lothar Späth and Oskar Lafontaine, and by certain representatives of business (witness the utterances of the president of the *Verband Deutscher Maschinen und Anlagenbau* in *Das Handelsblatt* of 31 December 1987).

Although the developments in the German Democratic Republic have overshadowed the ongoing debate for the time being, it is bound to surface again once the euphoria over German reunification is over, and a decision has to be reached over the macroeconomic strategy to be followed in the new Germany. It is striking that even Kohl, who eagerly played the nationalistic card during the elections, in concrete policy formulation stressed the idea of European political unity and European and Atlantic deliberations as the framework for the unification of Germany and of Europe. As we will see, this emphasis on European co-operation and political unity is an integral part of the new concept of control in the FRG.

MODERN LIBERALISM

The emerging new concept of control is most clearly expressed in the writings and political activities of Lothar Späth (CDU) and Oskar Lafontaine (SPD). Having often been cited as potential chancellors, they represent important orientations within their respective parties. The main elements characteristic of their thinking are:

1   That it is one of the central tasks of the state to support the international competitive position of German business through fiscal
policies, policies aimed at the flexibilization of the labour market,
provision of a good scientific infrastructure, support for fundamental research into new technologies, and support for the innovating small- and medium-sized firms;

2   That a relatively high level of taxation has to be accepted;

3   That a high level of wages has to be accepted, both to maintain
domestic demand and to ensure the required educational level of
the work-force;

4   That new ways of tying the highly skilled workers to their firms,
e.g. through paying part of the wages in the form of shares, have to
be stimulated;

5   That the social security system has to be privatized, with the
government only guaranteeing the basic minimum provision;

6   That the environmental crisis has to be solved through technological progress, with the state employing regulation and fiscal instruments to make introduction of these technologies possible without
endangering the international competitive position of German
capital;

7   That large-scale (European) agriculture has to be subjected to the
free operation of market forces;

8   That the service sector is to be considered an important pillar of
the economy;

9   That, internationally, a strengthening of European political unity is
to be combined with global free trade and with intensive economic
co-operation with Eastern Europe and what was the Soviet Union.

This concept of control seems to provide the basis for a new mode of
growth in which the new technologies, increased environmental awareness and the development of the service sector will be the central
stimuli, with their effects both on the supply side and on the demand
side of the economy.

Remarkable in this emerging new concept, and proof of its strength,
is the fact that it indeed incorporates elements of the anti-rationalization critique outlined earlier. That gives it a great potential public
support. Especially striking is the integration of environmental considerations. German policy seems more and more to perceive high environmental standards as deliberate means to stimulate technological
developments, as an incentive to make production more efficient, and
as an effective instrument to increase international competitiveness.

The incorporation of these critical elements does not, of course, mean that the critique itself and the desires for fundamental social change inspiring it will now be realized. Rather, social criticism is defused, the production process renewed, the workers integrated even stronger. But still, the integration of these developments into a new concept of control suggests that they have nevertheless contributed to the formulation of the new concept. Individualization and ecologically responsible production are no capitalist inventions, and a comparative analysis might throw light on the question to what degree non-economic, cultural factors influence the process of capitalist development.

Conversely, the new concept formulates clear demands for a change in the cultural identity of, in this case, the Germans. Creativity, identification with the company, flexibility, openness to new technologies and a cognitive structure capable of quick assimilation of technological change are elements of this new identity, which must be produced and reproduced through education and schools (cf. Rolff 1989).

Compared with the existing concepts, the new concept presented by Späth and Lafontaine can be considered as a mutation of corporate liberalism. The first mutation regards the economic role of the state, which shifts from a policy aimed at the general conditions of production and the maintenance of demand to the supply side. The new state intervention will be directed towards guaranteeing the international competitiveness of German business and supplying the scientific infrastructure needed to achieve this.

Second, class co-operation remains an important ingredient, but is intensified and transformed. Under corporate liberalism class co-operation took the form of tripartite co-operation between the state, the employers' organizations and the trade union movement at the national level. Now, co-operation is sought at the level of the individual through a range of instruments (such as 'skill dependent innovation' and profit-related wages), which makes people individually responsible for their situation, and which obfuscates the distinction between 'worker' and 'capitalist'.[6] The collective, corporatist element of corporate liberalism tends to disappear.

I propose to call this new modernized variant of corporate liberalism modern liberalism. It can be distinguished from both neo-liberalism (which in fact is the re-appearance of classical liberal internationalism) and from neo-mercantilism, which is characterized by a much greater degree of state intervention and protectionism (not in the national, but rather in the European context).[7] If we want to link these three concepts of control to the underlying structuration of capital, we might say (by way of hypothesis) that neo-liberalism is the expression of the money capital concept *par excellence*, and neo-mercantilism the expression of the productive capital concept. Modern liberalism, as identified above, would then be the specific expression of the interests of a tightly integrated, internationally competitive, finance capital (such as German finance capital) (see Figure 7.1).

CONCLUSIONS

In this chapter I have argued that the continued dominance of the engineering sector in Germany, based on its economic success, contributes to a considerable extent to an explanation of the continuity of West German politics. The changes in the political landscape taking place in the early 1980s cannot be explained by a changing balance of forces between different fractions of capital and a struggle between different concepts of control, but must rather be interpreted as adaptations in the hegemonic concept of control.

This hegemonic concept of control is carried by an industrially oriented finance capital in which the capital goods industry is predomi-

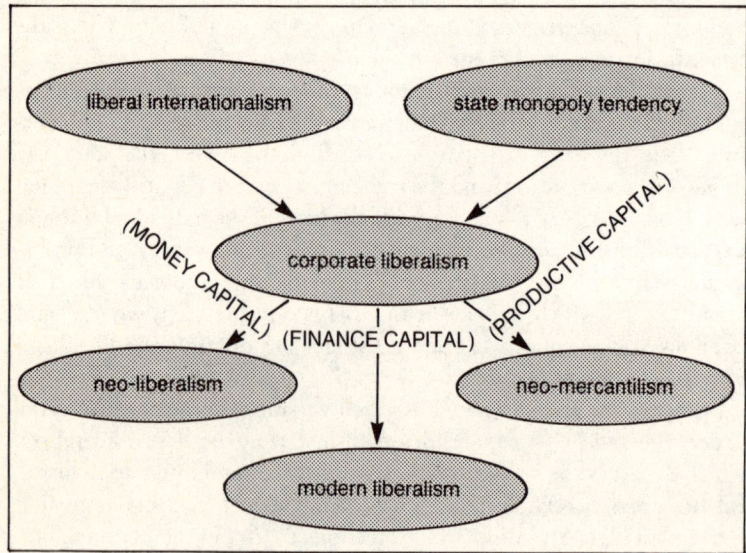

Figure 7.1 Concepts of control

nant. These firms were very successful in meeting the demands of the 1980s and did not require important changes in the regulation of their production process and labour supply. Therefore, these firms required no more than gradual adaptations in government policy and in the dominant concept of control as well. This explains why the new government formed by CDU's Helmut Kohl did not develop a neo-liberal programme in any meaningful sense (that is, if we disregard some of its rhetoric), even though there were forces in the CDU and in the new Cabinet arguing for such a programme. Instead, the particular configuration of forces in West Germany led to the transformation of corporate liberalism into what I have called modern liberalism, an adaptation to changing circumstances rather than a replacement by something essentially new. The unification of Germany with the concomitant boom in domestic demand for new capital goods will only strengthen rather than weaken this orientation.

NOTES

1   This chapter is largely based on a research project carried out in the second half of 1989 at the Department of International Relations of the University of Amsterdam. During this research, the stimulating support of Gerd Junne helped me a great deal to keep the project in full swing and made it possible for me to tackle a broad range of questions in a relatively short period of time. His help is gratefully acknowledged.

2   How unification will affect German class structures and politics in the long run can at the moment not be foretold. Much will depend on the swiftness and the methods with which the former GDR will be economically unified with former West Germany.

Two remarks, however, can be made. One is that according to a report by the Berliner Bank, the future economic structure of former East Germany will be rather different from the West German structure, with a stronger emphasis on the consumer goods industry (*Financial Times*, 6 February 1992). Since West German policy was largely based on the dominance of the investment goods sector, this development might significantly influence German policy in the future.

Secondly, the enormous costs of unification and the consequently growing social unrest both in Eastern and Western Germany might destroy the pact between labour and capital underpinning the successful economic performance of West Germany until very recently.

3   The two conservative parties concerned are the Christlich-Soziale Union (CSU), the party of the late Franz Josef Strauß, and the Christlich Demokratische Union Deutschlands (CDU) of Chancellor Helmut Kohl. The liberal party is the Freie Demokratische Partei (FDP) of Foreign Minister Hans Dietrich Genscher. The social-democratic party, finally, is the Sozialdemokratische Partei Deutschlands (SPD) of the former Chancellors Willy Brandt and Helmut Schmidt.

4　In the FRG, with its relatively highly skilled labour force, these problems are less urgent than in some other countries. The introduction of new technology in this situation is also simpler and hence more acceptable to the workers (cf. Junne 1989).

5　In the FRG the term 'corporatism' is primarily reserved for tripartite co-operation at the national level. Co-operation between employers and workers at the level of the firm is usually considered a precondition, not itself part of a corporatist arrangement (Kastendiek and Kastendiek 1985: 396).

6　This does not mean of course that the structural relation of domination disappears: rather it implies that this domination, the subjection to the 'logic of capital accumulation', must now be internalized by the worker if he she wants to hold on to the job.

7　The notions of neo-liberalism and neo-mercantilism roughly coincide with what Cox has called hyper-liberal capitalism and state capitalism respectively (Cox 1987: 285–98). Cox explicitly subsumes Germany under the state capitalist category, but we feel that to distinguish three variants gives us a more adequate understanding of what is indeed a complex reality.

8　Since these companies mainly produced very small series, traditional craftsmanship still plays an important role and has never been fully replaced by Taylorist production. This is a much better basis to master the new technologies and to introduce a new social organization of production than a highly Taylorized production system (as in the United States).

REFERENCES

Alber, Jens (1985) 'Modernisierung, neue Spannungslinien und die politische Chancen der Grünen', *Politische Vierteljahresschrift*, 26(3): 211–26.

Alber, J. (1986) 'Der Wohlfahrtsstaat in der Wirtschaftskrise – Eine Bilanz der Sozialpolitik in der Bundesrepublik seit den frühen siebziger Jahren', *Politische Vierteljahresschrift*, 27(1): 28–60.

Arbeitsgemeinschaft (1988) *Jahresbericht 1988* Frankfurt-am-Main: Arbeitsgemeinschaft der Deutschen Wertpapierbörsen.

Armingeon, K. (1988) 'Politische Regulierung industrieller Beziehungen. Vom Kaiserreich zur Bundesrepublik Deutschland' *Politische Vierteljahresschrift* Sonderheft 19, Staatstätigkeit (Vol. 29): 151–77.

de Beurs, M., Beijering, S., Dijkhuizen, E., Gibson, M. and van der Wurff, R. (1989) 'De Bondsrepubliek Duitsland en de Oost-West-technologietransfer', unpublished paper. Amsterdam: University of Amsterdam, Department of International Relations.

Bruder, W. and Hofelich, P. (1982) 'Interessengruppen und staatliche Forschungspolitik', *Aus Politik und Zeitgeschichte*, 16(35) 4 September: 19–33.

Bundesbank (1984) 'The share market in the Federal Republic of Germany and its development potential', *Monthly Review of the Deutsche Bundesbank* 36(4), April: 11–19.

Bundesbank (1986) *Report of the Deutsche Bundesbank for the year 1986*, Frankfurt-am-Main: Deutsche Bundesbank.

Bundesbank (1988) *Report of the Deutsche Bundesbank for the year 1988* Frankfurt-am-Main: Deutsche Bundesbank.

Bundesbank (1989) 'Longer-term trends in the banking sector and market position of the individual categories of banks', *Monthly Review of the Deutsche Bundesbank*, 41(4), April: 13–22.

Cox, R. W. (1987) *Production, Power and World Order. Social Forces in the Making of History*, New York: Columbia University Press.

Dolata, U. (1986) '"Überall sind Korrekturen nötig". Die Unternehmerverbände und die regierung Kohl', *Blätter für Deutsche und Internationale Politik* 31(4) April: 425–35.

Esser, J. (1986) 'State, business and trade unions in West Germany after the "political Wende"', *West European Politics*, 9(2) April: 198–214.

Esser, J. and Hirsch, J. (1984) 'Der CDU-Staat: Ein politisches Regulierungsmodell für den "nachfordistischen" Kapitalismus', *Prokla* 56: 51–66.

Feist, U. and Krieger, H. (1987) 'Alte und neue Scheidelinien des politischen Verhaltens. Eine Analyse zur Bundestagswahl vom 25 Januar 1987', *Aus Politik und Zeitgeschichte*, 12, 21 March: 33–47.

Fennema, M. and van der Pijl, K. (1986) 'International bank capital and the new liberalism', in M. Schwartz and M. Mizruchi (eds.) *Structural Analysis of Business*, 298–319, New York: Cambridge University Press.

Francke, H.-H. and Hudson, M. (1984) *Banking and Finance in West Germany*, London/Sydney: Croom Helm.

Gill, S. (1991) 'Reflections on global order and sociohistorical time', *Alternatives* 16: 275–314.

Grande, E. (1987a) 'Schwierigkeiten mit der 'Wende'. Neokonservatieve Ideologie und Politik in der Bundesrepublik Deutschland', *Österreichische Zeitschrift für Politikwissenschaft*, **16(3)**: 303–23.

Grande, E. (1987b) 'Neoconservatism and conservative-liberal economic policy in West Germany', *European Journal of Political Research*, 15: 281–96.

Hellema, D. (1980) 'De politieke karrière van Franz Josef Strauss', *Cahiers voor de Politieke en Sociale Wetenschappen* 3(2) October: 7–26.

Hirsch, J. (1985) 'Fordismus und Postfordismus. Die gegenwartige gesellschaftliche Krise und ihre Folgen', *Politische Vierteljahresschrift* 26(2): 160–82.

Junne, G. (1980) 'De vier aspekten van het "Model Duitsland": hun historische ontwikkeling", University of Amsterdam, manuscript.

Junne, G. (1989) 'Competitiveness and the impact of change: applications of "high techologies"', in P. J. Katzenstein, (ed.), *Industry and Politics in West Germany – Towards the Third Republic*, 249–74, Ithaca/London: Cornell University Press.

Kastendiek, H., and Kastendiek, H. (1985) 'Konservative Wende und industrielle Beziehungen in Großbritannien und in der Bundesrepublik', *Politische Vierteljahresschrift*, 26(4): 381–99.

Katzenstein, P. J. (1987) *Policy and Politics in West Germany – The Growth of a Semisovereign State*, Philadelphia: Temple University Press.

Kleinert, H. (1986) 'Noch wenig Chancen für einen "aufgeklärten Konservatismus", Zum Thema: Wie rechts ist die CDU?', *Blätter für Deutsche und Internationale Politik*, 31(5) May: 553–66.

Lafontaine, O. (1986) *Een Andere Toekomst – De Noodzaak van een Ecosocialisme*, Baarn: Ambo.

Lafontaine, O. (1988) *Die Gesellschaft der Zukunft – Reformpolitik in einer veränderten Welt*, Hamburg: Hoffmann und Campe Verlag.

Lafontaine, O. (1989a) 'Weniger Arbeit, mehr Demokratie', in O. Lafontaine, *'Das Lied vom Teilen' – Die Debatte über Arbeit und politischen Neubeginn*, 9–52, Hamburg: Hoffmann und Campe Verlag.

Lafontaine, O. (1989b) 'Rede des stellvertretenden Vorsitzenden der SPD auf dem Bundeskongreß der Jungsozialistinnen und Jungsozialisten vom 31 März bis 02 April 1989 in Osnabrück', 2 April.

Lafontaine, O. (1989c) 'Die Gesellschaft der Zukunft – Leitideen für den Entwurf eines neuen Grundsatzprogrammes der SPD, 4-10-1989', Köln: speech to 'Internationales Programmforum: Ökologisch und sozial verantwortliches Wirtschaften'.

Lampert, H. (1988) 'Die Soziale Marktwirtschaft in der Bundesrepublik Deutschland – Ursprung, Konzeption, Entwicklung und Probleme', *Aus Politik und Zeitgeschichte* 17: 3–14.

Meckel, H. (1988) 'Technischer Umweltschutz – ein Milliardenmarkt', *Umwelt* 11/12, December: 594–9.

Meißner, W. and Markl, R. (1988) 'Der Staat in der Sozialen Marktwirtschaft der Bundesrepublik Deutschland', *Aus Politik und Zeitgeschichte*, 17: 27–39.

Padgett, S. (1987) 'The West German Social Democrats in opposition 1982–1986', *West European Politics*, 10(3) July: 333–56.

Pijl, van der, K. (1984) *The Making of an Atlantic Ruling Class*, London: Verso.

Rolff, H.-G. (1989) 'Schule und gesellschaftlicher Wandel – Anforderungen an die Schule in den neunziger Jahren', *Aus Politik und Zeitgeschichte* 27: 14–25.

Roobeek, A. J. M. (1990) *Beyond the Technology Race – An Analysis of Technology Policy in Seven Industrial Countries*, Amsterdam/New York/Oxford/Tokyo: Elsevier Science Publishers.

Roth, R. A. (1988) 'Entwicklungstendenzen der politischen Kultur bei Jungwählern', *Aus Politik und Zeitgeschichte*, 30/31: 33–44.

Schirmeister, C., Grünert, H., Kruss, L., Weiß, R. and Burger, A. (1988) 'Finanzkapital in der BRD – ökonomische Macht und Eigentumsstrukturen', *IPW-Forschungshefte* 23(4), Berlin: Institut für Internationale Politik und Wirtschaft der DDR.

Schmid, T. (1986) 'Zwischen oder auf den Tankern? Der schwierige Weg der GRÜNEN in der Reformpolitik', *Aus Politik und Zeitgeschichte* 11: 3–15.

Späth, L. (1985) *Wende in die Zukunft – Die Bundesrepublik auf dem Weg in die Informationsgesellschaft*, Reinbek: Rowohlt Verlag.

Späth, L. (1987a) 'Neue Perspektiven für die Kulturgesellschaft', *Sonde* 3/4: 88–93.

Späth, L. (1987b) 'Vielfalt in der Einheit ist eine Stärke Europas', *Handelsblatt* 251(31) December: 17.

Späth, L. (1989a) *1992 – Der Traum von Europa*, Stuttgart: Deutsche Verlags-Anstalt.

Späth, L. (1989b) *Rede des CDU Landesvorsitzenden Ministerpräsident Lothar Späth anläßlich der 2 Ortsvorsitzendenkonferenz der CDU Baden Württemberg am 1 Juli 1989 in Reutlingen*, Stuttgart: Pressestelle des CDU Landesverbandes Baden-Württemberg.

Späth, L. (1989c) *Rede des CDU Landesvorsitzenden Ministerpräsident Lothar Späth vor dem 28 Landesparteitag der CDU Baden Württemberg am 28/29 April 1989 in Karlsruhe*, Stuttgart: Pressestelle des CDU Landesverbandes Baden-Württemberg.

SPD (s.a.) *Materialien – Arbeitsheft zum neuen Grundsatzprogramm der SPD, Entwurf März 1989*, Bonn: Vorstand der SPD, Referat Öffentlichkeitsarbeit.

Spohn, W. and Bodemann, Y. M. (1989) 'Federal Republic of Germany', in T. Bottomore and R. J. Brym (eds), *The Capitalist Class: An International Study*, 73–108, New York/London/Toronto/Sydney/Tokyo: Harvester Wheatsheaf.

Steil, A. (1987) 'Zwischen Traditionalismus und Moderne. Zur Binnendifferenzierung der politischen Rechten in der Bundesrepublik', *Blätter für Deutsche und Internationale Politik*, 32(3): 297–309.

Väth, W. (1984) 'Konservative Modernisierungspolitik – ein Widerspruch in sich? Zur Neuausrichtung der Forschungs- und Technologiepolitik der Bundesregierung', *Prokla* 56: 83–103.

8

THE NEO-LIBERAL
EXPERIMENT AND THE
DECLINE OF THE BELGIAN
BOURGEOISIE

André Mommen

Devo fare in una generazione
quello che altri hanno
fatto in tre.

Carlo De Benedetti

The neo-liberal experiment in Belgium lasted only seven years, but nevertheless fundamentally changed the way the economy was managed. Politically, the neo-liberal experiment reached an end with a crisis in autumn 1987, but the resulting coalition of socialists and Christian-democrats in fact built a broader mass base for austerity policies and supply-side economics. The obsessive idea was that salvation could only come from sound economic and financial policies and from a new consensus between capital and labour needed to make Belgian export less vulnerable to foreign competition. The end of the Keynesian road to full employment was a fact and this provided the basis for an enormous expansion of stock market speculation and other financial transactions.

At the same time, the transnational character of neo-liberalism was expresssed through the further decline of the Belgian bourgeoisie, particularly the old holding companies and the traditional industrial firms. This became obvious to the public at large when the Italian raider Carlo De Benedetti attempted to take over the Société Générale de Belgique in 1988.

THE CLASS BASE OF BELGIAN NEO-LIBERALISM

Neo-liberalism, in the Belgian context as much as anywhere, meant the

demise of the post-war policy of demand management and full employment, giving nineteenth century ideas of perfect competition and free
market capitalism a second youth. However, modern Belgian capitalism differed considerably from its early nineteenth century counterpart. Neo-liberalism appeared as a retro-idea giving birth to the illusion
that free market competition would lead to a dynamic industrial development and full employment in the long run. In this context it was not
too unrealistic; neo-liberalism could enlist the support of the old middle
class, of professionals and managers, and of a broad range of small
entrepreneurs and sub-contractors. Neo-liberalism even made inroads
into the labour movement, particularly among skilled workers, who
proved susceptible to the idea of an organic solidarity between big
capital and workers in the more competitive branches of industry
against the languid holding bourgeoisie and the workers in public
services. The result was a dwindling of solidarity among workers in
different branches of industry and a real demobilization of the Belgian
working class movement, known for its anarcho-syndicalist traditions.
Thus neo-liberalism also meant a breakup of corporatist conflict
management in industrial relations.

But neo-liberalism was never very influential among the traditional
Belgian bourgeoisie, which had already lost its economic and financial
power as a result of the large-scale penetration of international capital.
The dissemination of subsidiaries of multinational companies within
the traditional industrial structure during the 1950s and 1960s had
provoked a shift from coal and iron to the assembly of motor vehicles,
consumer electronics, and petro-chemical products. The remnants of
the Belgian holding bourgeoisie lost cultural and political hegemony
and suffered from repeated convulsions provoked by conflicts between
Walloon and Flemish interest groups and parties, leading to a steady
process of federalization and disintegration of the old centralized bourgeois state.

The Belgian neo-liberals never pretended to formulate an answer to
the ideological controversies about the state or the ethnic and linguistic
problems; they preferred to portray themselves as offering a purely
economic philosophy of industrial and financial recovery, making the
sphere of politics dependent on economic rationality. However, the
elaboration of a major political realignment around the neo-liberal
project necessitated an alliance of contradictory social groups and class
factions, such as the old middle classes, the professional new middle
class, skilled workers, managers, and some local interest groups, in
order to defeat the hegemonic coalition of organized labour and multi-

national capital and the pillarized system of interest mediation (*Verzuiling*) which had dominated Belgian politics since the early 1960s.

Big capital, i.e. the Belgian holding companies and the multinational subsidiaries, never fully backed the neo-liberal project. The suggestion that neo-liberalism was the project of large companies and big capital is surely wrong: the economic crisis and the fall of the profit rate obliged the multinationals and the Belgian holding companies to beg the helping hand of the state in order to 'socialize' their financial losses. Neo-liberalism was the project of a rather loosely organized network of economists, young ideologues and financial advisers who struck upon the idea of a new political strategy for economic and financial recovery.

Neo-liberalism was not an entirely new ideology of the right. In fact, the Belgian bourgeoisie was well known for its liberal economic philosophy. As long as the Belgian bourgeoisie was able to keep its hegemony over the middle classes and to defend its economic interests on the world market, liberalism sufficed as a rallying point for a consensus among all the property owning classes, excluding the working class and some layers of the intellectual urban middle classes. But during the 'golden sixties' at the very moment when the Belgian bourgeoisie lost its economic and cultural power, the liberal ideas faded away, giving birth to a new alliance of reformist social-democrats, Christian-democratic corporatists and multinational companies. So Keynesianism replaced the paradigm of liberalism as the ideology of capitalist hegemony.

The Belgian holding bourgeoisie

The rise of neo-liberalism has to be explained by the decay of the Belgian bourgeoisie within the capitalist world system. In the nineteenth century the economic and political power of the Belgian bourgeoisie had been built on steel and coal. The major steel factories in Wallonia were linked to investment banks which also controlled stock capital of the railway companies, electric power and light stations, urban transport firms, colonial mining companies and heavy chemical industry. The major instrument of financial control was the holding company. The large investment banks, such as the Société Générale de Belgique and the Banque de Bruxelles, owned specialized holding companies interested in such key activities as railways, coal mining, steel, plantations and non-ferrous metal factories, and mobilized a substantial part of the savings of the petty-bourgeois investors. Between 1890 and 1930 the Belgian bourgeoisie moulded its substantial economic interests into holding companies specialized in controlling electrical power stations and urban railway systems (SOFINA, Electrorail, Electrobel, Traction et Electricité, Electrafina), in mining activities (Forminière, Sibeka, Union Miniére), in industrial conglomerates (Poudreries Réunies de Belgique (PRB), Tabacofina, Union Chimique Belge (UCB), Fabelta, Papeteries de Belgique, Cimenteries et Briqueteries de Belgique (CBR)) and shipping (Compagnie Maritime Belge CMB) (Chlepner 1930: 77–112; Durviaux: 1947, 125–34; Joye 1960).

Two different kinds of financial and industrial empires developed with respect to the lines of international investment activities. The first category was the home-based industrial empire controlled by large banks financing their activities by loans and by purchasing their securities. The most powerful of these home-based empires was the group led by the Société Générale de Belgique. The Banque de Bruxelles succeeded in bringing together steel factories and coal mines when the owner of the Union Allumettière (a subsidiary of Swedish Match), Paul de Launoit, took over an important stake in it (Belart (n.d.): 90). Although they also controlled colonial mining firms and railway companies in several countries, the very aim of their internationalized activities was to provide their Belgian factories with cheap raw materials and export markets (Kurgan-Van Hentenryk 1971, 1982). It is noteworthy that cole and iron made up the core of these home-based financial empires. A second category of holding companies were the largely multinationalized groups specialized in holdings of urban power stations and transport systems. Its major exponent was the SOFINA linked with the German empire of AEG, but independent in its investment strategy around the world (Vanlangenhove (n.d.); De Boeck 1989).

After 1900 a central role was played by the Solvay family (with its relatives in both the Liberal and Catholic Party), which was on good terms with the leaders of the rising Belgian Labour Party, thus cementing a hegemonic bloc of big industrial capital and trade unions. An ill-fated 'democratic coalition' with the Solvay banker Albert-Edouard Janssen, which was in power during the winter of 1925–6, could not materialize Solvay's hegemonic project. During the economic depression of the 1930s the Solvay family tried to prevent the victory of a Popular Front and in 1937 they provided funds for the movement 'Belgique Toujours' led by the socialists Paul-Henri Spaak and Henri de Man. The role played by the Solvays has to be underlined because they were also present on the international scene. The Solvays had made their fortune in soda and they soon became aware of the necessity of internationalizing their industrial activities. As early as 1872, they financed the British firm Brunner Mond and Cy, and in 1926 they were present when the British heavy chemical industries were reorganized through the creation of Imperial Chemical Industries (ICI). The Solvay family held stakes in IG-Farben and US-based Allied Chemicals and Monsanto (Morphologie 1967: 237). On the European continent the family tried to establish a confederation of the chemical industry in order to develop the branch of plastic and viscose production (Daviet 1989: 194), a project which was aborted by the resistance of the French Government and Saint-Gobain.

In Belgium Solvay had to counter the ill-fated attempt of the Belgian banker Alfred Loewenstein, backed by the firm of J. Henry Schroeder, to establish a European monopoly of cellulose (Norris: 1987). Loewenstein failed in his speculative move to merge his Belgian firm Tubize with British Celanese and died in 1928 in mysterious circumstances when flying back in his private plane from London to Brussels.

World War I had shaken the economic and social power of the holding bourgeoisie. Notwithstanding the presence of some leading captains of industry and bankers in the bourgeois parties and in all the coalition governments, a hegemonic crisis destabilized bourgeois parliamentarism because the introduction of universal suffrage in 1919 gave the Belgian Labour Party a share of the popular vote rising to 40 per cent in 1925. In response, the bourgeois parties were transformed into mass parties to organize their lower-class voters. The holding bourgeoisie proved unable to unify the middle classes within one single conservative party. Flemish nationalists broke away from the Catholic Party and during the Great Depression a fascist party led by Léon Degrelle made some inroads into the petty bourgeois electorate in Wallonia and Brussels.

Individual savings sought an outlet in the direction of the stock markets, making speculation in high risk stock from different origins an exciting occupation for the urban middle class. Before World War I Argentinian railway companies, Russian coal and steel factories, Spanish mines (Asturienne des Mines, Rio Tinto), and later shares of Belgian colonial companies had flooded the Brussels stock market. Capitalism meant spreading risk over an ever increasing amount of stock capital, making investment in real estate less attractive than buying shares in industrial and colonial firms. But worrying ideas about the future of Belgian capitalism already began surfacing in books and academic journals because Belgian industry, especially the coal mines and steel factories, required more and more capital in order to with-

stand foreign competition. After World War I the Belgian holding bourgeoisie decided to use German reparation payments to increase
productivity of the steel mills and coal mines, instead of investing these
funds in more dynamic and profitable activities such as mechanical
works, electrotechnical plants or pharmaceuticals.

The lack of innovation was reinforced by the short-term interests of
rentier capitalists, mainly from petty bourgeois origins, who were
mainly interested in dividends, not in economic growth. Even prospec-
tive captains of industry appearing in the circles of high finance, were
not able to break the influence of rentier capital and of holding
companies owned by aristocratic families, leaving to the new generation of captains of industry a strictly technical role. After World War I
some critics of Belgian capitalism stressed the importance of Taylorism
and modern management, but they lacked all support from the core
groups within the holding bourgeoisie and the bourgeois parties.
Modernism remained the ideology of young technocrats around Henri
de Man in the Belgian Labour Party and some young university professors in the Catholic Party.

As a consequence of World War I Belgium had lost its status of 'neutral power' in Europe, obliging the government to redefine its position
within the realm of European politics. The dominant faction in the
holding bourgeoisie did not hesitate to choose a coalition with French
imperialism in order to ensure the defeat of German 'revanchism' and
to put the German government under optimal pressure. German reparation payments had to finance the Belgian economy and to provide the
holding bourgeoisie with new opportunities to invest in foreign countries. So German banks and industry had lost their holdings in Belgium
and important firms like the arms factory Fabrique Nationale d'Armes
de Guerre in Liège, the German commercial and shipping interests in
Antwerp, and also the metal refinery Société Métallurgique de
Hoboken went over into the hands of the holding bourgeoisie. In the
Grand-Duchy of Luxemburg the Société Générale de Belgique allied
itself with the French steel group of Schneider in order to control
ARBED (Jacobs 1988: 437–9). French and Belgian groups co-operated
in exploring the new coal fields in the Flemish province of Limburg and
they coalesced when taking control of the main industrial and mining
firms located in the successor states of the former Empire of Austria-
Hungary.

A drive towards cartelization of the basic industries convinced large
sections of the industrial bourgeoisie to merge its factories into large
trusts or cartels. An international cartel of the steel industry federated

the Belgian and Luxemburg steel firms. Support of the big banks could also solve the major investment problems of the cotton, tobacco, glass and cellulose industry by merging individual firms into trusts which were dominated by family capital. Of course, the Union Cotonnière (1919), Tabacofina (1928), Utexbel (1929), Univerbel (1930), Glaverbel (1931) and Fabelta (1932) allowed Belgian industrial capital to withstand foreign competition by protecting the internal market from cheap imports and by exporting their surplus abroad. But trustification was hampered by the narrow territorial boundaries of the Belgian state and the underdeveloped colonial markets in the Belgian Congo at a time when mass consumption was the only way out of the crisis of overproduction.

During the 1920s, the French-Belgian military treaty of 1920, which expressed the economic and political interests of the holding bourgeoisie and the petty bourgeois chauvinists, had to safeguard the imperialist partition of Europe. But this treaty soon became an object of discord in Belgian politics when the Flemish bourgeoisie started pleading for a neutral foreign policy, a better relationship with the Dutch government and economic collaboration with the Weimar Republic. German economic influence in Belgium was curtailed, but some companies like Siemens remained influential as providers of heavy capital goods. Finally in 1936 the Belgian government denounced its military alliance with France and returned to neutralism, but this time in a totally different international situation. French military supremacy in continental Europe had given to the Belgian holding bourgeoisie the short-lived illusion of playing an important military role in Europe, a situation that could only last until the moment Germany broke all its engagements. In Belgium this provoked a sudden breakdown of popular confidence in the ruling class and the prominent leaders of the holding bourgeoisie whose reputation had already been shaken by financial scandals and corruption.

FORDISM

The Flemish bourgeoisie

The absolute consensus about the primacy of heavy industry and rentier capital was eventually challenged by the Flemish entrepreneurs, who advocated the cultural and political emancipation of the Flemish people. As early as the beginning of the twentieth century, some university professors, urban shopkeepers and intellectuals already campaigned for a respectable role for the Flemish language in administration and business. The Antwerp-based industrialist Lieven Gevaert with his important factory of photographic paper provided the money, in 1926, for the foundation of the Flemish Economic League, the entrepreneurial pressure group of Flemish-speaking industrialists. But the Flemish Economic League proved too weak to challenge the hegemony of the holding bourgeoisie. For the same reason the Flemish bourgeoisie was easily penetrated by German and Dutch bankers and shipowners who subsidized Flemish newspapers and political parties.

Pleading for autonomy for the Flemish provinces meant the dissolution of the highly centralized Belgian state and challenging the political, economic and cultural hegemony of the holding bourgeoisie. Nevertheless the Flemish bourgeoisie argued that the holding bourgeoisie had betrayed its historical mission by refusing to invest in the Flemish economy and by using Flemish labour in Walloon coal mines and steel mills (Luykx: 1967). More autonomy for Flanders could be a solution but, unfortunately, the Flemish bourgeoisie lacked the capital base to supersede the holding bourgeoisie. This explains why the Flemish bourgeoisie in 1927 decided to invest in political power by sending its representatives to occupy the Department of Economic Affairs. The problem with this 'economic strategy' was that the holding bourgeoisie could integrate the Flemish bourgeoisie on the political level of the state by reinforcing its pressure on the financial sector of the economy.

The Flemish bourgeoisie proved its inability to influence the accumulation of capital or to build up a new power bloc. This inability became apparent when in 1926 a coalition government of socialists, Catholic workers, peasants and Flemish bourgeoisie was brought down by the coalesced power of the holding bourgeoisie and its international allies. From then on the Flemish bourgeoisie followed the example of the holding bourgeoisie, making of its 'economic strategy' a guiding principle. The Flemish bourgeoisie now allied itself with the Catholic Farmers' League in order to collect the savings of the farmers for some industrial and financial projects, an economic strategy that had to fail when the Great Depression hit the agrarian and industrial interests of the Flemish bourgeoisie. The bankruptcy of the Catholic Farmers' Bank (1934–5) proved the initial fragility of all initiatives which did not meet the support of the holding bourgeoisie (Van der Wee and Verbreyt 1985: 62–115). During the Great Depression an important part of the Flemish petty bourgeoisie and farmers was charmed by corporatism and fascism, making an alliance with the labour movement more problematic and provoking a fascist mass movement which supported the German occupation after 1940.

Although by then Taylorism and assembly line production had lost their exotic flavour, the few innovations that had been realized could not induce a decisive modernizing spasm into the lethargic structure of Belgian industry. Some Fordist firms had been moving into Belgium as early as the 1920s, but their impact remained rather limited. Automobile firms like Citroën, Renault, Ford Motor and General Motors established their assembly plants in Belgium primarily because of the high tariffs on imported automobiles. During the inter-war period and even until the late 1950s these assembly plants produced for the small Belgian market which mainly absorbed large and expensive American cars for a bourgeois public.

During the inter-war years the 'Fordist' pattern of consumption of the working-class was limited to the ownership of a bike, a radio set and of some electric lamps. The latter sector became the fief of Anton Philips, the owner of a fast-growing Dutch multinational, who in 1919 established his Société Anonyme La Lumière Economique in Brussels. Philips had to match the competition of Bell Telephone Manufacturing Company, founded in 1882 in Antwerp by local capitalists and the American Western Electric Company. Later on Bell Telephone became a powerful company monopolizing the market of telephones and sophisticated communication systems. After World War I Bell even penetrated into the quickly-growing market for radio sets and refrigerators. At the heyday of the boom of the gay 1920s the company employed more than 7,000 workers in its factories in Antwerp. In the same period Bell Telephone Manufacturing became a subsidiary of the International Telephone and Telegraph Corporation (ITT) (Bell 1982; Schoenberg 1985: 108, 114).

However, Bell's strategy soon reached the limits of the small Belgian market for home appliances. This demonstrated the inability of the Belgian holding bourgeoisie to set up large competitive companies in the consumer goods sector. Some minor Belgian companies such as the Société Belge Radio Electrique (SBR) only survived with the financial aid of the powerful Société Générale de Belgique, and after World War II Philips could easily establish its hegemony in the electric appliances branch. Thus protection of the internal market had had no positive effect at all on the development of either the motor car industry or the light electrical industry.

The Belgian working class in this period received low wages and lived in poor conditions of housing and nutrition. A Fordist restructuring of the working-class presupposes a functional separation between production and consumption, a concentration of the working-class population in large suburbs and a relatively high purchasing power in order to enable working class families to buy standardized products. All these features were absent in the Belgian case. Canned meat and processed food did not appear on the menu of the working-class families because a large part of the working class lived in the countryside growing its own vegetables and potatoes, holding a pig or a cow and combining the existence as a smallholder with being an industrial worker in the mines and factories of Wallonia. Their rural roots and their low wages kept the Belgian workers in a situation of semi-dependence on sources of income other than industrial wages, developing its particularism and resistance to capitalist inroads into its way of living. So capitalist firms in the sector of food processing remained small and weak and they had to concentrate their advertising on the more wealthy layers of the urban middle classes. In the industrial towns it was the socialist co-operative movement that organized the proletarian families, thus weakening the influence of the foreign multinational in the food industry. As long as the middle classes could afford aids in the kitchen and other personal services, they would not be eager to invest in expensive home appliances such as vacuum cleaners, freezers, dish washers and mixers. The middle classes, who were conscious of a direct relationship between opulence and food consumption, preferred the restaurant to a home cooked meal based on canned meat and frozen vegetables. The working classes also resisted the 'Fordist' way of living, preferring to spend money in the cabaret instead of eating a portion of frozen soup bought in a supermarket.

Keynesianism without Fordism?

If Fordism was to penetrate the Belgian economy, therefore, it would not be through the help of the holding bourgeoisie, but it would have to be imported from abroad by foreign multinational companies and it would have to be supported by other domestic social and political agents. The Belgian industrial conglomerates dominated by the holding bourgeoisie preferred to produce for the export markets and were only able to survive on a cartelized domestic market. After World War II the strategy of the holding companies remained largely unchanged. But on the social and political level some major adaptations were made under the influence of an increased strength of the left.

During the war the industrial bourgeoisie, represented by the leading

Flemish industrialist Léon Bekaert, had signed a secret Social Pact introducing corporatist industrial relations and proposing the establishment of a welfare state, which meant a virtual breakthrough of Keynesianism. But the Social Pact was also a class compromise, which promised that the hegemony of capital would not be challenged by the labour movement. And as long as the holding companies controlled the process of accumulation the Belgian government had to accept liberalism as the guiding principle for its economic policy. The result was an uneasy corporate-liberal synthesis.

The petty bourgeoisie and some layers of the industrial bourgeoisie in Flanders strongly supported corporatism, which was introduced by law in 1948. The 'Parity Commissions' (central commissions deciding on wage contracts) developed into real centres of social and economic power where labour and capital negotiated national and sectoral wage contracts. However, some of the corporatist institutions, e.g. the Central Council of Industry and the National Labour Board, were soon reduced to the status of simple advisory boards to the government.

The liberal climate was reinforced by a latent anti-tax mentality among the petty bourgeoisie and the entrepreneurs because of the rise in public spending for social programmes. This mentality found its mouthpiece in the small but influential Liberal Party. On the other hand, the conservatives in the Catholic Party neutralized the rising Catholic Trade Unions by stressing religious issues which had the virtue of dividing the working classes ideologically. Both political factions expressed the reluctance of the holding bourgeoisie to become involved in the shaping of a Keynesian Welfare State in Belgium. Financial capital (the holding bourgeoisie and the colonial interest groups) and the traditional layers of the liberal bourgeoisie (i.e. the still influential groupings of textile barons) remained committed to the pre-war economic policy of low wages.

Without a 'Fordist' drive a true Keynesian policy of fine tuning the economy had to fail. Slow growth became the fate of the Belgian economy after the Korean boom of 1950–3 in a period when the major capitalist powers were modernizing their factories and developing new products (Lamfalussy 1961).

The increasingly urgent question was how Belgian industry could be modernized and adapted to the changing conditions on the world market. The key was held by the holding bourgeoisie which dominated the uneasy coalition of steel firms and trade unions in Wallonia. This coalition preserved the dominant position of heavy industry by directing some $15 million of Marshall Aid towards the steel industry and the marginal coal mines, instead of closing down these collieries and building modern integrated steel mills near the seaports. The final outcome was that Marshall Aid reinforced the traditional structure of the Belgian economy instead of modernizing it, and increased the level of general costs while producers for the market of mass consumption were in great need of cheap energy and raw materials.

Trade unions and industrial consumers urged the government to intervene and nationalize the whole sector of energy and electricity. This threat of 'creeping nationalization' which would hit the holding bourgeoisie in its vital parts, was rebuffed by mobilizing the Keynesian consensus-producing apparatus. In 1955 a Committee of Control for the Production and Distribution of Electricity started to restructure the whole sector in line with consumers' needs. One might have thought that the holding companies were now losing control of the energy sector, because a semi-public control committee regulated investment and distribution. However, the public regulation of investment enabled the holding companies to collect enough capital to rationalize and concentrate the scattered production units, showing that a measure of public control could boost private profits in the short run.

In the long run, more fundamental changes in the energy sector were needed. The option of the Belgian government was to replace coal with nuclear power, which meant a huge effort of both government and holding companies in order to develop and build nuclear power units. A research centre sponsored by public funds was to develop a Belgian reactor, while a privately-owned company (Belgonucléaire) started in 1957 with some expensive experiments in the field of the enrichment of uranium. At the very moment, however, when the holding bourgeoisie decided to build high-performance nuclear power units in Belgium, French and American companies (Westinghouse, Framatome) moved in. In this way the holding bourgeoisie was deprived of control over a strategic basic sector. The process of transnationalization of the Belgian economy, and the concomitant decline of the Belgian bourgeoisie, had entered a new stage.

THE KEYNESIAN BREAKTHROUGH

In 1954 trade unions and entrepreneurs signed a Joint Declaration on Productivity, making it clear that the Keynesian income policy had to be paid out of higher productivity in industry and better export performances. However, the holding bourgeoisie was not prepared to consider the possibility of investment in new industrial activities beyond the realm of the heavy industry and the processing of colonial raw materials. Higher productivity was the accidental result of a defensive investment policy induced by the holding companies in order to strengthen their position in some key markets of non-ferrous metals, heavy chemicals and energy. Nonetheless, external influences and necessities generated by the general development of global capitalism required structural changes which would eventually occur in the years 1958–61.

First, the Schuman Plan (1950) obliged the Walloon coal mine owners and the holding bourgeoisie to reorganize. The Belgian government launched an emergency programme financed by the European Coal and Steel Community (ECSC) in order to save the depressed industrial areas, and helped the bankrupt pit-owners to rescue their holdings.

Second, the Treaty of Rome (1957) establishing the European Economic Community (EEC) obliged the Belgian holding companies and their subsidiaries to face foreign competition and to modernize their industries. The rivalry between the major holding companies, i.c. the group of Baron P. de Launoit (COFININDUS, Brufina, Banque de Bruxelles) and the Société Générale, was transformed into co-operation when in 1955 they merged their holdings in Cockerill and Ougrée-Marihaye into Cockerill-Ougrée. In the 1960s the Forges de la Providence, with their huge blast furnaces and coke-ovens in France, and Espérance-Longdoz, then controlled by the Baron Coppée, were also incorporated into Cockerill-Ougrée. In the end however, this continuous process of centralization could not preserve the Walloon steel works from total bankruptcy.[1]

Third, a real adaptation to the needs of the modern consumer goods industries was made by the commercial banks. The old tradition that the holding companies created their own commercial banks to collect cash money from their subsidiaries had always caused problems for innovating firms outside the orbit of the holding companies. With the huge amounts of cash money needed by the subsidiaries of the Fordist multinationals arriving in Belgium, the banking system could no longer cope and had to be reformed, an operation which provoked serious conflicts in the leading circles of the holding bourgeoisie.

Fourth, industrial activity in Wallonia declined and investment was directed towards the Flemish areas, mainly the port of Antwerp. For a long time, Antwerp had served as a transit harbour without industrial activity. After World War II a large investment programme modernized the harbour installations, allowing the petrochemical industry and the motor car plants of General Motors and Ford Motor to enlarge their operations. Chemical firms like Monsanto, Amoco, BASF, Bayer, Signal Oil, Esso, Shell, Texaco, Solvay and Petrofina enlarged the 'Fordist' industrial area with a well-paid 'new working class' of at least 50,000 workers in the petrochemical industry. Coal and iron ore were imported from overseas, dictating a relocation of the new steel mills and the coke-ovens near the North Sea. In 1961 SIDMAR (Sidérurgie Maritime) erected an important integrated steel factory near the sea canal of Ghent-Terneuzen.[2]

Fifth, the Christian-democratic modernizers were very successful in manoeuvring the conservative fraction of Walloon pit-owners and textile barons out of the leading circles of the Catholic Party. Léon Bekaert, surrounded by university professors and technocrats, and the modernizers of the financial bourgeoisie headed by the Solvay family and the investment banker Baron Léon Lambert, provoked a corporate-liberal breakthrough in the entrepreneurial organizations now dominated by multinational capital. In 1958 the Catholic Party had won the general election by promising 100,000 new jobs and a modernization of the whole agricultural sector, which would require public investment and regulation. A group of young Catholic technocrats around Fernand Nédée and Jacques de Staercke had defended this position when they rewrote the electoral programme of the Catholic party. In the same year both men founded the 'Tuesday Evening Group', which was an informal debating group of Keynesian and corporate-liberal modernizers. In the French-speaking wing of the Catholic Party the same point of view soon became prominent through 'La Relève', a journal led and sponsored by the investment banker Raymond Scheyven (Banque Allard, Solvay).

It was clear that the new electoral programme of the Catholic Party prepared the conditions for a corporate-liberal coalition urging the social-democrats and the modernizing wing of the Catholic Party to join hands. But the electoral victory of the Catholic Party only led to a pacification of clerical/anticlerical antagonisms, not to a 'Roman-Red' (= catholic-socialist) coalition government headed by Keynesian technocrats. The outcome, on the contrary, was a Catholic-Liberal government, giving the conservative bourgeoisie continued control over economic policy. Belgium was still waiting for major political and ideological changes.

Fordist hegemony

In 1958 unemployment suddenly rose above the 10 per cent margin. A spending deficit that was even worse was caused by the further decline of the coal and textile industry and called for a surgical intervention. In 1959 Prime Minister Gaston Eyskens installed a Central Planning Office, introduced a regional development programme and in 1960 installed a National Committee for Economic Expansion. At first obstruction from Liberal quarters and the influence of holding companies made these changes hollow. An unexpected popular revolt in the Belgian Congo in the early days of 1959 would, after bitter political strife, eventually lead to the demise of conservatism. The holding companies with their enormous mining interests initially urged Prime Minister Gaston Eyskens for 'une promenade militaire au Congo' (Eyskens 1988: 122). But the Government chose the path of decolonization. When in 1960 the decolonization process in Congo ended in disaster, a tightly knit group of aristocrats, Catholic right-wingers, conservative bankers, generals and Royalists led by Viscount Paul van Zeeland (Banque de Bruxelles, Banque Belge d'Afrique), Count Harold d'Aspremont-Lynden (Banque de Bruxelles, CMB) and Count Gobert d'Aspremont-Lynden (Grand-Marshal of His Majesty's Court) prepared for an abortive coup in a last attempt to stem the tides of change (Hoflack 1989: 73; Eyskens 1988: 127; Verhoeyen and Uytterhaegen 1981: 118–21).

Behind the scenes a Roman-Red coalition government was meanwhile being prepared during informal consultations at the dinner table of Baron Léon Lambert. Théo Lefèvre, president of the Catholic Party, and socialists like Paul-Henri Spaak (secretary-general of NATO), Antoine Spinoy and Henri Simonet (whose wife had joined the Banque Lambert) discussed with Baron Lambert the way a Roman-Red coalition government could take over (Hoflack 1989: 78).

In the autumn of 1960 the ailing government of Gaston Eyskens was finally toppled by a General Strike. Some layers of the working class in Wallonia believed that socialism was about to arrive (Deprez 1963; Féaux 1963; Meynen 1978). But the General Strike only preluded a new stage in the accumulation of capital and marked the end of classical anarcho-syndicalism, just as this episode marked the definitive turnaround in the fortunes of the holding bourgeoisie.

After the ensuing elections a new coalition led by Théo Lefèvre and Paul-Henri Spaak, with Antoine Spinoy at Economic Affairs, was formed, representing the modernizing forces of the bourgeoisie and the labour movement. The new Roman-Red government declared to stand for a policy of economic expansion, public intervention in the accumulation of capital and export-led growth. It opened the door for multinational companies and the influx of capital raised the average growth rate to between 4 and 6 per cent, leading to mass consumption of durable goods and to an increased standard of collective services. The government assigned to the state the role of regulator of the process of accumulation, and in 1961 a Directory of the Coalmines was installed in order to programme the closure of the marginal collieries. In 1962 the government installed the National Investment Corporation. This holding company led by the socialist technocrat Henri Neuman prepared for a more aggressive policy of industrial restructuring. The National Company for Industrial Credit and the state-owned General Savings Bank provided cheap credit to all multinational investors coming to Belgium.

The advent of the Roman-Red coalitions, and the influx of foreign capital, marked the further decline of the traditional holding bourgeoisie, and the erosion of its capacity to dominate the political and ideological arenas. The backward layers of the industrial bourgeoisie, engaged in obsolete branches (shoemaking, textile, wooden furniture, paper, railway equipment, heavy metal products) reacted by mobilizing all conservative forces against a government that had made 'creeping communism' its programme of action. As early as 1961 the Liberal Party had transformed itself into a Party for Liberty and Progress (PLP) mobilizing right-wing Catholics and Liberals against 'collectivism'. The PLP was led by Omer Vanaudenhove, an owner of a shoe factory, and clearly represented a bourgeoisie which was at odds with the unions and multinational capital. The PLP also represented the petty bourgeoisie and rentier capitalists by making rising inflation and taxation its major argument against the Keynesian Welfare State. In 1965 the PLP polled a fair 20 per cent of the vote, a doubling of the vote of the earlier Liberal Party. Nonetheless, the PLP failed to make a significant breakthrough into the socialist and Catholic electorate.

In 1966, the Roman-Red government resigned and a coalition of Christian-Democrats and Liberals, which stayed in power for only two years (1966–8), tried to reconcile the traditional bourgeoisie and rentiers with multinational capital. Prime Minister Paul Vanden Boeynants was inclined towards an authoritarian experiment, but he had to face the opposition of the Catholic trade unionists within his own party. Growing discontent in Flanders about the highly centralized Belgian state would soon give birth to regional linguistic parties challenging the 'traditional' parties. In the spring of 1968 Vanden Boey-nants had to resign as Prime Minister, in spite of his personal success in his electoral district in Brussels with his slogan 'J'ai besoin de vous!'. The defeat of the conservative reaction was consummated when Vanden Boeynants started talks with the PLP in order to realign all Belgian nationalists within one big party, and when Omer Vanauden-hove was removed from his presidency of the PLP. The influx of foreign capital had eroded the social, political and cultural influence of the holding bourgeoisie.

The hegemonic crisis provoked by the decline of the holding bour-geoisie made the rising Flemish bourgeoisie a natural and indispensable ally of trade unions and multinational companies within the emergent corporate-liberal coalition. Multinational investment in Flanders strengthened this process by the growing interpenetration of Flemish and multinational capital. The best-known example was the case of Gevaert Photoproducten, once a pioneering firm and organizer of Flemish economic recovery, which merged in 1962 with the German firm Agfa-Bayer to form Agfa-Gevaert.

The Flemish bourgeoisie also articulated reactionary ideas which harmonized with its vehement populism. In 1977 some prominent members of the Flemish bourgeoisie presided by the banker André Vlerick (Kredietbank) founded Protea, a friendly society organizing politicians of different political parties in order to defend the Apartheid in South-Africa (Verhoeyen and Uytterhaegen 1981: 100) and to ease the introduction of the shares of South African mining companies on the Brussels stock market.

As prominent promoter of industrial activities in Flanders the Flemish bourgeoisie had woven a pattern of financial ties, channelled through the Flemish Kredietbank and co-ordinated by Economic Coun-cils at the level of the provinces. Regional economic development spon-sored by public funds and articulated by neo-capitalist management represented a third step towards industrial recovery, providing the Fordist firms with well-trained managers, engineers and lawyers who could become agents of cultural and social change in Flanders. In one word, the Flemish bourgeoisie transformed itself into a true 'compra-dore' bourgeoisie, articulating its modernism and internationalism by stressing its Flemish identity. This strategy allowed the Flemish bour-geoisie to reconsider its relation with the holding bourgeoisie and French financial groups like Paribas and the Compagnie Lambert, forcing them to accept Flemish-speaking managers in leading posi-tions.[3]

Once the Flemish bourgeoisie held power and dominated the Roman-Red coalition governments, and once the issue of its emancipation was no longer of overriding importance, an anti-étatist and anti-union sentiment developed within the Flemish entrepreneurial organization and started criticizing Keynesianism and 'creeping socialism'. The very reason for this early neo-liberal criticism is to be found in the strategy the socialist trade union movement adopted after 1970. The socialist union argued that a reinforced role of the public investment companies could prevent an anarchic process of accumulation, and that public control of the basic industries would provide better opportunities for the working class to achieve economic democracy within the firms. Finally it was in 1974 and on impulse of the Flemish bourgeoisie and the entrepreneurial federation for the oil industry that the Christian-Democratic Party decided to break up the Roman-Red coalition. The Flemish bourgeoisie could not accept the 'socialist' project for a state oil company. The year 1974 marked the end of the Keynesian idyll and the beginning of a gradual drive towards mitigated liberalism.

THE NEO-LIBERAL TAKEOVER

The breakdown of the Roman-Red coalition governments laid bare the congenital weakness of Keynesianism and Fordism. With a view to their concrete economic interests, the Flemish entrepreneurs chose lower taxes, lower wages, less state intervention, and unorganized labour, measures which enabled them better to withstand fierce international competition. Thus the Flemish bourgeoisie gradually moved towards a supplyside stance.

In 1981 the Christian-Democrat Party made up its mind: a coalition with the Liberal Party became a 'natural alliance', necessary to save the country not from rampant socialism, but from economic and financial disaster. In 1981 the spending deficit of the Belgian government had reached 14.5 per cent of GNP and total state expenditure had climbed to 57 per cent of GNP. The financial burden of public debt became an ever-growing snowball obliging the Treasury to borrow heavily. In 1984 total foreign debt totalled some US$18 billion and unemployment reached a peak of 546,000 people, i.e. 14 per cent of the total workforce.

Some major ideological changes had been articulated through the channels of the entrepreneurial networks and newspapers. In 1972 Jacques de Staercke, who was a notable admirer of the New Deal and key figure of the Tuesday Evening Group, became managing director of Fabrimétal, the employers' organization of the motor car and electrical industries. De Staercke pleaded for a restrictive wage policy and for supplyside virtues on behalf of the exporting firms. In 1976 he developed the idea that the 'Belgian disease' had been caused by too high a level of industrial wages. High taxes and generous social insurance schemes resulted in an expensive Welfare State the Belgian industry could not subsidize. Some 300,000 people were earning their living in the firms organized by De Staercke's federation, a fact any government had to consider. De Staercke vigorously opposed the proposals by the trade unions for a shorter working week to create more work for the jobless (Carbonelle 1987: 71–99), a point of view which was also defended by a generation of young Catholic technocrats (De Grauwe 1986; Van Rompuy 1979, 1984) and in some aspects surpassed by the spokesmen of the Flemish entrepreneurial organization.

For the time being the neo-liberals made little headway. Because they had to work within the existing organizations, and because, under the pressure of linguistic quarrels, the liberal PLP had split into a multitude of factions, they were confined to the margins of governmental power.

But the unsuccessful Keynesian attempt to cope with growing unemployment and worsening terms of trade led to unpopular measures which the unions were reluctant to accept and the socialists could not impose without eroding their social base. The end came when in 1981 a balance of payments deficit forced the Roman-Red coalition to resign. The neo-liberal forces could now finally prepare the ground for a political and ideological revolution.

Around this time, the Flemish neo-liberal Guy Verhofstadt translated popular neo-liberal writings (Milton Friedman, Public Choice writers) and published a 'Radical Manifesto', which in 1979 was adopted by the Flemish Liberal Party (Raes: 1983). 'Monetarism for the masses' appeared more and more in the speeches of the leading liberal politicians and entrepreneurs and a merger of the French-speaking Liberals of Wallonia and Brussels under the leadership of Jean Gol strengthened the new trend. Next, Flemish- and French-speaking Liberals purged themselves from social liberalism and absorbed the anti-tax party RAD-UDRT. Neo-liberal think-tanks sponsored by the International Chamber of Commerce (Moden and Sloover 1980: 279–84) and 'Entreprise et Société' flourished and created a revival of liberal economic theory in the universities (Mommen 1987: 11–12).

Wilfried Martens, who had led between 1977 and 1981 four consecutive Roman-Red coalition governments, in 1981 agreed to lead a Liberal-Catholic coalition with an outspoken neo-liberal programme. But the group supporting Wilfried Martens was eager to confine the neo-liberal revolution within the limits of the Keynesian Welfare State and they also opposed a neo-conservative drive headed by the CEPIC (Centre des Indépendants et Cadres Chrétiens), an organization which was led by Paul Vanden Boeynants (whose name had been mentioned in several affairs of corruption) and financed by the remnants of the French-speaking holding bourgeoisie.[4]

The new government formed by Martens in 1981 presented a programme of economic and financial recovery, and emphasized the necessity of obtaining 'special powers' to neutralize the trade unions. Martens devalued the Belgian franc by 8.5 per cent and froze wages and social allowances. Martens further tried to reduce the public spending deficit (13 per cent of GNP in 1982). His target was to lower this deficit to 7 per cent of GNP by 1985. However, despite severe budget cuts public debt soared and the parliamentary elections of 1985 opened the way for even stronger neo-liberal pressure. Guy Verhofstadt, the young political leader of the Flemish Liberals, removed the old guard from leading positions and became Minister of Budget Control in a new Liberal–Christian-Democratic coalition government led by Wilfried Martens.

The neo-liberal faction led by Verhofstadt pressed for deep cuts in social allowances and for privatization of state-owned companies in the sector of transport (ports, ferries, aviation), steel (Cockerill-Sambre) and credit. The neo-liberals aimed to dismantle the Keynesian Welfare State and to privatize the social security system by introducing Milton Friedman's system of negative income tax (Mommen 1987).

The neo-liberal economic policy clearly favoured the export industry and rentier capital. Profits were boosted, while the average wage earner lost 15 per cent of his/her purchasing power. In the same period (1982–7) profits increased about 10 per cent a year. After 1984 productive investment increased by 8 per cent annually while in 1974–81 the growth of productive investment had stagnated. So industry was able to finance its investment from cash flow and could easily award substantial dividends to the share holders, which provoked speculation on the stock markets. For the first time since the oil crisis of 1973 the public was eager to subscribe to new emissions in a climate of soaring market quotations.

In that speculative climate the shrinking faction of the old holding bourgeoisie disappeared as an autonomous faction of the Belgian bourgeoisie. Within a period of ten years all the prestigious holding companies (Empain, Coppée, Bruxelles-Lambert, Société Générale) fell into foreign hands. As early as 1978 Baron Ede-Janos Empain was moved out of his Parisian headquarters by a coalition of French insurance companies and the group Paribas (Empain 1985).

In 1980 the Groupe Coppée-Rust, once the most powerful firm specializing in cokes and steel, was compelled to merge with the French Lafarge (Dubois 1987: 253–5). In 1982 the Lambert family invited the Walloon steel baron Albert Frère and his foreign allies (Pargesa, Power Corporation, Paribas-COBEPA) to save his ailing holding Groupe Bruxelles-Lambert (GBL). Five years later Baron Léon Lambert was relieved from all his functions, and he retired to New York to enjoy his famous collection of modern paintings (Baumier: 1988).

The process of the Frenchification of the Belgian economy was completed in 1988 when, during an epic battle against Carlo de Benedetti, the French Suez group took control over the largest Belgian holding company Société Générale de Belgique. French companies now dominate the Belgian insurance market through their stake in Royale Belge, Assurances Générales and Assubel, while important banks like Bruxelles-Lambert and Banque de la Société Générale de Belgique operate under supervision of Paribas and Suez (Turani 1988; Cuypers 1988; Vanden Driessche 1988; Raid 1988; Dethomas and Fralon, 1989). Of course, one could still name a number of independent industrial firms under Belgian control, but these too might become the victims of a leveraged buy-out. During the boom on the stock market major firms like Côte d'Or, Sucre Tirlemont, Interbrew, Solvay, Bekaert, etc. raised new capital by putting shares up for sale.

In this way, however, they made themselves vulnerable to unsolicited take-over bids. Alternatively, as was the case with Côte d'Or in 1987 and Sucre Tirlemont in 1989, major private shareholders could decide to sell their holdings to foreign multinational companies anticipating Europe 1992.

TOWARDS A POST-FORDIST COMPROMISE?

The triumph of neo-liberalism was not consummated during the second Liberal/Christian-Democratic coalition government led by Wilfried Martens (1984–7). The Catholics feared that unpopular measures would alienate their working-class voters, a fear they saw confirmed in the rising popularity of the Socialist Party.

When Verhofstadt pressed his colleagues for still lower taxes and new cuts in social expenditure, a political crisis which had been growing latently for some time brought the coalition government down on 19 October 1987, the day of the crash on Wall Street. The following elections confirmed the general trend in favour of a new Roman-Red coalition. The socialist political family now outnumbered the Christian-Democrats in votes and in seats. Within the socialist trade unions, furthermore, a pragmatic current representing the better paid workers gained the upper hand and sought a compromise with the Catholic unions and the Christian-Democrats. A Roman-Red coalition, finally, was also backed by leading spokesmen of the Catholic bourgeoisie (De Ridder 1989: 57). This constellation of forces could not but lead to a broader compromise on the necessity of marrying supplyside economics to some reformed version of Keynesianism. In that case it would be necessary to oust the hard core neo-liberals such as Verhofstadt.

The new Roman-Red government, which was once again headed by the political chameleon Wilfried Martens, promised to break with neo-liberalism. A booming economy (a growth rate of GNP of 4.2 per cent over 1988 and 4.5 per cent over 1989, see Table 9.1) enabled industry to concede higher wages and the government to increase civil servants' pay. This process of accommodation was eased by the fact that from 1987 the trade unions and the entrepreneurial organizations agreed on the necessity of re-establishing a system of collective bargaining on the national and sectoral level, and on the return of a technical form of automatic wage indexation. It was also agreed that wages had to follow increased productivity and that one had to lower interest rates in order to boost investment. In this way internal demand could grow along with soaring external demand. Extremely high profits made by the exporting industry had to be prevented by higher wages, which in turn would induce higher internal demand.

In order to secure the Welfare State the Roman-Red coalition government also broke with the neo-liberal philosophy that only privatization could rescue the bankrupt publicly-owned pension funds. A system of broader fiscalization of the financing of the Welfare State now met the sympathy of the Christian-Democrats who, inspired by their innate corporatist leanings, had always stressed the importance of insurance schemes and solidarity among the workers. The economic boom gave the Roman-Red coalition considerable leeway. Nevertheless, in 1989 there still persisted a spending deficit of 6.5 per cent, combined with an overall public debt of BFrs7,800 billion (US$176 billion or 121 per cent of GNP). An unemployment rate of 10 per cent proved that the end had not yet been reached. Job creation at an average of 50,000 new jobs a year meant that the reserve army of 419,000 people could not be absorbed by a Keynesian policy mix. A major problem for the Roman-Red coalition government was how to preserve a positive balance of trade, which had to compensate the traditional deficit on the balance of payments due to the massive tax-evading export of capital. The government decided to counter this capital flight by tax reduction on dividends, a policy the neo-liberals had also pleaded for. Industrial investment and the expanding construction activities of the private sector became substitutes for public investment which remained at an extremely low level. Soaring profits enabled the entrepreneurs and the banks to boost the chemical industry and to restructure the energy sector, the non-ferrous metal industry and the telephone manufacturing firms.

The government initiated several new large investment projects and allowed the state-owned airline company SABENA to find a foreign partner (KLM and British Airways and later on Air France). A programme for heavy investment in an extension of the French high-speed railway system (TGV) to Brussels (and on to Amsterdam) received top priority.

Of course, 'Fordist' multinational firms remained the backbone of the Belgian economy, but their relative importance diminished as the service sector speeded up. There was still a declining tendency in industrial employment (a decrease from 1,081,000 jobs in 1981 to 920,000 in 1987) while employment in the service sector expanded (from 1,039,000 jobs in 1981 to 1,138,000 in 1987). This helps to explain

Table 8.1 Main indicators for the Belgian economy (real growth in %)

	1984–7	1988	1989	1990
Private consumption	2.2	2.4	3.8	3.9
Public spending	–	−0.5	−2.0	0.2
Public consumption	1.4	−0.7	−0.7	0.5
Public investment	−8.6	1.5	−12.4	−2.0
Building activities	4.1	22.3	18.9	7.0
Industrial investment	6.0	16.8	16.3	9.0
GDP	2.4	4.3	4.0	3.7
Export	4.9	8.2	7.6	4.0
Import	5.9	8.3	8.7	3.8
GNP	1.8	4.2	4.0	3.7

Source: National Bank, Reports 1989 and 1990

why the trade unions gradually moved towards a less radical point of view and were ready to acquiesce in growing flexibility rather than endanger the social security system. The particular stance taken by the Belgian socialists narrowed the gap between orthodox Keynesian policies and neo-liberal reforms in favour of private capital. In their eyes private initiative became as precious as public control of investment, a strategy which enabled them to assuage the still hesitant right wing of the Christian-Democratic party and to undermine the neo-liberal rhetoric. Less State and higher individual purchasing power could be combined with a Welfare State providing a decent social standard of living to everybody. Because the Treasury had to serve an enormous public debt, increases in the salaries of the public servants could only be financed by borrowing abroad. This the socialists were no longer prepared to do: they accepted the limitations on public spending which the new post-Fordist era implied, and now preferred financial orthodoxy to Keynesian deficit spending.

This left move towards the centre of the political spectrum protected the Roman-Red coalition from severe attacks from the entrepreneurial organizations. As cunning tacticians the leading socialists and Christian-Democrats manoeuvred the radical neo-liberal spokesman Verhofstadt off the political stage. After two years of opposition the neo-liberal leaders had to concede they were losing ground and within both the Flemish and the Walloon Liberal parties discontent was growing against the leading cliques. So, when in November 1991 the Roman-Red coalition suffered an important electoral set-back, this was not due to an increased impact of neo-liberal demagogy, but the result of a generalized malaise caused by anti-parliamentarian feelings gaining popularity in the wake of an anti-immigrant campaign launched by the fascist Vlaams Blok party in Flanders and the Front National in Brussels and Wallonia.

CONCLUSION

Neo-liberalism in Belgium succeeded in reorganizing the Keynesian Welfare State and in fundamentally changing the relationship between labour and capital. Indeed, multinational capital called for lower wages and greater 'flexibility', which would make labour relations and social practices less subject to trade union vetoes. The Keynesian Welfare State also came under fire from the neo-liberal ministers who influenced the governments of the centre-right (1981–8). However, it did not succeed in destroying the strongholds of the trade unions who adopted a low profile in order to convince the leading industrial circles that complete abolition of the fundamentals of the Welfare State was not necessary nor politically desirable.

The neo-liberal drive towards more market and less State was in fact a conjunctural phenomenon accompanying the process of concentration and rationalization within the industrial and financial sectors still dominated by the Belgian holding bourgeoisie. In the course of this process, the holding bourgeoisie was bought out by foreign capital and was reduced to the status of a rentier class excluded from the corridors of economic power. Repeatedly some reactionary factions of the holding bourgeoisie tried to go against the tide by destabilizing the parliamentary institutions in an attempt to install an authoritarian regime. These plans for a coup all failed, because their social and political base was shrinking with the diminishing economical and cultural power of the holding bourgeoisie. In addition, the modernizing neo-liberals never considered a coalition with the Catholic Old Right or with the anti-parliamentary pressure groups led by Vanden Boeynants.

However, through speculative stock market operations and leveraged buy-outs rentier capitalism increased its popular impact and spread the free market ideology. Belgian rentier capital now multinationalized as a consequence of its search for higher profits and lower taxes. In order to stop rampant tax evasion and some fraudulent practices the neo-liberals wanted to lower income taxes and taxation on profits and dividends. This operation, which was later continued by the Roman-Red coalition, liberalized the Belgian capital market and eased the position of the Treasury still in financial need.

The ever-increasing public debt and high unemployment combined with an export-led growth imposed important constraints on all Keynesian velleities some social-democrats were still showing. Economic recovery (1983–6) and expansion (1987–9) did not expand industrial employment, but translated into an expanding service sector. The decline of heavy industry (steel and coal) was speeded up by the closing down of the remaining coal mines in Limburg and the old steel mills and blast furnaces in Wallonia. Even the Roman-Red coalition was inclined to subordinate its social and economic policies to the interests of the multinational companies by promoting more flexibility and adopting a 'liberal' attitude. The basic economic philosophy of the Roman-Red coalition does not differ from the neo-liberal one: the social-democrats now even support the idea that the State needs to privatize state-owned companies (after having reorganized them).

NOTES

1 In 1981 a final merger gave birth to the steel giant Cockerill-Sambre (CS) in which the Belgian state became the majority share holder. This meant the end of the industrial domination of the holding bourgeoisie in Wallonia.

2 ARBED (S.A. des Aciéries Réunies de Burbach-Esch-Dudelange) and the main Belgian steel companies and their shareholders controlled SIDMAR, but they had accepted the financial backing of the government (Meynaud *et al.* 1965, 287–320).

3 Fordism bolstered a network of shared interests in the private and public sectors and enabled (socialist) technocrats and politicians to start or end their careers in multinational firms or state-owned financial groups. Bell–ITT and Ford Motor Company Belgium were led by a socialist, and even Paul-Henri Spaak, towards the end of his career, became an adviser of ITT.

4 The CEPIC was a meeting point for some aristocrats, conservative intellectuals of the Opus Dei (Van Bosbeke 1985: 15), politicians grouped within the CEDI (Centre Européen de Documentation et d'Information) led by Otto von Habsburg, the Cercle des Nations (founded by Count Hervé d'Ursel and Baron Adelin van Ypersele de Strihou) (de Bock 1981: 129, 137), and army generals. All these groups were preparing a *coup d'état*, which the Belgian Gendarmerie and the World Anti-Communist League (Verhoeyen and Uytterhaegen 1981: 76) would support. A central position in this connection was held by Baron Benoit de Bonvoisin, the grandson of a governor of the Société Générale.

After the dissolution of CEPIC in 1981 the so-called 'Gang of Nivelles', which organized terrorist attacks on supermarkets, appeared on the scene in an effort to destabilize the parliamentary system. Soon one could presume these terrorist activities were backed by individuals involved in illegal arms trade, drugs trafficking, and the Belgian secret services. In 1989 this chapter of terrorism ended with the mysterious kidnapping of Vanden Boeynants. Most likely, some members of the 'Gang of Nivelles' were operating on their own account.

REFERENCES

Baumier, J. (1988) *La Galaxie Paribas*, Paris: Plon.

Belart, U., Keller, K. and Heinertz, H. B. (n.d.) *Opkomst en Ondergang van Ivar Kreuger*, Amsterdam: Allert de Lange.

Bell (1982) *Bell Telephone Manufacturing Company 1882–1982*, Antwerpen: Bell Telephone Mfg Co. N.V.

Carbonelle, C. (1987) *Jacques de Staercke. Opdracht: Ondernemen*, Tielt: Lannoo.

Chlepner, B.-S. (1930) *Le Marché Financier Depuis Cent Ans*, Bruxelles: Librairie Falk.

Cuypers, P. (1988) *Het bod op België. Carlo de Benedetti's Greep Naar de Generale Maatschappij*, Wommelgem: Uitgeverij Den Gulden Engel.

Daviet, J.-P. (1989) *Une Multinationale à la Française. Histoire de Saint-Gobain 1665–1989*, Paris: Fayard.

De Bock, W. (a.o.) (1981) *Extreem-rechts en de Staat*, Berchem: EPO.

De Boeck, A. (1989) 'La SOFINA (société de transports et d'entreprises industrielles), 1989–1914', *Présences Belges dans le Monde à l'Aube du XXe Siècle*, 21–40, Louvain-la-Neuve/Bruxelles, Academia/Univers-Cité.

De Grauwe, P. (1986) *De Zichtbare Hand. Het Conflict Tussen Economie en Politiek*, Tielt: Lannoo.

Deprez, R. (1963) *La Grande Grève (Décembre 1960–Janvier 1961). Ses Origines, son Déroulement, ses Leçons*, Bruxelles: Fondation J. Jacquemotte.

De Ridder, H. (1989) *Sire, Geef me Honderd Dagen*, Leuven: Davidsfonds.

Dethomas, B. and Fralon, J.-A. (1989) *Les Milliards de l'Orgueil. L'Affaire de la Société Générale de Belgique*, Paris: Gallimard.

Dubois, L. (1988) *Lafarge Coppée 150 Ans d'Industrie. Une Mémoire pour Demain*, Paris: Belfond.

Durviaux, R. (1947) *La Banque Mixte, Origine et Soutien de l'Expansion Économique de la Belgique*, Bruxelles: Etablissements Emile Bruylant.

Empain, Baron E. J. (1985) *La Vie en Jeu*, Paris, J.C. Lattès.

Eyskens, G. (1988) *Het Laatste Gesprek. Herinneringen Aan 40 Jaar Politiek Leven*, Kapellen/Brussels: DNB/Uitgeverij Pelckmans/IPOVO.

Féaux, V. (1963) *Cinq Semaines de Lutte Sociale. La Grève de l'Hiver 1960–1961*, Bruxelles: Editions de l'Institut de Sociologie de l'Université Libre de Bruxelles.

Hoflack, K. (1989) *Theo Lefèvre, Staatsman*, Antwerpen-Baarn: Hadewijch.

Jacobs, D. (1988) *Gereguleerd Staal. Nationale en Internationale Economische Regulering in de Westeuropese Staalindustrie 1750–1950*, Enschede: Sneldruk.

Joye, P. (1960) *Les Trusts en Belgique. La Concentration Capitaliste*, Bruxelles: Société Populaire d'Editions.

Kurgan-Van Hentenryk, G. (1971) *Léopold II et les Groupes Financiers Belges en Chine. La Politique Royale et ses Prolongements (1895–1914)*, Bruxelles: Académie Royale de Belgique.

Kurgan-Van Hentenryk, G. (1982) *Rail, Finance et Politique: les Entreprises Philippart (1865–1890)*, Bruxelles: Editions de l'Université de Bruxelles.

Lamfalussy, A. (1961) *Investment and Growth. The Case of Belgium*, London: Macmillan.

Luykx, T. (1967) *Geschiedenis van de Economische Bewustwording in Vlaanderen, 1926–1966*, Antwerpen: De Nederlandsche Boekhandel.

Meynaud, J., Ladrière, J. and Perin, F. (eds) (1965) *La Décision Politique en Belgique. Le Pouvoir et Les Groupes*, Paris: Librairie Armand Colin.

Meynen, A. (1978) 'De grote werkstaking 1960–1961', *Belgische Tijdschrift voor Nieuwste Geschiedenis*, 9(3–4): 481–513.

Moden, J. and Sloover, J. (1980) *Le Patronat Belge. Discours et Idéologie (1973–1980)*, Bruxelles: CRISP.

Mommen, A. (1987) *Een Tunnel Zonder Einde. Het Neo-liberalisme van Martens V en VI*, Antwerpen: Kluwer.

Morphologie (1967) *Morphologie des Groupes Financiers*, Bruxelles: CRISP.

Norris, W. (1987) *The Man Who Fell from the Sky*, New York: Viking.

Raes, K. (1983) *Aan hen de Keuze? Een Kritisch Essay over de Ideologie van het*

Neo-liberaal Bezitsindividualisme, Ghent: Masereelfonds.

Raid (1988) *Raid sur la Générale*, Bruxelles: Edition de l'Echo de la Bourse.

Schoenberg, R. J. (1985) *Geneen*, New York: Warner Books.

Turani, G. (1988) *L'Ingegnere. Carlo De Benedetti e l'Assalto ai Cieli della Finanza*, s.l.: Sperling & Kupfer Editori.

Van Bosbeke, A. (1985) *Opus Dei in België*, Berchem: EPO.

Vanden Driessche, M. (1988) *Poker d'enfer. O.P.A. sur la Générale de Belgique*, Paris: Fayard/Marabout.

Van der Wee, H. and Verbreyt, M. (1985) *Mensen Maken Geschiedenis. De Kredietbank en de Economische Opgang van Vlaaderen 1935–1985*, Brussels: Kredietbank.

Vanlangenhove, F. (n.d.) 'Heineman Dannie-N.', *Biographie Nationale*, 40, suppl. 12: 382–420.

Van Rompuy, H. (1979) *Op de Kentering der Tijden. Getuigenissen van een Dertiger*, Tielt/Amsterdam: Lannoo.

Van Rompuy, H. (1984) *Hopen na 1984*, Leuven: Davidsfonds.

Verhoeyen, E. and Uytterhaegen, F. (1981) *De Kreeft met de Zwarte Scharen. 50 Jaar Rechts en Uiterst Rechts in België*, Ghent: Masereel Fonds.

9

CANADA IN THE CRISIS

Transformations in capital structure and political strategy

William K. Carroll

INTRODUCTION[1]

If with O'Connor (1987) we view crisis not as an apocalytic breakdown but as an historic 'turning point' in the political economy of capitalism, in appraising the present period we are led to consider the practices through which the terrain of politics and economics in the capitalist democracies has been reshaped since the early 1970s. The crisis can be theorized as a series of interconnected transformations in the structures and strategies of capitalist class power, particularly in the characteristic form of the circuit of capital, in the predominant regime of accumulation, and in the hegemonic concept of control in terms of which strategies for political regulation are constituted. The development of a fully transnational finance capital, the deepening crisis of Fordist accumulation, and the collapse of the corporate-liberal synthesis which informed national policies and international relations in the era of Pax Americana are dimensions of a global crisis, evident in varying degrees in all of the capitalist democracies. In this contribution I examine these processes of restructuring as they have occurred in Canada. The recomposition of 'Canadian' finance capital, the shift away from an intensive regime of 'permeable Fordism', and the rise of a 'continental neo-liberal' concept of control mark far-reaching changes which are at once nationally specific and expressive of developments at the global level.

I first discuss the predominant tendencies in the organization of capital and the strategy of bourgeois hegemony during the era of North-Atlantic Fordism, and the connections between the crisis of Fordism, the recomposition of finance capital and the rise of neo-liberal political strategy. Secondly, I analyse the changing structure of finance capital and the crisis of Fordism in Canada in the 1970s and 1980s, a period in which the incipient adoption of monetarism and neo-liberal deregulation has combined with domestic centralization of share capital and rapid expansion abroad to consolidate a set of financial groups whose business strategies tend to privilege a money-capital orientation that is international in scope but continental in emphasis. Thirdly, I trace the associated rise of neo-liberal business activism which has paralleled developments in Britain and the United States in endeavouring to build support for the new accumulation strategy and for broader transformations. In this respect as in others, the historical specificity of the Canadian political economy must be acknowledged. In contrast to Thatcherism and Reaganism, neo-liberal restructuring in Canada has taken shape less as a 'national' hegemonic project than as a passive revolution in which the federal government has sought to 'manage change' without disowning the 'sacred trust' of the post-war settlement.[2]

DIMENSIONS OF CRISIS: FINANCE CAPITAL, FORDISM, NEO-LIBERALISM

The concept of finance capital represents advanced capitalism's economic structure as a circuit in which the growing interdependence of large-scale industrial and financial capital finds expression in institutionalized relations between the credit system and the industrial sector, 'by means of a series of links and relationships between individual capitals' (Overbeek 1980: 102). While the notion of finance capital as a 'coalescence of capitals' is unobjectionable, it is important to acknowledge the inherent dynamic of fractionation vs. integration within which finance capital moves (Overbeek 1988: 283). Since the total circuit of capital requires a ceaseless metamorphosis of value across money, commodity, and productive forms, the 'coalescence' always incorporates a contradiction between capital as abstract labour (in particular, mobile money capital) and capital as surplus-value production, i.e. productive capital (Shortall 1986). As Harvey puts it,

> The analysis of finance capital as a flow reveals the underlying unity and antagonism between financial and surplus value-producing operations. The accumulation cycle ... suggests a balance of power between industrial capital and banking capital over the course of the cycle.
>
> (Harvey 1982: 319).

Such a dynamic conception of finance capital allows for an analysis of bourgeois politics which breaks from the mechanical notion of a preconstituted ruling 'monopoly' fraction, yet retains a capacity to appreciate the practical connections between accumulation and politics. The shifting balance of power between productive and money capital provides a basis for the articulation – within an overall integration of capital circuits – of distinct fractional perspectives. Industrial capital will be principally interested in the continuity of production and sale of its product, and therefore in the neutralization of capital/labour conflict; money capital will be especially concerned with unimpeded circulation, including the convertibility of currencies, and will gravitate towards a classical-liberal perspective (Overbeek 1988: 24). For this reason, in the era of finance capital 'certain conflicts within the capitalist class remain traceable to the different fractions persisting in the context of apparent fusion' (van der Pijl 1984: 7).

Van der Pijl goes on to analyse the 'money-capital' concept and the 'productive-capital' concept as ideal-typical frames of reference in terms of which bourgeois hegemony has been internationally articulated in the twentieth century:

> These two concepts capture the common denominators in the antinomous positions from which capitals, actively or passively, were engaged in the international circulation of capital; either as functionaries of fictitious capital or as managers of real capital. ... [They] constituted the vantage-points from which historically specific, and increasingly synthetic, strategies for adjusting bourgeois rule and international relations to the ongoing process of internationalization were developed.
>
> (*idem*: 9)

In the regime of intensive accumulation that developed in the North Atlantic under American hegemony, productive capital was structurally prioritized in several respects. The Fordist pattern of mass production for mass consumption, reinforced and amplified by the state's commitment to macroeconomic demand management, harmonious industrial relations, and expansive social welfare 'implied a subordination of independent bank capital and the rentier element in the bourgeoisie to an integrated, state-supported finance capital' (van der Pijl 1986: 26). New Deal legislation and comparable measures elsewhere separated commercial and investment banking and regulated the circulation of share capital on stock exchanges. During the long post-war boom, industrial capital enjoyed considerable room to manoeuvre, as corporations were able either to self-finance their expansion or to obtain loan capital from multiple, competing financial institutions. Concomitantly, the pre-war centralization of share capital within investment banks was supplanted by a tendency towards share dispersal which further strengthened the fractional position of industrial managers. Pax Americana's Atlantic ruling class was thus constituted on the basis of a contingent 'unity' in the predominant regime of accumulation, in the ascendent strategy of political regulation, and in the form of the circuit of finance capital.

John Scott has provided a detailed account of the last of these developments in his analysis of the 'common move' within the advanced capitalist countries 'towards bank hegemony of a loosely structured kind' (Scott 1987: 227). Scott (1985) holds that within this post-war system of 'polyarchic financial hegemony' the dominant stratum of the capitalist class has been reorganized around a distinct institutional structuring of allocative power over the flow of money-capital and strategic control over large corporations. On the one hand, multiple financial institutions have taken up powerful capital-allocative positions *vis-à-vis* large corporations, knitting the major companies of each national economy into a more or less integrated network, with the financial institutions positioned near the centre. In this structure, finance capitalists influence the mobilization of capital, and thus corporate strategies, through their directorships in the hegemonic financial institutions. On the other hand, the strategic control of corporations has become 'depersonalized': the wealthy shareholding families of the early twentieth century have been displaced by more complex 'constellations of interests' – loose coalitions of families and institutional investors too diverse to act in concert yet too important to be ignored by corporate managements (Scott 1987, 222). This structuring of capital allocation and control has tended to mitigate against the segmentation of finance capital into coherent financial groups: the interlacing of institutional investments and the tendency for large corporations to deal with multiple banks have helped sustain relatively integrated national networks of corporations and financial institutions.

As an account of the predominant tendencies in the organization of finance capital during the long post-war wave of accumulation, Scott's analysis has considerable plausibility. Yet if the system of loosely-structured financial hegemony was tendentially convergent with the Fordist pattern of accumulation – within which money capital was structurally subordinated to productive capital and circuits of capital were still nationally focused – its basis has been cumulatively undermined by developments in the 1970s and 1980s. The crisis of Fordism, the eclipse of 'national' economies, and the associated rise of neo-liberal policies have set in motion a restructuring of relations within the dominant stratum of the bourgeoisie.

These transformations became acutely visible in the 1980s, but their origins can be found in the early 1970s, when the American abrogation of Bretton Woods and the rise of the Eurodollar effectively 'privatized' the international monetary system, freeing money capital from national regulation by central banks (Edwards 1985: 181). The generalized international recession of 1974–5 forced banks further into the international arena in the competition for new customers, including a host of Third World debtor states (MacEwan 1986: 194). In the process

> the existing relation between money capital and productive capital broke down and was replaced by a hypertrophy of the international circuit of money capital managed by the international banking system [as] ... monetary authorities were unable to maintain the Keynesian nexus between money capital and productive capital at the international level.
>
> (Fennema and van der Pijl 1987: 305)

In conjunction with the ongoing internationalization of productive capital and the emergence of a new international division of labour, this breakup of nationally integrated, state-regulated finance capital has in the 1980s pressed towards a recomposition along the lines theorized by Andreff (1984). Newly transnational banks not only came to speculate in Eurodollars and to extend massive loans to debtor states; they also established closer relations with multinational corporations, in order to draw a share of profit through relations of credit, influence or control. The result has been an emergence of transnational finance capital, within which 'money capital and productive capital are organically linked in their internationalization' (ibid.: 66).

This recomposition of finance capital represents more than a trend towards the coalescence of capitals at the international level, for it is money capital that now occupies the strategically dominant position in the circuits of transnational finance capital. The resurgence of money capital *vis-à-vis* productive capital is evident in each of the major capitalist economies. It can be seen in (1) the increased external financing of industry, (2) the rapid internationalization of bank capital in the 1970s, (3) the supersession of New Deal financial regulation by policies of deregulation, (4) a general shift in the distribution of profits from productive to money capital, and (5) a reorientation, even among 'industrial' corporations, towards the financial sphere, with increased holdings of liquid assets, including intercorporate financial participations

(Fennema and van der Pijl 1987: 307–10).

The political mobilization of the new right around a neo-liberal concept of control has occurred in concert with this recomposition of finance capital. As part of the resurgence of money capital,

> the disintegration of the industry-trade union compromise supporting the Fordist order politically was replaced by bank power and rentier interests as the dominant group in the new configuration. Thus rentier interests – in the broad sense of the word – were crucial in the formation of a new power bloc which rose to political power after 1975.
>
> (ibid.: 310)

Neo-liberalism, in expressing the preference for 'free' labour and un-impeded international circulation, presents the perspective of money-capital as a general interest around which the immediate sectoral interests of different capital fractions can be assembled (van der Pijl 1986: 3). It is in this sense that, under the weight of crisis and un-relenting capitalist internationalization, the altered balance of power between money and productive capital has had its political corollary in the hegemonic projects of Thatcher, Reagan, and their lesser emulators.

CANADA IN THE CRISIS: THE RECOMPOSITION OF FINANCE CAPITAL

These structural and strategic transformations can be observed in the case of Canada. An indication of the recomposition of finance capital can be gleaned from aggregate economic statistics and from an analysis of the changing interlocking-directorate network of the largest corporations in Canada. The enhanced position of money capital within the circuit of finance capital is evident firstly in the shifting distribution of national assets since the 1960s. By 1984 financial institutions accounted for 22.1 per cent of total national assets, up from 15.5 per cent in 1961. Concomitantly, highly-mobile portfolio investments came to comprise a larger share of Canada's international debt: as a proportion of the Canadian bond market, foreign-held bonds grew from 23.8 per cent in 1961 to 44.4 per cent in 1984 (O'Hagan 1986). In the 1970s and 1980s the composition of foreign investment in Canada shifted dramatically in the same direction, as the Bank of Canada's high interest rate policy made Canadian bonds and treasury bills attractive particularly to Japan-based capital.[3] By 1988, portfolio investment constituted 47 per cent of total foreign investment, up from 29 per cent in 1970, while the percentage claimed by direct investment – typically a vehicle for controlling productive capital – had shrunk from 52 to 28 (Drohan 1989).

The recessions of the 1970s and early 1980s also provoked a massive centralization of capital, as surplus funds were diverted from new fixed capital investment to struggles for control of existing sites of valorization. With the 1981–2 slump productive-capital investment dropped from one-quarter of GNP to one-fifth, and has not subsequently rebounded (see Table 9.1). Meanwhile, capital became more concentrated within the 100 leading enterprises, which by 1985 controlled 52 per cent of all non-financial assets, and non-financial corporations became more deeply implicated in circuits of financial

Table 9.1 Trends in capital accumulation in Canada, 1872–86

Year	Productive-capital investment[1]	Concentration of corporate assets[2]	Increase in long-term financial debt[3]	Increase in long-term financial claims[4]
1972	23.0	–	24.7	10.6
1973	24.5	–	33.6	8.2
1974	26.3	–	35.7	11.7
1975	25.6	46.5	39.0	8.7
1976	25.2	46.5	33.6	6.9
1977	24.4	47.6	43.2	14.7
1978	23.6	48.6	54.4	23.1
1979	25.4	48.6	45.6	24.7
1980	24.0	48.2	52.1	22.8
1981	25.3	49.2	86.6	39.0
1982	19.8	51.9	83.1	25.1
1983	20.1	52.2	33.3	6.8
1984	20.4	51.3	36.3	16.7
1985	20.6	52.0	34.9	22.4
1986	20.9	–	64.7	29.7

Notes:

1 Expressed as a percentage of GNP. Investment comprises Gross Fixed Capital Formation plus Increase in Stocks. Source: IMF (1987, 166–7).

2 Percentage of total non-financial assets controlled by 100 leading enterprises. Source: Statistics Canada Cat. # 61-210, various years.

3 Expressed as a percentage of retained income. Long-term debt includes long-term borrowing and bond issues, plus share issues. Source: OECD (1988, 26–7).

4 Expressed as a percentage of re-investment in productive capital. Long-term financial claims include holdings of long-term bonds and loans plus shares. Productive-capital re-investment includes increases in fixed assets and stocks. Source: OECD (1988, 28–9).

capital, as both debtors and investors. Between 1972 and 1982 Canadian corporations resorted more to long-term debt as a source of funds, and invested a greater share of funds in long-term financial claims relative to productive-capital re-investment. Although recovery from the 1981–2 recession temporarily reversed this trend by boosting non-financial profitability, by 1986 long-term debt and investment in long-term financial assets (particularly corporate shares) were again on the rise among non-financial firms. Indeed, by 1989 non-financial corporate debt, which had reached a high point of 50 per cent of GNP in 1981, had risen back to a level of 45.7 per cent (*Globe and Mail*, 13 November 1989).

Alongside the shift from productive to money capital, a second aspect of recomposition has been associated with the further internationalization of finance capital. Like their counterparts elsewhere, in recent years Canadian banks have increased their presence in other countries by opening foreign subsidiaries and, in the case of the Bank of Montreal, acquiring in 1984 Harris Bankcorp, a medium-sized American bank. Between 1976 and 1985 the big five Canadian chartered banks increased their foreign subsidiaries from a mean of 22.6 to a mean of 39.0.[4] An expanding share of the chartered banks' net income derives from international operations which include extensive dealings in the Eurocurrency market (Kaufman 1985; Mittelstaedt 1985).

These developments have been matched by transformations in the structure of productive capital. The eclipse of American hegemony in the early 1970s brought changes not only to the international financial system, but to the network of transnational corporations. The relative decline of US-based transnationals and commensurate rise of transnationals based elsewhere have effected a cross-penetration of capital among the major economies (Portes and Walton 1981; Fennema 1982). In Canada this has been evident in two respects:

1   a decline of the US-based comprador bourgeoisie (Niosi 1981) as Canadian capitalists repatriated control of many foreign-held firms, decreasing the foreign control of non-financial corporate assets from 37.0 per cent in 1971 to 23.4 per cent in 1985 (Canada 1987b: 70);

2   an expansion of Canadian-based corporations into other advanced economies (particularly the US), as well as into the periphery (Niosi 1985a).

From being a net importer of (mostly US-based) foreign direct investment in the period of American world hegemony (1946–74) Canada became a net exporter. Accompanying this reversal was the United States' decline after 1980 from a large net exporter to the major importer of direct investment in the world economy. Thus, as part of a worldwide redirection of capital flow, between 1975 and 1984 total Canadian direct investment in the US expanded by 438 per cent, a growth rate much stronger than that of Canadian direct investment in Europe (150 per cent), Australia (114 per cent), Africa (81 per cent) and South/Central America (16 per cent), and only exceeded by the rate of expansion in Asia (600 per cent). The attraction of the world's largest and most politically stable market, immediately to the south, has been an irresistible force in structuring Canadian business strategies. As of the mid-1980s the US absorbed almost four-fifths of Canadian exports and over 70 per cent of Canadian direct investment abroad (Rugman 1987: 5–7, 72).

A more concrete appraisal of the recomposition of finance capital can be derived from a longitudinal comparison of the 'Top 100' corporations in Canada, their interlocks and financial participations.[5] From 1976 to 1986, a proliferation of investment companies effected both a centralization of capital into family-controlled financial empires and a repatriation of foreign-controlled corporations. The number of investment companies controlling major corporations grew from seven to nineteen, fifteen of which were ultimately controlled by a handful of wealthy Canadian families and individuals. In the same decade, the number of top-ranked industrial corporations under Canadian rather than foreign control grew from thirty-one to forty-nine, and among these, the number of companies controlled ultimately by shareholding families or individuals as opposed to 'constellations of interests'[6] grew from nine to twenty.

A serviceable indicator of relationships between individual capitals is provided by interlocking directorates, particularly strong primary interlocks whereby a pair of firms share two or more inside directors. These links, which tend to persist through changes in executive personnel (Ornstein 1984; Stokman and Wasseur 1986) mark an especially advanced coalescence of top management. Table 9.2 presents the results of successive clique analyses[7] performed on the network of strong primary ties in 1976 and 1986, to reveal the densely-interlocked subgroups of firms at the heart of the network.

In 1976 the largest connected network – the so-called dominant component – contained forty-six corporations, thirty-eight of which belonged to one or more of seven major cliques; in 1986 the dominant component consisted of forty-eight companies, forty-four of which

Table 9.2 Composition of intercorporate cliques, 1976 and 1986

Lead company	Size	Density	nBanks	nOFinl	nIvtCo	nSubs	nInd	nProp
1976								
1 Can. Pacif.	12	0.30	1	2	1	8	7	1
2 Bank. Comm.	10	0.22	1	1	1	2	6	
3 T.D. Bank	8	0.25	1	3	2	6	5	1
4 Argus. Corp.	7	0.48	1	4	1	3	2	
5 'London'	6	0.53					1	
6 Bell Tel.	5	0.40	2	1	1	2	3	
7 Brascan	5	0.10				2	2	
1986								
1 Brascan	12	0.41		2	6	12	3	1
2 Brascan/OY	11	0.42		2	5	11		2
3 Olymp. York	7	0.62		1	2	7	2	2
4 Thomson	7	0.52	1		1	4	4	
5 OY/Thomson	7	0.57			2	4	4	1
6 Brascan/Eaton	6	0.73			4	5	1	
7 Power Corp	6	0.40		2	2	5	2	1
8 Bell Enterp.	6	0.33	1		1	5	2	1
9 T.D. Bank	6	0.33	1				2	1
10 Bank N.S.	5	0.50	1	1			3	
11 CEMP	5	0.50	1	1	1	3	1	1
12 Can. Pacif.*	8	0.29	1	1		5	6	

Key

nBanks: number of chartered banks in clique
nOFinl: number of other financial institutions in clique
nIvtCo: number of investment companies in clique
nSubs: size of largest component of intercorporate ownership relations in clique
nInd: number of industrial corporations in clique
nProp: number of property development companies in clique
*This clique is not part of the 1986 dominant component of strong primary ties.

belonged to at least one of eleven major cliques. In the former year, the chartered banks were prominent in five of the seven intercorporate groupings, yet investment companies played key roles in only two. Two of the larger cliques of 1976 formed star-like configurations, each with a chartered bank at its centre radiating ties to various other firms suggestive of loosely-structured financial hegemony.

The eleven major cliques of 1986 show the increased prominence of investment companies and weakened position of chartered banks in the network of strong primary interlocks. Whereas in 1976 all of the 'big five' banks were in the network's dominant component and four were direct participants in the major intercorporate groupings, by 1986 the dominant component contained only two banks, and with one exception the banks were isolated from the component's larger cliques. On the other hand, investment companies and intercorporate financial participations were profuse in nine of the cliques. Other financial institutions in the 1986 cliques tended not to be widely-held but were in several cases under the strategic control of leading capitalist shareholders. Also, the cliques at the centre of the 1986 network tended to be composed of fewer industrial corporations and of more urban real estate developers.

A final point of comparison concerns the ultimate control of the capital represented within these groups. In 1976, with the exception of one group, most of the corporations in the seven cliques were ultimately 'widely held', i.e. strategically controlled by complex constellations of interests. By 1986 the largest seven cliques in the dominant component depicted either financial empires under the ultimate control of a few wealthy families: Edward and Peter Bronfman, the Reichmanns, the Thomsons, and the Desmaraises, or interfaces between one family's holdings and another's.[8] The first three of these families, among the four wealthiest in Canada, had personal fortunes prior to October 1987 estimated at C$10 billion (Reichmanns), C$6.6 billion (Thomsons) and C$1.7 billion (Bronfmans). Indeed, of the nine Canadian families estimated to have personal fortunes of at least C$500 million six were direct participants in the cliques making up the 1986 dominant component.

At the heart of the network of finance capital we witness: (1) the consolidation of a family-based holding system entailing an enormous centralization of strategic control; (2) a shift from industrial to financial-rentier investments; and (3) a commensurate weakening of the system of loosely-structured financial hegemony as the corporate network is restructured more along lines of strategic control than along lines of multilateral capital allocation. This is not to say that the ascendant family-controlled financial empires have entirely displaced other mechanisms of capital integration, particularly those associated with widely-held banks and life insurers. The strong primary interlocks which form the basis for intercorporate cliques provide only the barest skeleton for the entire corporate interlock network. Analysis of weaker and secondary interlocks indicates that while the major investment companies, property development companies and owner-controlled industrials gained centrality in the network of strong primary interlocks after 1976, the major chartered banks and other widely-held financial institutions continued to hold central positions in the overall network, particularly by virtue of their manifold secondary interlocks. Banks continue to serve as bridges between distinct capitalist interests (cf. Mintz and Schwartz 1985) and, at least in the 1970s, came to occupy more central positions in the international network of interlocks, reflecting the growing allocation of money capital on an international basis (Fennema 1982). By 1983 Canadian chartered banks held on average 42.5 per cent of their total assets in foreign currency holdings (Canadian Bankers Association 1985: 6). Further, as I shall argue, the recent entry of the chartered banks into investment-banking activities may ultimately lead to stronger relations between banks and Canadian-based industrial capital, as the former come to dominate corporate underwriting.

What is clear in all of this is a significant recomposition of finance capital, from a system of loosely-structured financial hegemony to a system within which power is wielded in deregulated and increasingly international circuits by means of strategic concentrations of money capital.

FROM PERMEABLE FORDISM TO CONTINENTAL NEO-LIBERALISM

Accompanying these transformations in the circuit of capital have been significant changes in both the regime of accumulation and the concept of control in terms of which capitalist hegemony is strategically constructed. The Trudeau era of Liberal dominance in federal politics (1968–84) began at the climax of Fordist regulation, embodied in Keynesian economic policies and the social-democratic rhetoric of the 'Just Society'. But as the Bank of Canada adopted monetarist policies in the 1970s and the federal government introduced deflationary wage controls, tentatively in 1975 and more comprehensively in the '6 and 5' programme of 1982–4, a drift towards neo-liberalism set in (Wolfe 1984). As elsewhere, these moves comprised a macroeconomic volte-face, from state-supported valorization of productive capital around the mass worker–consumer, to a policy perspective that prioritized the restoration of 'sound money' so as to force 'sound micro-economic reasoning . . . upon the state and society as a whole' (van der Pijl 1987: 23).

In the same period the orientation of the state towards the regulation of capitalist enterprises showed some parallel transitions. The first tentative moves to restructure the financial sector came with the 1967 Bank Act revisions, which allowed trust companies to function as deposit-accepting near-banks (Richardson 1988: 3–4). In the 1970s, as conglomerate mergers and takeovers raised popular concerns about the concentration of economic power, a Royal Commission on Corporate Concentration was appointed. Its report, reflecting the emerging neo-liberal ethos, gave a green light to further centralization of capital by strongly endorsing the move towards an economy organized around large, internationally competitive enterprises (Canada 1978: 407).

In these respects, Canadian neo-liberalism can be seen to have followed a course similar to the rise of the new liberalism elsewhere. Yet it is equally important to take account of the historically specific conditions in which the transition from corporate liberal to neo-liberal strategy occurred in Canada. In the first place, the regime of accumulation that had been consolidated in the post-war boom period nurtured by conscious political policies and by copious flows of direct investment from the United States in the 1950s and 1960s was an especially permeable Fordism (Jenson, 1989). Canada's accumulation strategy in the era of Pax Americana was that of mass production for mass consumption within a continental framework of resource exports, capital imports, and the branch-plant production of consumer goods (cf. Houle 1983; Holmes, 1988: 34–6). This permeability meant, firstly, that Keynesian policies were adopted alongside a continuing commitment to an open, trading economy whose very openness would introduce 'an important element of instability into the implementation of the post-war political compromise' (Wolfe 1984: 48). Secondly, to ameliorate the uneven nature of resource-based, export-oriented industry, Keynesian measures would have to be supplemented by regional development policies. Post-war programs of Fordist regulation thus arose as a series of attempts to mediate the tensions of federalism: to build a consensus around a strong state that could provide guidance in a large, dispersed and fragmented country (Jenson 1989: 83).

These elements of permeable Fordism set the stage for a singularly Canadian retreat in the 1970s, as global stagflation set in and as international demand for Canadian exports fell. Continued fiscal stimulation tended to boost domestic demand for imports, exacerbating a current account deficit that was already ballooning from dividends and interest remitted to foreign-based capital (Wolfe 1984: 64–71). General problems of demand management were thus complicated by 'a steadily worsening balance-of-payments problem that seriously constrained the government's abilities to pursue the goals of the Keynesian welfare state' (ibid.: 48–9). As the federal government and Bank of Canada began to beat their retreat from Keynes in 1975, the increasingly continental circuit of mass production for mass consumption prefigured the even greater permeability that would prevail in a deregulated post-Fordist environment; indeed, in the 1980s it came to serve as the structural premise for the Free Trade strategy, as the choice for Canada came to be posed between long-term stagnation or taking 'that leap of faith' into a fully continental market.[9] The discourse of Fordist nation-building which had organized consent during the post-war expansion was meanwhile transformed into a crisis of federalism. As the economy fragmented and the post-war 'nation-building' development strategy was disputed by 'province-builders' such as the governments of Alberta and Quebec, the Fordist paradigm 'crumbled in the face of new and fragmenting collective identities based on language and region' (Jenson 1989: 85).

The related transition to a neo-liberal concept of control can also be seen to have taken a specific course in Canada. Developing in tandem with permeable Fordism, the corporate-liberal rendering of a general interest during Pax Americana was indelibly continental. In the 1960s economist Harry Johnson expressed the views of many Keynesians that 'Canada is an American nation', but that Canada's open door should be enclosed by generous social programmes and by some measure of industrial policy to facilitate the efficient use of capital and full employment of labour (Johnson 1963: 32, 103, 265).

In the early years of the crisis, the turn towards monetarism and wage controls was likewise tempered by a productivist, state-capitalist emphasis on the integrity of the 'national economy', a construct at the heart of Keynesian regulation (Radice 1984). Federal initiatives such as the Foreign Investment Review Agency (FIRA), the Canada Development Corporation (CDC), and the National Energy Program (NEP) emphasized domestic control over capital, the first by means of screening potential foreign investments to ensure their net contribution to domestic economic well-being (at least through increased employment), the latter two by means of direct state intervention in strategic sectors. If by the early 1980s many of the Keynesian strategies of macroeconomic regulation had been renounced, the prevailing 'continental nationalist' accumulation strategy still included a productivist interest in extra-market planning and state intervention. It thus constituted a compromise worked out between the more conservative elements of Canadian business, who wanted less government intervention, and the more nationalist wing of industry and the upper state bureaucracy, who advocated a full-fledged industrial policy (Niosi 1985b: 63).

By enhancing domestic control of industry without, however, 'nationalizing' the circuit of capital, the strategy of continental nationalism helped consolidate the hegemonic position of Canadian-based finance capital, even as its reliance on access to the American market deepened (Wolfe 1989: 119). Further erosion of American competitiveness in the 1980s brought recurring threats of protectionism, against which the Free Trade option evolved in the dialogue between Canadian business associations and the MacDonald Royal Commission (Drache and Cameron 1985). Its final report, issued in September 1985, recommended a fundamental change in the relationship between governments and markets, a permanent reduction in social welfare expenditures, and free trade with the United States (Drache 1989: 25).

It has been the project of the Conservative government of Brian Mulroney, first elected in 1984, to complete the transition to neo-liberalism begun by the Trudeau Liberals. The Conservatives' discussion paper, *A New Direction for Canada: An Agenda for Economic Renewal*, released in November 1984, called for a wide-ranging reorientation of public policy in the direction of less regulation, smaller government, more self-reliance by individuals and businesses, the encouragement of growth, and the building of a new national consensus (Drache 1989: 24). In 1985 the FIRA was converted into 'Investment Canada', its screening function all but replaced by a new mandate to attract new investment on a worldwide basis. The NEP was also repealed; the CDC and several other crown corporations privatized. Within the federal state apparatus these 'destructivist' changes eliminated much of the residual productive-capital orientation towards an integrated national economy.

With regard to the circuit of capital, however, the key neo-liberal initiatives have been in the deregulation of capitalist enterprises (particularly in the financial sector) and the negotiation and implementation of a comprehensive Free Trade Agreement (FTA) with the United States. The former, pursued both at the federal and provincial levels, removes many of the restrictions on money capital that were in effect throughout the Fordist era, in particular protection of banking from foreign competition and the regulated segmentation of the financial system into 'four pillars' of commercial banking, insurance, trust and mortgage lending, and investment banking. These measures terminate the state-sponsored hegemony of the chartered banks which since Confederation had been reproduced by limiting the fiduciary activities of other financial institutions (Neufeld 1972). But the same measures free the banks to engage in corporate underwriting, clearing the way for a movement from loosely-structured financial hegemony to German-style universal banking on an increasingly global scale. By early 1989 five of the six largest Canadian chartered banks had bought controlling interests in major investment banks, and the sixth, Toronto-Dominion, had created its own investment bank subsidiary (McNish 1989). In making a similar purchase in 1987 the Deutsche Bank took advantage of provisions in the same legislation for foreign banks to play a larger role in the Canadian market. The federal government's precedent-setting decision in 1989 to grant a full-fledged bank charter to American Express Company carried similar implications in further eroding the basis for a nationally-focused system of loosely-structured financial hegemony while promoting the consolidation of transnational finance capital.

Lastly, the FTA, 'the centrepiece of the Conservative policy agenda in the late 1980s', has removed many restrictions on the continental flow of capital and commodities. In a climate of bellicose protectionism among influential fractions of American industry this agreement ostensibly secures Canadian access to the US market. But its real political significance lies in the mechanism that the emerging common market provides for shifting the balance of class forces in Canada to the advantage of capital. In this sense, US–Canada Free Trade forms the linchpin of an accumulation strategy of continental neo-liberalism, which expresses the specific interests of 'Canadian' capitalists in an era of transnational finance capital.

CONTINENTAL NEO-LIBERALISM: AN ACCUMULATION STRATEGY FOR CANADIAN CAPITAL

It is this specifically continentalist rendering of the money-capital concept politically crystallized in the FTA which has become hegemonic within the Canadian bourgeoisie, and for good reason. 'Canadian enterprise is increasingly continental both in terms of market orientation and in terms of investment patterns' (Niosi 1985b: 63). Whether their capital is valorized within the newly consolidated financial groups or in units of more modest size many capitalists in Canada have had an immediate stake in securing long-term access to the market that absorbs most of their substantial exports. Canadian finance capitalists, typically with substantial investments in US industry, real estate, commerce, and the financial sector, have an especially strong fractional interest in promoting the free flow of capital and commodities across the 49th parallel.

But the continentalist 'free trade' option goes beyond the fractional level in representing a more general interest of capital in Canada. In contrast to one likely scenario for economic unification in western Europe where the class power of enhanced capital mobility may be tempered by guarantees of minimum social rights across all the participating countries there is no potentially social-democratic subtext to the politics of US–Canada Free Trade. As the circuit of capital becomes more fully continental, investment will flow to the cheapest and most compliant sections of the North American workforce. In effect, the larger and organizationally decimated American working class and the sub-subsistence workforce of the maquiladora industry along the US–Mexican border will set the standards for proletarian subsistence in Canada. Moreover, the 'harmonization' of policies required in order to remove non-market trading advantages will over time require the Canadian state to abandon many of its palliative interventions into the circuit of capital: the marketing boards, regional development grants, crown corporations, social programs, etc. In a deregulated North American market-place where capital is increasingly mobile, factors like minimum wages, levels of unionization, unemployment rates, and unobstructive labour laws will become critical components of corporate investment decisions (Lynk 1988: 28). Just as American employers in the North have long been able to use a 'Southern strategy' threatening to relocate in the low-wage Sunbelt in order to extract concessions from their employees and from local states, pressure to erode Canadian labour laws and social programs will come from Canadian business. In giving Canadian corporations US citizenship rights, the Free Trade grants Canadian capital the same structural power to threaten 'capital strikes' against local workforces and governments in Canada. The effect, in Lynk's terminology, will be 'forced harmonization', as states such as Texas (minimum wage US$1.40; unionization rate 12.5 per cent) compete directly for new investment capital with provinces such as Ontario (minimum wage C$5.00; unionization rate 33.7 per cent) (Kumar 1988: 773).

Understandably, capital pressed hard in 1987 and 1988, particularly through the Canadian Alliance for Trade and Job Opportunities, for a comprehensive free trade agreement as a means of establishing a regime of continental neo-liberalism (Warnock 1988). As if to provide a text-book example of its newly-enhanced structural power, two months after the FTA began to take effect the Canadian Manufacturers Association argued in a brief to the Canadian Finance Minister that the Agreement 'makes it more urgent that we tackle the outstanding issues that affect our competitiveness'. To this end, the Association advocated substantial deficit reduction through cut-backs in social programs and the elimination of universal access, and warned that the lack of such action would lead to a 'crisis of confidence' far worse in its effects than the recessionary implications of the cut-backs themselves. The same brief, however, called for a variety of tax breaks for manufacturers to improve their international competitiveness (*Globe and Mail*, 1 March 1989). Meanwhile, other centres of business activism have busied themselves with elaborating additional components of the neo-liberal project. In the crisis-ridden 1970s three such organizations appeared. The Business Council on National Issues (BCNI), Fraser Institute, and National Citizens Coalition (NCC) represent a turn towards business activism that has also been noted in the US and UK (Useem 1984). Tied to finance capital via funding and interlocks (see Table 3), these groups express the shift to a money-capital perspective within which trade unionism, welfarism, and state regulation are viewed as structural rigidities that undermine international competitiveness and personal freedom.

The BCNI, the most 'moderate' of the three, was created in the 1970s expressly as a vehicle for developing a new consensus on national policy among the major sections of monopoly capital. It con-tinues to be comprised predominantly of high-level executives in major corporations, has had a strong influence on federal economic policy, and was particularly active in the Canadian Alliance for Trade and Job

Table 9.3 Number of dominant corporations interlocked with the directorates
of neo-liberal political organizations

	1976	1986
Business Council on National Issues	45	53
Fraser Institute	12	42
National Citizens Coalition	*	5

*In 1976 the National Citizens Coalition apparently had not yet formed a board
of directors.

Opportunities during the Free Trade debates (see Langille 1987;
Warnock 1988: 114–16).

The Fraser Institute and National Citizens Coalition have been
important in giving a social base to more extreme right-wing positions.
In itself, the entry of these positions into public debate has shifted the
ideological spectrum by making other neo-liberal groups, like the
BCNI, look moderate (Fillmore 1986: 10). The proliferation of
corporate interlocks to the Fraser Institute a consistent exponent of
privatization, deregulation, and full-scale monetarism since its formation in 1974 (Stainsby and Malcolmson 1983; Swankey 1984) testifies
to the neo-liberal movement in the higher circles of Canadian business.
Through dozens of book-length publications and hundreds of news-
paper columns and public addresses, the Fraser Institute has focused on
building favourable public and elite opinion around a neo-liberal accumulation strategy. The Institute also has close ties to neo-liberal organizations elsewhere, such as the Mont Pelerin Society and the British
Institute for Economic Affairs, and in this sense forms part of what
Gill (1990) has termed a developing transnational historic bloc of economic and political forces rooted in the structural power of internationally mobile capital.

The National Citizens Coalition with the fewest ties to major
corporations has been more active in mounting 'political actions' to
advance neo-liberalism as a hegemonic project. Its leaders have pursued
a right-populist strategy, and claim to have built up a membership of
over 30,000. Through strategic placement of full-page 'open letters' in
high-circulation newspapers, the NCC has generated revenue for itself
and thousands of protest letters for the federal government from irate
citizens worried about the supposed dangers of Asian immigration,
progressive tax reform, Soviet expansionism, etc. (Fillmore 1986: 10–
11). The Coalition had also financed a major legal challenge to the

political use of union dues, and in 1986 formed an alliance with small capital and anti-feminists to oppose the Ontario government's pay-equity legislation. As NCC leader David Somerville remarked, 'There's nothing in the Constitution that says you should be repealing the law of supply and demand' (*Globe and Mail*, 17 May 1986; 8 July 1986).

Despite such libertarian overtures towards broadening the money-capital concept of control beyond the economic realm, the decisive strategic thrust in Canadian neo-liberalism has been the Free Trade initiative. Deregulated continentalism provides a formula for integrating the circuit of North American capital in such a way that Canadian-based financial groups can become direct participants on an equal footing with their American-based counterparts in a lucrative and polit-ically stable field of accumulation. The concept of continental neo-liberalism projects this fractional concern into a cosmopolitan conception of the 'national interest'. For the middle and working classes in Canada the benefits are presented not in terms of concessions to the mass worker/mass consumer, but within a vision of the *atomized consumer-worker* enjoying the lower prices and increased job opportu-nities that a deregulated common market will allegedly yield.

Yet as Jessop (1983) points out, the construction of such a 'general interest' in an accumulation strategy is not yet tantamount to the successful articulation of a hegemonic project. It is on this issue, which takes us beyond the structure of capital to consider the broader strategy of bourgeois hegemony, that we can discern some instructive differ-ences between neo-liberalism in Canada and its 'triumph' in Canada's Anglo-Atlantic allies.

Owing to the legacy of Britain's and then America's central posi-tions in world capitalism, the Thatcher and Reagan governments were in the 1980s able to tap deep nationalist sentiments in order to build support for policies which actually enhance the power of essentially stateless, internationally mobile capital. Nationalism has thus provided an ideological cover for the de-nationalization of capital, 'creating an appearance of a unified interest between fractions of capital, and between capital and the national working class, so ensuring the hegemony of an international elite' (Atkins 1986). This authoritarian–populist ideological offensive has endeavoured to replace the Fordist equation of nation-state and national economy with a general interest constructed around the 'ethnic nation', struggling to survive in a hostile international environment (van der Pijl 1986). In Canada, however, a bi-national country which has long occupied a secondary-imperialist location in world capitalism, no 'tribal demons of national chauvinism' can be summoned to build support for neo-liberalism. Canadian nationalism, traditionally bifurcated into Anglo and Quebecois versions, cannot be credibly invoked as legitimation for attacks on unions, welfare recipients, etc. (Whitaker 1987: 223). In fact, the continentalist content of Canadian neo-liberalism has rendered it particularly vulnerable to nationalist critique. In the Free Trade election of 1988 concerns about the further erosion of political sovereignty and cultural autonomy briefly imperilled the Conservatives' re-election prospects, prompting an unprecedented political involvement of the capitalist class (Brodie 1989).

Two further comparisons serve to demarcate neo-liberalism in Canada from the higher-profile projects of Thatcherism and Reaganism. First, in contrast to Britain the Canadian state is a federated apparatus with a division of powers that mandates provincial control over important elements of accumulation (e.g. resource rents and labour law) and social reproduction (e.g., health, education and welfare), exercised within a framework of highly uneven regional economic development. This division has tended to displace the more class-charged elements of the crisis of Fordism on to the provinces (as in struggles over trade union rights and social services), making it difficult to articulate a truly comprehensive concept of control on a national basis, à la Thatcherism.

In Ontario, where most of the manufacturing sector is located and the internal market is quite large, there has been a continuing basis for Fordism, as shown by the expansive reforms of the current Liberal government. In the more resource-based and export-oriented provinces such as British Columbia, Saskatchewan and Newfoundland, greater fluctuation in international demand, increasing competition from other exporters, and a weak multiplier effect have undermined the basis for Fordism and increased the appeal of neo-liberal 'solutions' to the crisis.

In these provinces, as in the parallel case of Sweden, the dominant export-oriented fraction of capital 'stands to lose more than it gains from a welfarist recovery based on domestic demand stimulation, since this would increase labour costs without significantly increasing final demand' (Pontusson 1987: 24). In British Columbia there has been a particularly militant mobilization of neo-liberalism within the ruling Social Credit Party which has, with direct advice from the Fraser Institute, led the way in implementing Thatcher-style policies of austerity, authoritarian labour legislation, and privatization (Carroll and Ratner 1989). Within Canada's federated state structure, British Columbia has acted as a role-model for like-minded provincial governments such as that of Saskatchewan, which has since deployed similar programmes. The more peripheral provinces, the poor cousins of Ontario-centred Fordism, have thus become a vanguard of neo-liberal attacks on trade unionism and the welfare state. The federal government has pursued a separate but complementary agenda of stricter market discipline through Free Trade, deregulation and a high interest rate policy which shores up the dollar and dampens inflation in southern Ontario, but which further exacerbates regional economic disparities by choking the prospects for recovery in the peripheral provinces (Black and Landry 1989).

Of course, the American state apparatus is also federated, and state-level politics, particularly in California, have been an important breeding ground for the new right (Davis 1986: 158). To grasp the crucial difference between neo-liberalism in Canada and the US we must look not to the structure of the state but to the balance of class forces. The crisis of Fordism in the United States has been pre-eminently a crisis of business unionism, as union density has plummeted to below 20 per cent of the non-agricultural workforce (ibid.: 145–8). Yet in Canada the 1970s was a period of intense organizing, particularly of public-sector workers, and the 1980s have seen major industrial unions such as the Auto Workers and Woodworkers break away from US-based 'internationals' over the issue of concessionary bargaining. And, while the influence of American unions in the Democratic Party has waned, in Canada the social-democratic New Democratic Party (NDP) has continued to represent the reformist views of its chief sponsor, organized labour. As Huxley *et al.* have observed,

> the most striking difference between the Canadian and American movements during the past two decades is the increasing importance of more adversarial and political unionism in Canada, marked above all by the interdependence and effective mutual aid between key unions and the New Democratic Party in English Canada, and analogous developments in Quebec involving a more electorally amorphous and even an extra-parliamentary left.
>
> (Huxley *et al.* 1986: 131)

Ironically, the perennial status of the NDP as a strong 'third party' within parliament also seems to have distanced it from what is elsewhere called the 'crisis of social democracy'. Through its left-nationalist criticism of the policies of both bourgeois parties, the NDP increased its popular support at the federal level between 1984 and 1988, and in the process held the more extreme aspirations of the right in check.

Indeed, notwithstanding the efforts of the BCNI, Fraser Institute, and National Citizens Coalition, the mobilization of neo-liberalism in Canada has been somewhat less vigorous than its American counterpart, which has been able to access an ideological matrix of institutional racism, nationalistic anticommunism, and evangelical Protestantism in sections of the white middle strata and working class. But the US–Canada difference has not been merely a matter of working-class organization and political culture; it is also rooted in the social organization of the capitalist class. In Canada, neo-liberal business activism did not rise upon a separate fraction as in the peripheral grouping of predominantly Southern and Western capitalists at the core of the American new right (Davis 1986: 157–80). It developed as a more temperate transition within the inner circle of monopoly capital, as in the corporate elite's collective sponsorship of the BCNI. In this respect, Canadian neo-liberalism's lower profile can be partly attributed to the highly centralized structure of Canadian finance capital, which has made it possible to achieve political ends through less visible means.

While American business leaders had to undertake a broader and more vociferous ideological campaign on account of the dispersal of power in their system, their Canadian counterparts were able to rely on a more organized form of 'elite accommodation'. The Business Council on National Issues has been able to exercise an even more pivotal role than its American counterparts, the Business Roundtable and the Committee for Economic Development, largely because power is more concentrated in Canada (Langille 1987: 55).[10]

For all these reasons the difficulty in articulating continentalist neo-liberal policies to a national-chauvinist discourse, the federal-provincial division of powers and regional unevenness of economic crisis, the relative strength of social democracy and less visible mobilization of the extreme right; in Canada neo-liberalism appears less as a 'national' hegemonic project marking a conscious break from Fordist regulation and more as an uneven process of passive revolution, punctuated by intensified class struggle in the peripheral provinces and by a lingering national question at the federal level.

This strategic mix is not, however, without its advantages. Unburdened by American-style alliances to the religious right and commitments to a bloated military-industrial complex, Canadian neo-liberalism has been able to present itself in the federal political field as a rational, progressive, and cosmopolitan force, attuned to the seemingly inevitable logic of capitalist internationalization. Thus, for example, in attempting to build support for the Free Trade Agreement, the Department of External Affairs posed 'a choice between building bridges to other lands, or looking inward and building walls around our country' (Canada 1987a: 12). Within this discourse, Canadian–American partnership is depicted not as a renunciation of sovereignty but as the leading edge of a 'constructive internationalism' that holds out new opportunities for enterprising Canadians.[11]

Similarly, the apparent vulnerability of continental neo-liberalism to left-nationalist critique must be considered in light of the effects of the Americanization of popular culture in Canada. Modern Canada has been profoundly shaped by the early and pervasive spread of both Fordism and the mass cultural industries from their epicentre in the USA (Carroll 1986: 207–9). These economic and cultural forces 'have cumulatively changed the notion of what constitutes the Canadian national interest' (Clarkson 1988: 28). Although for many Canadians Americanization has inspired a cultural nationalism which cuts against the continentalist grain, for many others, detached from aspirations for cultural autonomy, the continentalist dimension of subjectivity has by now attained the certainty of 'common sense'. Those possessed of a North American identity are already predisposed to view continental neo-liberalism as part of a seemingly natural evolution towards a North American society. To the extent that full-scale economic integration takes hold while state support for indigenous cultural production continues to wither, the politico-cultural balance can be expected to tip towards the latter forces. The inelegance of reorganizing consent around a 'national' interest that is in substance continental must in this sense be weighed against the prospects for cumulatively narrowing the basis for a Canadian left-nationalism. Here again, the metaphor of passive revolution seems appropriate: popular support for neo-liberal transformation is recruited not by promoting a new 'national policy' but by enhancing the pre-existing cultural trend towards Americanization.

As several scholars have suggested, the appropriate strategy for countering a passive revolution is to conduct an anti-passive revolution, 'based on an extension of class struggles and popular-democratic struggles so as to mobilize ever-wider sections of the population for democratic reforms' (Simon 1982: 49; Buci-Glucksmann 1979). The groups which in 1988 coalesced into the Pro-Canada Network in the struggle against Free Trade provide a prime example. Their actions are the latest in a series of collective responses to the crisis, reaching back to the Canadian Labour Congress's Day of Protest against wage controls in 1976.

Historically, the terrain on which these groups have struggled has been framed by the Canadian state. If, however, the passive revolution is successful in establishing a fully continental field of deregulated accumulation, the political terrain will also have shifted. In that event, future movements will need to become more 'continental' in their own strategic outlook, if not their activity. This is a daunting thought in view of the disorganized state of the American left. But in a world order where ruling-class strategies are increasingly global and where historic blocs necessarily cross borders, the prospects for significant social transformation on a strictly 'national' basis are limited, particularly in a country whose permeable border joins it to the dominant capitalist power. The conclusion Mike Davis draws from his study of the American working class may hold great pertinence for Canadians, and for Mexicans. If socialism is to arrive one day in North America it will most likely be 'by virtue of a combined, hemispheric process of revolt that overlaps boundaries and interlaces movements' (Davis 1986: 314).

NOTES

1 This chapter draws upon earlier papers (Carroll 1989, 1990). It has benefited from comments by Warren Magnusson and by participants in the *After the Crisis* seminar at the University of Amsterdam, particularly Meindert Fennema, André Mommen, Henk Overbeek, John Rhijnsburger and Kees van der Pijl. I also appreciate the research assistance of Peter Atamanenko, Charles Partridge and Matt Stables.

2 In campaigning for federal election in 1984, Conservative leader Brian Mulroney described Canada's social programmes as a 'sacred trust' that could not be violated. 'Managing change' was the symbol around which the Conservative government defended its record and presented its agenda in the election of 1988. In the month before the election was called, Mulroney described the US–Canada Free Trade Agreement as 'the instrument to ensure that we can manage change in the national interest' (*Globe and Mail*, 3 October 1988, p. A9). On the day parliament was dissolved, Mulroney promised the key issue in the election would be 'who can manage change in the years ahead' (*Canadian News Facts* 23 (18), 19 October 1988, p. 3883).

3 Between 1985 and 1988 the spread between the Canadian Bank Rate and the US Discount Rate – traditionally a lever for attracting money capital to Canada – increased from 1.9 per cent to 3.4 per cent (Black and Landry 1989).

4 Calculated from *Who Owns Whom*, North American Edition, 1977 and 1986.

5 The 'Top 100s' are composed of the seventy largest industrial firms, twenty largest financial institutions, and ten largest retail or wholesale merchandizing companies (all ranked by assets) for the years 1976 and

1986. To each 'Top 100' two further sets of large corporations were added: (1) companies as large as the 70th ranked industrial and engaged in urban property development, a booming sector for speculative investment; and (2) investment companies owning strategically significant blocs of shares in at least one of the 'Top 100' firms (see Carroll 1986 for a detailed statement of methodology). The rationale for selecting investment companies according to their shareholdings in other dominant corporations is that due to complex pyramiding arrangements the actual assets of an investment company may be far less than the capital under its strategic control. It is precisely the latter that is relevant in a study of finance capital. The sample excludes crown corporations under majority-control of the state, though it includes several firms in which the federal or Quebec governments hold a minority interest.

6   In the present analysis a holding of at least 5 per cent of voting shares (in the absence of other, larger blocs) was deemed sufficient to enable a shareholding interest to exercise strategic control. As Scott (1985) has shown, large corporations whose shares are 'widely held' are not necessarily under 'management control', but often are controlled by constellations of interests: institutional investors and wealthy families, no one of which holds at least 5 per cent of voting shares.

7   In the present context a clique refers to a (maximal) subnetwork of at least five corporations, within which each pair of firms is connected by one or more strong primary interlocks, either directly or at one remove (cf. Alba 1973). This definition allows for the possibility of multiple cliques within a single, connected network, and of overlapping clique memberships. Detailed description of the changing network structure can be found in Carroll (1989).

8   The most important interfaces linked (1) the Brascan-Bronfman group with the Olympia and York-Reichmanns, through joint ventures in finance and real estate, and (2) the Reichmanns to the Thomson group, through the strong commercial relation between Thomson Newspapers and its main newsprint supplier, Reichmann-controlled Abitibi-Price. Since 1981 the Reichmanns and Kenneth Thomson have been joint owners of a newsprint mill in Georgia, further cementing their commercial relation (Goldenberg 1984: 75–6).

9   As Donald MacDonald (the Chairman of the Royal Commission on the Economic Union and Development Prospects for Canada) put it, 'either we stay still and do nothing, or we make that leap of faith' (*Toronto Star*, 20 November 1984).

10   On the decentralized structure of the American corporate network and the centralized structure of the Canadian network compared to other advanced capitalist countries see Ornstein (1989).

11   The phrase was employed to describe one of the principal goals of the Canadian government in the Throne Speech of 27 April 1989 (Howard 1989).

REFERENCES

Alba, R.D. (1973) 'A graph-theoretic definition of a sociometric clique', *Journal of Mathematical Sociology*, 3: 113–26.

Andreff, W. (1984) 'The internationalization of capital and the reordering of world capitalism', *Capital and Class*, 22: 58–80.

Atkins, F. (1986) 'Thatcherism, populist-authoritarianism and the search for a new left political strategy', *Capital and Class*, 28: 25–48.

Black, E. and Landry, G. (1989) 'Guess who wants higher interest rates?', *Canadian Dimension*, 23(3): 15–18.

Brodie, J. (1989) 'The "Free Trade" election', *Studies in Political Economy*, 28: 175–82.

Brym, R.J., (ed.) (1985) *The Structure of the Canadian Capitalist Class*, Toronto: Garamond Press.

Buci-Glucksmann, C. (1979) 'State, transition, and passive revolution', in C. Mouffe (ed.), *Gramsci and Marxist Theory*, 207–36, Boston: Routledge & Kegan Paul.

Canada (1978) *Report of the Royal Commission on Corporate Concentration*, Ottawa: Minister of Supply and Services.

Canada (1987a) *The Canada–US Trade Agreement in Brief*, Ottawa: Minister of Supply and Services.

Canada (1987b) 'Corporations and Labour Unions Returns Act', *Report, Part 1: Corporations*, Ottawa: Statistics Canada.

Canadian Bankers Association (1985) *Concentration of Power in the Financial Services Industry*, Toronto: Canadian Bankers Association.

Carroll, W. K. (1989) 'Neoliberalism and the recomposition of finance capital in Canada', *Capital & Class*, 38: 81–112.

Carroll, W. K. and Ratner, R.S. (1989) 'Social democracy, neo-conservatism and hegemonic crisis in British Columbia', *Critical Sociology*, 16(1): 29ʟ–53.

Carroll, W. K. (1986) *Corporate Power and Canadian Capitalism*, Vancouver: University of British Columbia Press.

Carroll, W. K. (1990) 'Restructuring capital, reorganizing consent: Gramsci, political economy, and Canada', *Canadian Review of Sociology and Anthropology*, 27: 390–416.

Clarkson, S. (1988) 'Continentalism: The conceptual challenge for Canadian social science', in *The John Porter Memorial Lectures 1984–1987*, 23–43, Montreal: Canadian Sociology and Anthropology Association.

Davis, M. (1986) *Prisoners of the American Dream*, London: Verso.

Drache, D. (1989) *The Deindustrialization of Canada and its Implications for Labour*, Ottawa: Canadian Centre for Policy Alternatives.

Drache, D. and Cameron, D. (eds) (1985) *The Other MacDonald Report*, Toronto: James Lorimer.

Drohan, M. (1989) 'Foreigners avoid direct investment', Toronto *Globe and Mail*, 20 October, pp. B1, B4.

Edwards, C. (1985) *The Fragmented World*, New York: Methuen.

Fennema, M. (1982) *International Networks of Banks and Industries*, Boston: Martin Nijhoff.

Fennema, M. and van der Pijl, K. (1987) 'International bank capital and the new liberalism', in M. S. Mizruchi and M. Schwartz (eds) *Intercorporate*

Relations. The Structural Analysis of Business, 298–319, New York: Cambridge University Press.

Fillmore, N. (1986) 'The right stuff: Inside the National Citizens' Coalition', *This Magazine*, 20(2): 4–11,19.

Gill, S. (1990) *American Hegemony and the Trilateral Commission*, Cambridge: Cambridge University Press.

Goldenberg, S. (1984) *The Thomson Empire*, Toronto: Bantam Books.

Harvey, D. (1982) *The Limits to Capital*, Chicago: University of Chicago Press.

Holmes, J. (1988) 'Industrial restructuring in a period of crisis: An analysis of the Canadian automobile industry, 1973–83', *Antipode*, 20(1): 19–51.

Houle, F. (1983) 'Economic strategy and the restructuring of the Fordist wage-labour relationship in Canada', *Studies in Political Economy*, 11: 127–47.

Howard, R. (1989) 'Conservative agenda remains unclear', *Globe and Mail*, 23 May, p. A8.

Huxley, C., Kettler, D. and Struthers, J. (1986) 'Is Canada's experience "especially instructive"?', in S. M. Lipset (ed.) *Unions in Transition*, San Francisco: Institute for Contemporary Studies.

International Monetary Fund (1987) *International Financial Statistics Yearbook*, Washington: IMF.

Jenson, J. (1989) '"Different" but not "exceptional": Canada's permeable Fordism', *Canadian Review of Sociology and Anthropology*, 26: 69–94.

Jessop, R. (1983) 'Accumulation strategies, state forms, and hegemonic projects', *Kapitalistate*, 10–11: 89–111.

Johnson, H. (1963) *The Canadian Quandary*, Toronto: MacGraw-Hill.

Kumar, P. (1988) 'Estimates of unionism and collective bargaining coverage in Canada', *Relations Industrielles*, 43: 757–9.

Kaufman, M. (1985) 'The internationalization of Canadian bank capital (with a look at bank activity in the Caribbean and Central America)', *Journal of Canadian Studies*, 19(4): 61–81.

Langille, D. (1987) 'Corporate statesmen: The Business Council on national issues and the Canadian state', *Studies in Political Economy*, 24: 41–85.

Lynk, M. (1988) 'Free trade and the forced harmonization of labour law', *Canadian Dimension*, 22(5): 28–32.

MacEwan, A. (1986) 'International debt and banking: Rising instability within the general crisis', *Science and Society*, 50: 177–209.

McNish, J. (1989) 'T-D securities unit emerges industry winner', *Globe and Mail*, 11 February, p. B4.

Mintz, B. and Schwartz, M. (eds.) (1985) *The Power Structure of American Business*, Chicago: University of Chicago Press.

Mittelstaedt, M. (1985) 'Banks and trust companies', *Report on Business Magazine*, 2(1): 34–40.

Neufeld, E. P. (1972) *The Financial System of Canada: Its Growth and Development*, New York: St. Martin's Press.

Niosi, J. (1985a) *Canadian Multinationals*, Toronto: Garamond Press.

Niosi, J. (1981) *Canadian Capitalism*, Toronto: James Lorimer.

Niosi, J. (1985b) 'Continental nationalism: the strategy of the Canadian bourgeoisie', in R. J. Brym (ed.) (1985) *The Structure of the Canadian Capitalist Class*, 53-66, Toronto: Garamond Press.

O'Connor, J. (1987) *The Meaning of Crisis*, Oxford: Basil Blackwell.

O'Hagan, P. (1986) 'Structure, trends and fluctuations on the balance sheets of the major sectors of the economy, 1961–1984', *Canadian Statistical Review*, 60(11): vii–xxxv.

Organization of Economic Cooperation and Development (1988) *Non-Financial Enterprises Financial Statements 1987*, Paris: OECD.

Ornstein, M. (1984) 'Interlocking directorates in Canada: Intercorporate or class alliance?', *Administrative Science Quarterly*, 29: 210–31.

Ornstein, M. (1989) 'The social organization of the capitalist class in comparative perspective', *Canadian Review of Sociology and Anthropology*, 26: 151–77.

Overbeek, H. (1980) 'Finance capital and the crisis in Britain', *Capital and Class*, 11: 99–120.

Overbeek, H. (1988) *Global Capitalism and Britain's Decline*, Doctoral dissertation, University of Amsterdam.

Pontusson, J. (1987) 'Radicalization and retreat in Swedish social democracy', *New Left Review*, 165: 5–33.

Portes, A. and Walton, J. (1981) *Labour, Class, and the International System*, Toronto: Academic Press.

Pijl, K. van der (1984) *The Making of an Atlantic Ruling Class*, London: Verso.

Pijl, K. van der (1986) 'Neoliberalism vs. planned interdependence. Concepts of control in the struggle for hegemony', Paper presented at the conference on Interdependence and Conflict in the International System, Polemologisch Instituut, University of Groningen, November 19–21.

Pijl, K. van der (1987) 'Capitalist class formation at the international level', paper presented at the 1987 Annual Meeting of the American Political Science Association, Chicago.

Radice, H. (1984) 'The national economy: A Keynesian myth?', *Capital and Class*, 22: 111–40.

Richardson, R. J. (1985) 'A structural-rational theory of the functions of directorship interlocks between financial and non-financial corporations', in R. J. Brym (ed.) (1985) *The Structure of the Canadian Capitalist Class*, 103–16, Toronto: Garamond Press.

Richardson, R. J. (1988) '"A sacred trust": The trust industry and Canadian economic structure', *Canadian Review of Sociology and Anthropology*, 25: 1–22.

Rugman, A. M. (1987) *Outward Bound: Canadian Direct Investment in the United States*, Toronto: Canadian–American Committee.

Scott, J. (1985) *Corporations, Class and Capitalism*, second edition, London: Hutchinson.

Scott, J. (1987) 'Intercorporate structures in western Europe: A comparative historical analysis', in M. S. Mizruchi and M. Schwartz (eds) (1987) *Intercorporate Relations. The Structural Analysis of Business*, 208–32, New York: Cambridge University Press.

Shortall, F. C. (1986) 'Fixed and circulating capital', *Capital and Class*, 28: 160–85.

Simon, R. (1982) *Gramsci's Political Thought*, London: Lawrence and Wishart.

Stainsby, C. and Malcolmson, J. (1983) *The Fraser Institute, the Government, and a Corporate Free Lunch*, Vancouver: Solidarity Coalition.

Stokman, F. N. and Wasseur, F. W. (1986) 'National networks of 1976: A structural comparison', in F. N. Stokman, R. Ziegler and J. Scott (eds), *Networks of Corporate Power*, 20–44, Cambridge: Polity Press.

Swankey, B. (1984) *The Fraser Institute: A Socialist Analysis of the Corporate Drive to the Right*, Vancouver: Centre for Socialist Education.

Useem, M. (1984) *The Inner Circle*, New York: Oxford University Press.

Warnock, J. W. (1988) *Free Trade and the New Right Agenda*, Vancouver, New Star Books.

Whitaker, R. (1987) 'Neo-conservatism and the state', in R. Miliband, L. Panitch and J. Saville (eds), *Socialist Register 1987*, 1–31, London:The Merlin Press.

Wolfe, D. (1984) 'The rise and demise of the Keynesian era in Canada: economic policy 1930–1982', in M. S. Cross and G. S. Kealey (eds), *Modern Canada 1930–1980s*, 46–80, Toronto: McClelland and Stewart.

Wolfe, D. (1989) 'The Canadian state in comparative perspective', *Canadian Review of Sociology and Anthropology*, 26: 95–126.

10

NEO-LIBERALISM AND THE SHIFT TOWARDS A US-CENTRED TRANSNATIONAL HEGEMONY

Stephen R. Gill[1]

INTRODUCTION

Much of the discussion of international relations in the 1970s and 1980s has tended to focus on the question of American decline. In so doing, many writers have tended to ignore or overlook the transformation of both US hegemony and the global political economy. US hegemony has changed from an outward projection of US 'national' hegemony. What is emerging is a necessarily incomplete form of transnational, neo-liberal dominance, one which is nevertheless anchored in US political and military centrality. At the level of world order, then, the world is undergoing a shift from a relatively hegemonic to a post-hegemonic world order. Although this is not a crisis in the dominance of the United States *per se*, its policies have been intimately bound up with the transition, albeit in a contradictory manner.

In the 1980s and 1990s, globalizing economic forces are serving to integrate important aspects of material life on the planet, whilst simultaneously disintegrating other forms of state and material and social organization. The changes in East and Central Europe, the disintegration of the Soviet Union, the transformations in the Third World and in the metropolitan heartland of capitalism are part of a general process of global restructuring of forms of state and social relations. Such global changes are driven by, amongst other forces, intensifying competitive pressures, and economic innovation and transformation. Economic and political change has been punctuated and accelerated by recessions of deepening severity in the 1970s, 1980s and now in the

1990s. Indeed, for many parts of the world, there has been chronic economic depression since the early 1980s, a depression which may well continue for much of the 1990s.

This essay attempts to help explain aspects of these transformations by drawing on the concepts of the structural power of capital, hegemony, historic bloc and organic intellectuals. In the essay I hope to show the dialectical and contradictory aspects of these transformations in the emerging world order, and in so doing, go beyond state centric and reductionist conceptions of international relations.

Some of the contradictions discussed relate to the social and economic trajectory of the neo-liberal counter-revolution which has occurred on a global basis over the last twenty years, in the context of a deepening global economic crisis. Social forces within the United States have been crucial to these developments, in conjunction with their counterparts in other major capitalist states, in what can be called an emerging neo-liberal transnational historic bloc. The most recent manifestation of the international politics of this historic bloc concerns the attempt to reconstruct the successor republics to the Soviet Union, so as to integrate these post-communist societies into global capitalism. This transition is taking place under the aegis of the Group of Seven major capitalist states, the IMF, the European Bank for Reconstruction and Development, and a range of organic intellectuals associated with neo-liberalism (for example, Paul Volcker, the former Chairman of the US Federal Reserve, who is now helping to supervise the reconstruction of banking and finance in Russia).

From the vantage point of 1992 (that is, in the context of the deepest global recession since the 1930s, and of the debt deflation following the financial excesses of the 1980s), the political appeal and legitimacy of the vanguard class forces in this bloc would appear to be less hegemonic (in a Gramscian sense) than that which prevailed in the West and Japan in the 1950s and 1960s during the Cold War. This is not only because of rising unemployment, but also because the social basis of hegemony may be narrowing, as capitalist politics and US leadership appear to be increasingly based less on consent and the inclusion of subordinate interests, and more on dominance, coercion (economic and military), conflict and harsh competition. This marginalization of growing numbers of the population calls into question the economic and political sustainability of the brave new world of liberal transnational capitalism, at least on present trends.

Before we can discuss this possibility further, however, we need to explain the changes which have brought the post-1945 order to its present conjuncture. For purposes of exposition, the article is divided into three sections: the crisis of post-war hegemony, the transnationalization of the world economy and its significance, and the creation of a US-centred transnational hegemony.

THE CRISIS OF POST-WAR AMERICAN HEGEMONY

The origins of post-war American hegemony

The careful planning for, and creation of, a US-centred post-war order sought to create a *Pax Americana*, involving the political, economic and social reconstruction of the defeated axis powers, the regeneration of Western Europe under the Marshall Plan, the militarization of US–European relations through NATO, and the ideological and politico-strategic rivalry with a new expanded world communism in the form of a Cold War primarily directed against the Soviet Union. What Geoffrey Barraclough has called the era of 'contemporary history' resulted in something which some nineteenth century thinkers had suggested was likely: the eclipse of Europe and the rise to global power of the United States in the West and Russia – temporarily the Soviet Union – in the East (cf. Barraclough 1967).

As a response to the inter-war crisis, and because of worries concerning America's continued prosperity after the war, the US government, from the 1944 Bretton Woods conference onwards, sought to create an integrated, liberal international economy, one which would give maximum scope to the expansion of economic forces, particularly those centred in the US. This would provide the basis for a new world order, building upon, and evolving from the different variants of the 'welfare-nationalist' form of state (cf. Cox 1987).

The social model for this, at least in the metropolitan, Atlantic heartlands of the system, was the 'internationalisation of the New Deal' (cf. van der Pijl 1984). In the European context this took the form of rebuilding or creating liberal democracy, encouraging the political centre, class compromise and corporatism, and the use of Keynesian forms of macroeconomic management. At the level of production the system was premised on the Fordist mode of accumulation: the system of mass production organized in assembly lines under Taylorist principles of 'scientific management'. The macroeconomic aspects of the system involved growing effective demand, by virtue of rising real wages and thus mass consumption, exemplified by the growing automobile and electrical industries, allied to the military-industrial complexes in an era of cheap energy.

With regard to international money and finance, the system was driven by the supply of international liquidity in the form of US capital exports, overseas military expenditures and direct transfers. The hub of the international monetary system was the gold-dollar standard, and international trade and payments were lubricated by the supply of dollars as the US ran consistent balance of payments deficits. Nevertheless, the mobility of international financial capital, which had been an important destabilizing feature of the inter-war system, was placed under some control in the post-war order. Both Keynes and Harry Dexter White, the principal architects of the Bretton Woods agreements, were critical of the power of rentier (money) capital, and they sought articles in the IMF agreements to ensure that financial flows across borders would serve mainly to lubricate international trade and more broadly, the movement of factors of production. In this regard, Keynes distinguished between 'virtuous', that is productive, and 'vicious', that is speculative movements of hot money and flight capital. The latter he saw as profoundly destabilizing to government policies and economic activity more generally. Indeed, White's boss at the New Deal stronghold in the US Treasury, Secretary Morgenthau, was committed to making finance the 'servant', rather than the master of 'production'. Nevertheless, financial interests associated with Wall Street and their counterparts in Europe managed to dilute any substantial attempt to impose stronger state controls and tighter forms of international economic co-operation in matters of international finance. This later opened the way for a renaissance in the power of financial capital, especially after the return to convertibility of the major European currencies in the late 1950s, and as the offshore financial, or Euromarkets, began to grow rapidly in the 1960s (see Strange 1976; for later developments, Frieden 1987).

The onset of crisis in the post-war order

While the world economy expanded, and the mobility of international capital, notably financial capital, was restricted, the world order was more or less hegemonic, at least in its core areas, as both left-wing and extreme right-wing forces were marginalized and the political centre was consolidated. Since the 1970s, the balance between these complex forces has begun to break down, so that we have entered a period which corresponds to a crisis of hegemony for the post-war world system. One indicator of this is that US leadership was increasingly based upon a narrow view of its interests. The retreat from economic universalism was signalled by the shift towards a more aggressively nationalist stance in the form of the Nixon 'shocks' of August 1971. These changes were designed to protect US jobs, in the context of a decline in productivity growth and competitiveness. The United States suspended the convertibility of the dollar into gold, and imposed import surcharges (hitting the interests of European, Third World and especially Japanese exporters), forcing adjustment on the rest of the world.

After 1971, the world monetary system thus rested on a pure dollar standard, and fixed exchange rates were abandoned. These changes occurred at the same time as there was substantial growth in offshore Eurodollar markets: markets outside formal political jurisdiction. Indeed the US government did little to stop the growth of these markets since they provided another means to internationalize the costs of its domestic policies, as well as a vehicle for the domestically-regulated US banks to make larger profits (the Euromarkets were not subjected to interest rate ceilings as were US domestic financial markets). Also the Euromarkets were a means by which US transnational companies could raise finance more readily for their international investments and operations more generally.

US macroeconomic policies were inflationary (which helped internationalize the costs of financing both the Great Society and the Vietnam War by devaluing the dollar and thus causing a depreciation in foreigners' dollar-denominated holdings). These policies were, in David Calleo's phrase, characterized by 'malign neglect' of the interests of the rest of the world and part of a package of wider political and strategic measures, including the Nixon doctrine (which included the idea of building up the power of the Shah of Iran as a 'regional policeman') to allow the US to have 'hegemony on the cheap' (cf. Calleo 1982). Finally, US hegemony suffered enormous blows to its political and military prestige – the defeat in Vietnam, the humiliations following the Iranian revolution, the apparent rise to military parity of the Soviet Union.

The recessions of the 1970s and 1980s and their effects

The 'Nixon shocks' initiated a wave of 'mercantilist' reactions to the global recessions of the 1970s and 1980s throughout the capitalist world. The scale of recession in the 1970s and 1980s is revealed in

Figure 10.1, showing severe recessions in 1974–5 and 1980–2, the latter much the deepest. The secular trend was a slowdown in the growth of output among all country groups between 1963–72 and 1973–82.

The growth in per capita output of industrial countries between 1973–82 was 1.7 per cent per annum, in contrast to 3.7 per cent in the former period, and that of the oil-exporting countries fell from 5.6 to 3.8 per cent in the two periods. The non-oil developing countries' per capita growth rates fell from 3.6 to 2.7 per cent. In the Western hemisphere, the growth in per capita output in 1973–82 was 2 per cent, compared with 3.3 per cent in the previous decade. In the United States, the 1979–82 recession was the worst since the 1930s and it saw, in the summer of 1981, a prime rate of interest of 20.5 per cent, which broke the usury laws of some of the American states. The effects of the slowdown were particularly severe for less-developed and indebted nations, especially in Africa and Latin America (see Table 10.1).

What was crucial, at least in ideological terms, was that recession helped activate the reappraisal concerning the role of the public sector and the appropriate 'mix' of intervention and market in a capitalist economy. These recessions also led to changes in expectations about international relations, for example, the likelihood of concessions by the developed countries to less-developed countries and the viability of commodity agreements and cartels such as OPEC. The pressure of

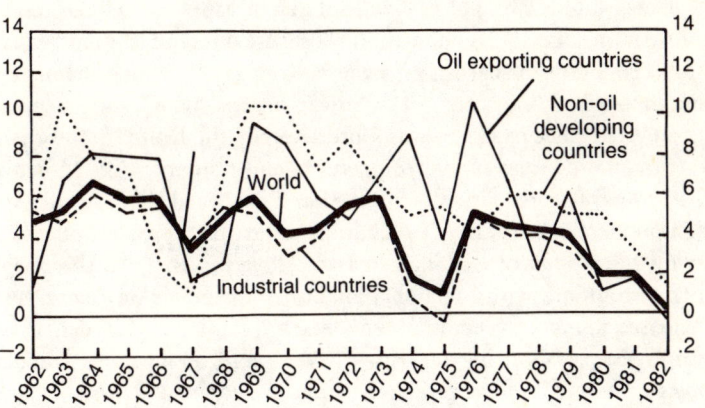

Figure 10.1 Real gross domestic product by region, 1962–82 (per cent change over previous year)

Source: International Monetary Fund, *International Financial Statistics*, supplement on output statistics (Washington DC, International Monetary Fund, 1984), p. x.

Table 10.1 Developing countries' real rates of growth, GDP per capita,
1968–85

	1968–77	1977–81	1981–5
15 heavily indebted nations	3.9	1.4	−1.7
Latin America	3.6	1.7	−1.5

Source: International Monetary Fund, *World Economic Outlook, 1986* (Washington DC, International Monetary Fund).

recession, an acceleration in the fall of real prices of commodity exports (see Figure 10.2) coupled with very high real interest rates in the late 1970s and early 1980s (see Figure 10.3) forced many indebted nations to turn to the International Monetary Fund, which in turn pressed these countries to liberalize their economies and cut the size and growth of the public sector. In addition, since 1981, the Soviet Union was weakened relative to the major capitalist states because of the rapid fall in the price of oil, its major source of foreign exchange.[2]

These recessions had obvious short-term purgative effects associated with a downswing in the business cycle. This promoted a general restructuring of capital, and capital-labour relations. For example, during 1979–82 there were record numbers of bankruptcies, and the decline of older, less-competitive industries was accelerated.

Thus, noteworthy links between different aspects of global restructuring in the late 1970s and early 1980s were discernible. In many ways the recession of the early 1980s can be seen as facilitating the material and ideological renovation of American hegemony. This might appear unexpected since recession was more severe in the United States than it was for its main economic competitors and military rival. Moreover, the Federal Reserve virtually initiated and deepened the recession with tight monetary policy (1979–82) at the same time as real oil prices rose following the fall of the Shah of Iran. However, in 1982 the Reagan 'boom' took off, with a combination of fiscal stimulus (involving vastly increased military expenditures entailing a spiralling budget deficit) and supply-side, tax-cutting measures (these were designed to stimulate investment and improve productivity and the competitiveness of certain sectors of the American economy).

America's capacity to expand out of recession in this way contrasted with the other major capitalist states which exercised strict controls on growth of public spending. This was an aspect of America's continuing

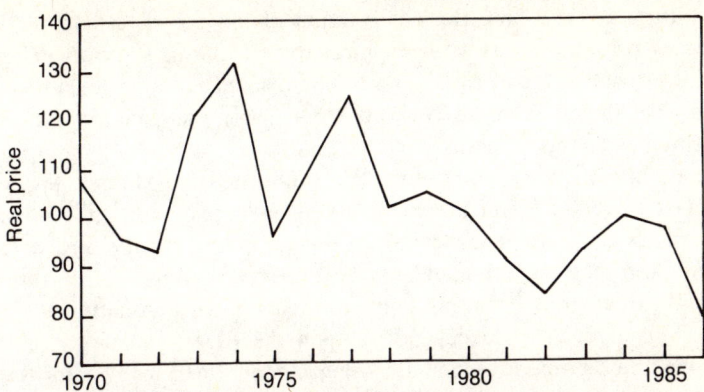

Figure 10.2 Real prices of developing country commodity exports, 1970–85, (1980=100)

Source: Feldstein *et al.*, *Restoring Growth in the Debt-Laden Third World* (New York, Trilateral Commission, 1987), discussion draft, p. 13a. Based on OECD and IMF statistics.

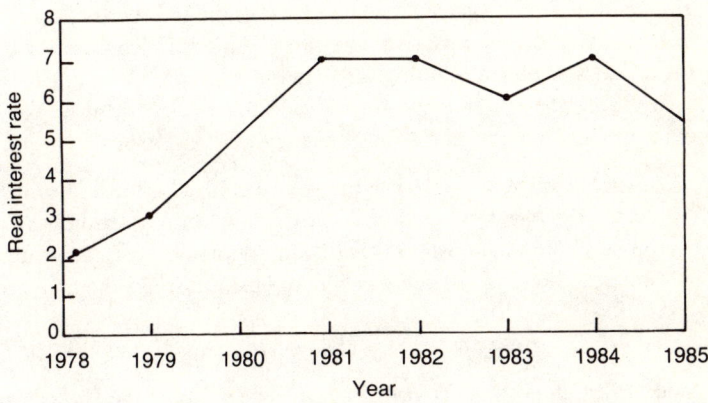

Figure 10.3 Real interest rates, 1978–85 (Eurodollar rate minus US GNP deflator)

Source: Feldstein *et al.*, *Restoring Growth in the Debt-Laden Third World*, p. 13b.

economic exceptionalism. A second element of exceptionalism, that is Reaganite populism, provided much of the justification for the policies which helped generate the post-1982 boom. Reaganism was in tune with, as well as a catalyst for, the resurgence of possessive individualism and hostility towards statist paternalism. Along with the Reaganite stress on the need for a 'strong America' these themes served to vindicate tax cuts, the deregulation of industry and banking, an attack on union power (for example the sacking of Patco members), and provided part of the context for the spread of a 'get-rich-quick', speculative and increasingly short-term mentality in America (and to a certain extent elsewhere).

From the vantage point of the late 1980s the United States appeared much more successful in restructuring major sectors of its economy than Western Europe, as least with respect to job creation, investment and profit growth, although less so with respect to improving its rate of productivity growth. In this context, foreign-based transnationals were becoming much more dependent upon the American market at the same time as American manufacturing capital shifted many of its assets towards high-profit sectors like energy reserves, financial services, real-estate, emergent technology, and defence.

With respect to labour, the 1980s witnessed substantial shift in the balance of power between organized labour and capital. This was true in most major capitalist states and was reflected in lower wage claims, falling union membership, lower resistance to technical change and attempts by capitalists to eliminate overstaffing and, partly as a consequence, in 1983–5, higher profit rates (American corporations had their highest profit rates for a decade in the mid-1980s).

In 1986, the real average weekly earnings of American workers by contrast were 8.5 per cent lower than they were in 1970:

American wage and salary earners have enjoyed no real improvements in living standards for 20 years now – a misfortune which can be found in almost no other country outside Africa and Latin America. Most of the fall in US earnings occurred from 1979 to 1982.

(*Financial Times*, 20 January 1987)

Since 1983, important sectors of organized labour in the United States accepted real wage cuts, with much lower pay levels for new employees than for established workers. This created a two-tier wage structure. American labour unions jeopardized their long-term solidarity and strength, whilst union membership continued to decline:

While inflation has been slowing, so has the escalation in pay settlements [in the US]. As a result, there are now millions of US workers for whom an annual pay cut – in actual money wages, not just in 'real terms' – is a fact of life.

(ibid.)

Key reasons for this trend were both an increase in foreign competition and, of much greater significance, the impact of more and more American producers operating with non-unionized labour. Perverse though it may seem, many non-unionized American workers actually enjoyed consistently higher pay rises than their unionized counterparts after 1982. These developments should be seen in a context where there was no strong socialist movement, in contrast to Western Europe and to a lesser extent Japan. Capitalist hegemony appeared more firmly embedded in the United States, and to have strengthened in the last decade, despite the Reverend Jesse Jackson's attempts to organize a Democratic coalition of the disadvantaged during the decade along left-liberal principles.

A similar story can be recounted for Japan. Here the once powerful Japanese trade union movement rapidly lost influence, its membership declined. In the 1940s, over half the work-force in Japan was unionized, whilst in 1986 only 28.9 per cent were unionized. In 1985 the number of working days lost through strikes (already very low by American and West European standards) fell to its smallest level since the war. Between 1980 and 1986 manufacturing sector efficiency rose by 30 per cent, whilst wages increased only 10 per cent (*Guardian*, 1 July 1986). Japanese corporations began to lay off workers, cut overtime and reduce traditional twice-yearly bonuses, and large-scale redundancies became commonplace. Not only blue-collar but also white-collar employees took pay cuts. For example in April 1986 Nissan Motor's 2,300 middle managers took a 5 per cent cut and its 48 top managers a 10 per cent cut (*Financial Times*, 20 January 1987).

To sum up, the advanced countries moved towards more information-based, high-technology, 'post-Fordist' production. Traditional forms of organized labour were placed in the defensive. Sensing they were gaining the upper hand, right-wing forces pressed for policies which would begin to reverse the tendencies towards the growth in the size and resources of the state, partly to eliminate the tendency towards fiscal crisis. Keynesian ideas came under attack and the utility of the welfare state was increasingly questioned as stagflation and recession, with growing unemployment, began to place financial constraints on state budgets, as well as growing strains on the post-war political consensus. In essence, this consensus had presupposed consistent economic growth and an international division of labour organized primarily between countries, understood as 'national economies', or national producers, interacting and competing internationally, with the US pump-priming the system's liquidity through the international use of the dollar. By the 1970s the era of cheap energy was over, the rise of transnational companies and the rise of the newly-industrializing countries heralded the onset of dramatic changes in the international division of labour as well as the collapse of corporatist bargains, and the possibility of Keynesian policies on a national level was increasingly undermined, by these changes and the growing scale, power and mobility of financial capital.

THE TRANSNATIONALIZATION OF THE GLOBAL ECONOMY

Transnational versus national social forces

How do we understand the nature of some of the forces of integration/ disintegration noted above, and their effects in terms of transformations occurring in the post-war world order? Although there is no simple or straightforward way to do this, it is important to focus on some of the crucial elements of world order which are often neglected in the conventional explanations which tend to characterize the crisis in terms of a decline in US national and international power.

Our starting point here is to examine the new dynamics of the capitalist global economy. In the past decade, the forces of transnationalization and globalization (for example, transnational companies favouring and embodying international production and exchange and capital mobility) have steadily expanded, and have been engaged increasingly in a struggle *vis-à-vis* more nationalist and protectionist blocs of forces – that is those seeking to assert or maintain some form of social control over key aspects of economic and political life at the national level.

The transnationalization process is at its most developed form in the wealthiest capitalist nations, especially the 'Trilateral' countries. For example, in 1987, 30 million of the 90 million manufacturing workers of the member countries of the Organization for Economic Co-operation and Development (OECD) were directly employed by transnational companies, with many millions of others indirectly dependent on the activities and production of transnationals for their jobs (UNCTC 1988). However, as debates on the 'new international division of labour' reveal, the process is a global one, although in manufacturing it is concentrated, outside the OECD, in a limited number of 'newly-industrializing' nations, such as South Korea and Taiwan.

Transnational firms, through transfer pricing and intra-firm trade, minimize tax liabilities and maximize global profits, implying a narrower tax base for governments than would be the case if production were organized along national lines. (This would appear to be the only really novel way in which transnational capital is able to increase the extraction of the social surplus.) Firms also cut down on transaction costs by integrating activity in one firm, thereby tendentially internalizing the 'world market for commodities, finished products and finance' (Hoogvelt 1987: 75). Ankie Hoogvelt estimates that by the late 1980s perhaps 40 per cent of total world trade was in the form of intra-firm trade by transnationals, although the 1988 United Nations survey puts the figure closer to 30 per cent. The globalization of production has also been facilitated by technological developments, for example enabling the breaking down of production into discrete and increasingly unskilled tasks. The co-ordination and control over the production process has been facilitated by improved communications and transportation.

For most of the post-war period the transnational phenomenon was mainly confined to extractive industries and manufactures, with most firms financing expansion through internal sources of capital. Since the late 1960s this situation changed, with productive companies becoming more dependent on banks and the burgeoning offshore financial (Eurodollar) markets for supplies of finance. In addition, many productive corporations have been internally restructured in ways which have given their financial divisions more influence over corporate strategy. An important variable in this equation was the internationalization of American banks, and the development of innovations in financial services designed to circumvent national banking regulatory systems. Partly as a result of such developments, banks have become increasingly important in influencing and (in some cases controlling) the operations of transnationals in mineral extraction and manufactures.

These trends suggest that transnational companies are playing a growing role in the world economy. Let us now discuss these developments with respect to trade, production and finance. World trade since World War II has grown rapidly, both in absolute terms and as a percentrage of world GNP, as Table 10.2 shows. Growth in output stopped during the recession of 1979-82, and no growth in trade in real terms occurred in 1981. From 1982 trade grew again, and reached 9 per cent in 1984, falling to about 3 per cent growth in 1985 (*Financial Times*, 26 November 1985). Trade may have had an accelerationist effect on growth in output (Cline 1983: 5).

From this table we can also see the predominance in world trade of

Table 10.2A Exports, FOB, billions of current $US

	1950	1960	1970	1980
Trilateral	34.0	81.0	214.0	1,224.3
United States	10.1	20.4	42.6	220.7
Japan	0.8	4.1	19.3	130.5
W. Europe[a]	20.1	51.0	136.0	806.1
W. Europe[b]	n.a.	25.6	44.1	256.1
West Germany	2.0	11.4	34.2	192.9
United Kingdom	6.3	10.6	19.3	115.2
World total	60.8	128.3	313.9	1,855.7

B Exports	as % of GNP				as % of world exports	
	1950	1960	1970	1980	1950	1980
Trilateral	7.3	8.8	10.5	17.2	55.9	66.0
United States	3.5	4.0	4.3	8.4	16.7	11.9
Japan	5.6	9.4	9.5	12.5	1.3	7.0
W. Europe[a]	13.8	15.5	17.8	25.1	33.1	43.4
W. Europe[b]	n.a.	7.8	5.8	8.0	n.a.	13.8
West Germany	8.5	15.8	18.4	23.5	3.3	10.4
United Kingdom	17.0	14.7	15.6	22.2	10.4	6.2
World total	11.7	11.3	12.6	21.2	100.0	100.0

Source: N. Ushiba *et al.*, *Sharing International Responsibilities* (New York, Trilateral Commission, 1983), pp. 81, 93, based on UN and Eurostat statistics.
Notes: Trilateral = USA, Canada, EEC and Japan. [a]Western Europe: including intra-European trade. [b]Western Europe, excluding intra-European trade. 'World' total excludes inter-trade amongst the following: China, Mongolia, North Korea, and North Vietnam (from 1976, Vietnam).

the Trilateral countries. The share of world trade as a percentage of world GNP rose from 11.7 per cent in 1950 to 21.2 per cent in 1980, with the substantial increase in world trade between 1970–80 mainly due to the oil price rises. The larger shares for Japan and West Germany more than compensated for the declining shares of the United States and Britain. This growth has been accompanied by the increasing interpenetration of capital, initially mainly in the form of direct investment from America to the other Trilateral countries, and then later, and particularly in the 1980s, from them to the United States. During the 1970s and 1980s there was also an increase in portfolio investment. This has served to increase the transnationalization of capital.[3] The mutual stakes invested in each of the blocs of the Triad (the United States,

Japan, and the EC), as well as their respective growth rates, are illustrated in Figure 10.4.

The transnationalization process was initially mainly the result of an outflow of investment from the United States to Western Europe (1945 to the mid-1970s); then increasingly from Western Europe and Japan into the United States (especially in the 1980s). What has failed to occur is a comparably significant amount of overseas direct investment into Japan. The transnational phenomenon remained very much dominated by the United States. The pattern of overseas direct investment shown in Figure 10.4 reveals, first, the underdeveloped nature of the process of transnationalization in Japan when compared with other Trilateral countries, and second the magnetism of the American economy since the late 1970s for investors from other countries.

By the mid-1980s Japan was awash with available capital to invest, and there was a surge in Japanese foreign direct investment. The massive revaluation of the yen against the dollar since mid-1985 (by

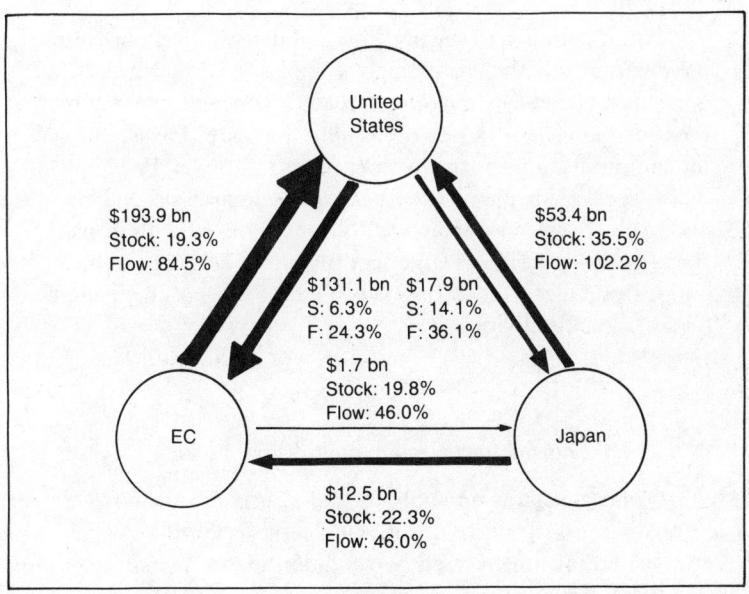

Figure 10.4 Intra-Triad foreign direct investment, 1988
Source: UNCTC World Investment Report 1991 (New York, UN), p. 40.
Note: Dollar figures show 1988 outward stock; percentages show average annual growth rates, stocks and flows. Stock growth rates are for 1980 to 1988. Flow growth rates are for 1985 to 1989.

perhaps 50 per cent up to March 1987) propelled Japanese trans-national companies up the table of the top 100 companies very rapidly indeed. Japan had seven of the top ten banks in the world by the end of 1985 (*Wall Street Journal*, 29 September 1986).

However, the stock of Japanese direct investment abroad is still small by United States and European standards, but in the late 1980s manifested a rapid growth. Japanese companies, measured in terms of the numbers of employees abroad, are still not very transnational when compared with their United States and West European counterparts. The last few years have further seen a relative slowdown in the interna-tionalization of Japanese capital, although more so in the financial sphere than in the productive sphere where the threat of protectionism continues to fuel the drive to the further internationalization of Japan's transnationals.

Irrespective of country of origin, what is clear is that transnational firms have become dominant forces in the transfer of capital, produc-tion, and technology in the global political economy. Robert Kudrle summarizes some of the implications:

> The [transnational company] exemplifies the era of trans-nationalism and the increasingly complex problems nearly all governments face in devising effective, coherent international economic policies. From 1960 until the late 1970s, annual foreign production of [transnationals] grew at over 10 per cent, while world trade grew at 9.5 per cent and world production at about 8 per cent .... Moreover, the enormous growth in world trade has taken place in large part under the aegis of the [trans-nationals]. Over half of US exports are now accounted for by [transnational] activity.
>
> (Kudrle 1986: 175)

Transnationalization, politics and the state

The movement of large amounts of capital between countries, in the form of direct foreign investment, short-term capital flows and long-term portfolio investment, acts to condition the behaviour of govern-ments, firms, trade unions and other groups. By large, I mean relative to the size of any potentially countervailing elements. Thus these capital flows are now vast relative to the size of trade flows, the foreign exchange reserves of central banks, and to the potentially counter-vailing resources of national capital and labour organizations.

What exactly is the relationship between changes in the material structures of the global political economy and changes in class formations and state structures? How are such changes related to prevailing ideas in political economy in the non-communist world?

First, evidence indicates there is indeed a developing transnational capitalist class faction within a wider 'trilateral establishment'. The elite within this class fraction can be said to be at the zenith of an emerging transnational historic bloc, whose material interests and key ideas (within a broader political consciousness) are bound up with the progressive transnationalization and liberalization of the global political economy. Among its key members are top owners and key executives of transnationals; central and other international bankers; many, though not all, leading politicians and civil servants in most advanced capitalist countries, and some in certain developing nations. Although not members of a capitalist class in the strict Marxist sense of the term, some of the élites of the (former) communist states could be considered as members of this wider international establishment. Thus, in 1987, the Soviet Union announced measures designed to accelerate inflows of foreign direct investment, while China's 'four modernizations' were well under way. The growth of this class fraction has been facilitated by improved transport and communications, and increasingly by 'private' as well as 'public' institutions fostering dialogue and interaction between élites. Such dialogue and interaction may serve to promote a transnational 'identity' and a shared consciousness which fosters a closer identification of interests. This promotes conditions where this faction becomes, to use Marx's phrase, more a class 'for itself' as opposed to merely a grouping of disorganized material forces.

Second, the strengthening of some of these links and associated networks has gone hand in hand with the 'transnationalization' of the state. By this I mean a process whereby state policies and institutional arrangements are conditioned and changed by the power and mobility of transnational factions of capital.

The growth and scale of such mobility intensifies the need for governments, competing to attract foreign capital under recessionary conditions, to provide an appropriate business climate for overseas investors. A state will be judged in terms of its comparative hospitality to foreign capital. Thus the policies of the state towards the market, to labour-capital relations, towards the provision of an appropriate social and economic infrastructure, are incrementally recast in an international framework as the cumulative process of transnationalization, like a snowball rolling down a mountain side, gathers pace and size. In consequence the policies of deregulation of financial markets which arose in the United States in the 1970s and 1980s provoked similar changes overseas, the net effect of which was to liberalize the financial structure of the system as a whole (cf. Strange 1986).

In the 1970s and 1980s this gave increased weight to certain parts of government, notably finance and economics ministries relative to foreign and defence ministries, as well as the private offices of Prime Ministers or Presidents. (For example, the 'sherpas' who plan and co-ordinate the seven-nation economic summits are drawn from the staff of the heads of government.) More crucially, state agencies linked to industry, employment and welfare tended to be downgraded as the competition for foreign capital intensified amid recessionary conditions. The corporatist agencies identified with the post-war Keynesian consensus were increasingly marginalized, the political role of organized labour declined and smaller scale 'national' manufacturing industry was put under pressure from international competition. Key individuals within the financial and economics ministries were linked to networks of international organizations and international interests represented in institutions such as the Trilateral Commission, and thus are part of an informal structure of international influence. Apart from the fact that a large number of Trilateral Commissioners were significant figures in the political establishments of their own countries, of the world's largest 100 companies in 1985, at least sixty had Commission members. Commission members were associated with major productive transnationals as well as banks and firms dominating the world's rapidly growing financial services markets (*Wall Street Journal*, 29 September 1986).

These transnational networks should also be understood in the context of the way recessionary conditions have intensified the fiscal crisis of the state at various levels in the system (national, provincial, local), further forcing governments to compete to provide an attractive 'investment climate' relative to each other. The competition to each other. The competition to attract scarce supplies of capital (for example to finance public expenditure) has thus also been accompanied by privatization of state assets and by competitive changes in regulations and tax structures, effectively shifting the tax burden away from capital and towards the lower-skilled and less mobile members of the labour force. One indicator of this is the general shift away from direct, progressive, and towards more indirect and regressive forms of taxation.

Third, these changes in economics and politics have gone with changes in the prevailing ideologies and in the terrain of contestability concerning appropriate policy. For example, the degree to which such changes were reflected in a growing international consensus on the direction of state economic policies was revealed in a speech given to the Trilateral Commission by Paul Volcker, Chairman of the Federal Reserve Board between 1979 and 1987. Volcker was for many years a senior banker at Chase Manhattan, and a former member of the Commission and the Council on Foreign Relations:

> there is an economic strategy ... maybe not well coordinated, maybe not implemented as smoothly as it could have been ... that is internationally shared, for almost the entire time I've been in this office.... We had to create stability in a price sense, in a monetary sense, if we were going to have a foundation for progress in other directions. You can raise questions about how it has been implemented ... but there is a remarkable reduction in inflationary pressures around the world ... and there has also been a very considerable convergence, so even the highest inflation countries ... are much closer to the pack than ... five years ago.
>
> There is another element of common strategy too that's been persistent for some years. It's a harder one to describe: more emphasis on market orientation in economic policies, more concern and effort to reduce the proportion of government in GNP, more emphasis on private initiative. Obviously that matches a lot of rhetoric and oratory in the United States. But what is really startling is the rhetoric and oratory in France that parallels this kind of broad orientation of policies. It is even true in much of the developing world.[4]
>
> (Volcker 1985)

Such liberal ideas and practices are intended to promote market efficiency; the virtues of free trade and investment; flexible exchange markets; the control of inflation and public expenditure; and the private sector relative to the public; and labour market flexibility (and the dangers of trade union monopoly power which may obstruct the introduction of new technology and hold up real wages at a level incompatible with full employment). Given that these ideas became more widely accepted during the late 1970s and 1980s, they also served to restrict the ability of subordinate classes to analyse the nature of the political economy, and construct alternatives. A dramatic instance of this was Prime Minister Thatcher's claim, made in the context of her aim of eradicating socialism from Britain, that there was 'no alternative' to her supply-side monetarist policies. Thus this structure of thought manifests the positive and negative aspects of class ideology.

The hegemony of transnational finance capital

Notwithstanding these shared ideas, there may be conflicting as well as complementary interests between different factions of transnational capital. For example, energy corporations prefer a high oil price, whereas most other transnational corporations prefer a low oil price. This example also illustrates the interdependence between different factions of capital in that some leading banks made loans to oil-exporting nations like Mexico, Venezuela and Nigeria, who, of course, needed buoyant oil revenues to service their debts to the banks. Also, the very distinction between national and transnational capital is a matter of degree, that is, as to the proportion of investment and sales outside the parent country.

Firms whose assets are heavily concentrated in one country will be more vulnerable to an appreciation of that country's exchange rate than will be the case for firms who have a small proportion of their assets invested in that country. Another important distinction is that between financial and industrial factions of capital, the former of which seems to be less concerned about a rising exchange rate or high interest rates. The high liquidity and mobility of most financial capital contrasts with the higher opportunity costs for, and the constraints on, industrial transnationals when relocating production (Gill and Law 1988: 81–102). Moreover, the time horizons of financial and productive factions of capital are often different, the former usually being shorter than those of manufacturing companies.

The growing predominance of transnational finance capital can be analysed in terms of a transnational coalition of forces which actively seeks to shape a range of state policies, but it can also be analysed in terms of a set of social forces which include the extension of the structural power of market discipline. In practice, this was partly based on the liberalization of foreign exchange and capital markets, a process fostered by the lobbyting of transnational factions of capital, especially financial capital. This process was propelled by the competition between different national financial centres, especially that between New York, Tokyo and London.

What do these developments mean for the overall thrust of our argument? In modern financial markets, the relatively high degree of international mobility of capital is bound up, at the institutional level, with the nature of local financial markets and the opportunities afforded across a range of states for freedom of capital flows. Such flows can have dramatic effects, not just on the foreign exchange markets, but also on commodity and stock markets. In the 1980s, financial experts were predicting a 'brave new world' for the international banking industry (*Financial Times*, World Banking Special Supplement, 22 May 1986: p. 1).

The globalization of markets means that decisions to shift capital do not need to be co-ordinated in order to have dramatic effects. Apart from the potential constraints these shifts create on the actions of government and labour, they can also have unintended consequences; for example, the large loans by banks to certain less-developed countries in the 1970s helped create the conditions for the emergence of the debt crisis of the early 1980s, and a major threat to the solvency of many of the self-same lenders. Indeed, apart from ethical questions, many commentators have noted the destabilizing effects of these rapid, and sometimes highly volatile flows of financial capital.

More generally, this suggests that the process by which the structural power of financial factions of capital has been extended has not been a stable one. Susan Strange (1986) warned that the growing uncertainty, volatility, and speculation in the markets might undermine the respect for 'ethical values ... upon which a free democratic society relies'. Her arguments also anticipated the October 1987 stock market crash, which started in New York and spread rapidly to markets elsewhere (at one point the People's Republic Bank of China stepped in to bail out the commodity futures market in Hong Kong). Strange traces the origins of this new situation to 1973 when, coincientally, the Trilateral Commission held its first meetings. 'The year 1973 stands out as a benchmark, a turning point when the snowball of change from the leisurely 1960s to the hectic yo-yo years of the 1970s and 1980s began to gather momentum' (Strange 1986: 5).

As Strange points out, the new banking fraternity resembles less and less the stereotypical image of cautious, conservative, sober-suited patricians. Today's bankers are increasingly risk-takers, gamblers in a global financial casino, whose waking moments are dictated by distant time-zones. Computer monitors and modems are the most obvious links between these individuals and firms. Are there deeper links? From the point of view of a transnational coalition of forces, some writers have commented on the existence of a 'banking complex', in the major capitalist states, centred in the United States. This complex, analogous to an internationalized military–industrial complex, comprised a network of private and central banks, other financial institutions, policy-oriented academics in certain think-tanks and prestigious universities, as well as influential members of the (financial) media (see Amen 1985: 181–200).

The interests of financial factions of capital are especially well provided for in terms of (organic) policy intellectuals, since they have access to massive data bases, droves of political risk analysts, many publications of their own, and have endowed élite universities with well-paid posts and large research funds to generate a wider basis for the practical forms of knowledge needed to make profits. These intellectuals, and their banker counterparts, are often the best brains that money can buy.

Such thinkers try to maintain a long-term political vision which goes beyond the short-term outlook and apparent anarchy of the financial casino. Thus these organic intellectuals operate both within and outside the banking complex, developing the capacity to theorize the conditions of existence for capitalist hegemony as a whole, as well as the technical expertise to master often difficult (e.g. financial) issues. For Gramsci, the degree of 'organicity' in this respect is related to the relative proximity of the intellectual to the organization of the forces of production and exchange, and to the occupation of senior positions in state bureaucracies which relate to the maintenance of stable political conditions within which such forces operate. With respect to the banking complex, the most organic intellectuals are the leaders of transnational financial corporations (rather than the major shareholders), key financial institutions such as the International Monetary Fund, central banks and economics and finance ministries, especially the United States Treasury and Federal Reserve. The Trilateral Commission involves a wider and more diverse group of intellectuals with expertise in political matters more generally.

The degree to which such a transnational complex of interests moves towards an increased degree of co-operation rests, in part, not only on a congruence of material and institutional forces, but also on the extent to which its key intellectuals share a common outlook. It also rests upon the degree to which such shared ways of seeing and interpreting the world are diffused and shared amongst personnel at lower levels within the organizations in question, and, to an extent, within the population at large. As is indicated in the public choice literature, the wider the sets of issues and problems, the more difficult this will be.

The moment of hegemony occurs if and when there is a widespread acceptance of the key principles and political ideas of a leading class fraction or constellation of interests. When this happens, the policies which embody these principles will appear to be more natural and legitimate to broader elements within civil and political society. What is crucial to this argument, however, is that such a nucleus of ideas is not simply a form of direct ideological domination, but rather a structural force which conditions and constrains class and other social forces.

If the hegemonic capitalist class faction is internationally oriented, its key principles would typically include the view that the market mechanism is the most efficient form of global economic organization, that capital mobility and free trade increase global welfare, and that the long-term improvement of the condition of the planet and its inhabitants would be best served by strengthening the capitalist states *vis-à-vis* communism.

TOWARDS A US-CENTRED TRANSNATIONAL HEGEMONY

In this final section, we will see how the specific character of this new world economic and political order took shape under Reagan in the 1980s, and what its prospects are in the 1990s.

The Reaganite reconstruction of US leadership

In contrast to the Carter Administration's avowed goals of overhauling Trilateral relations and moving towards 'world order politics' through co-ordinating economic policies with its allies and with Third World regional influentials such as Saudi Arabia and Brazil, the Reagan Administration initially pursued a different, and some claimed incoherent, economic strategy, lecturing the representatives of these states at the 1981 Cancún North–South conference on the need for more 'market place magic'. Critics of Reaganomics such as the Director of the Institute for International Economics, Fred Bergsten (whose views find resonance with many American Trilateral Commissioners), reproached Reaganomics for jeopardizing the long-run health of the United States economy. Reagan (like his Californian predecessor Richard Nixon) has failed to understand 'the international consequences of US actions' (Bergsten 1985: 138). By contrast, according to Georgetown's more conservative former Reagan staff member, Henry Nau, Reagan's policies were quite cognizant of international forces. Nau argued that Reagan's moves were designed to project America's structural economic power and set the conditions for its economic relations with other states (Nau 1984–5: 22–3; see also Nau 1985).

Nau's argument dissents significantly from neo-realist and liberal wisdom concerning hegemonic decline. Nau suggests that at least since World War II, and probably since the 1930s, the United States has been structurally dominant in the world economy. Indeed, one can go further and suggest that American economic power, whilst showing relative decline in aggregate terms, is in fact enormous when compared to that of any other country, and has an international aspect which gives the United States government an unparalleled prerogative *vis-à-vis* the rest of the world. What seemed to be at issue was the question of whether American leaders were able to perceive the implications of such structural dominance and harness it in their policies.

Reagan's policies, particularly in his first administration, corresponded graphically to a realist concept of unilateralism in that they showed a willingness by the United States government to reorient the policies of other states so that they became more open to American economic penetration. In Giovanni Arrighi's terminology, this reflected a long-term transformation in United States' strategy away from a formal (political, military) to an informal (market-based) system of control (Arrighi 1982). As has been indicated, this process was much more painful for other countries than for the United States, since Reagan's policies siphoned capital from abroad, raised the dependence of other states on the American market, and globalized the financing of American military programmes. Premised initially on domestic remobilization, Reaganomics had the effect of strengthening transnational forces, through promoting the further interpenetration of capitals, the liberalization of markets, and deepening the interdependence between American and other states' macroeconomic policy-making conditions.

The Achilles heel of Reaganomics was, of course, the contradiction between growing military expenditures and the relative narrowing of the American fiscal base. Reaganomics has proven to be a perfect recipe for long-term fiscal crisis. This meant that, in order to finance the budget deficit, the United States had to offer relatively high yields on Treasury bonds, which kept interest rates high, not only in the United States, but world wide. Apart from aggravating the debt servicing problems of the developing nations, this also tended to depress world investment, whilst simultaneously the United States attracted a vast influx of capital. Although this may have appeared to make domestic sense to United States policy-makers, it had serious global macroeconomic consequences, at least if one took a long-term view.

At a secondary level, the Reagan boom was accompanied by a massive surge in imports, causing the United States trade deficit to rise to unprecedented levels (partly because world demand was depressed elsewhere, and also because of the high level of the dollar). This generated substantial protectionist pressure in Congress, which in turn gave an added impetus to foreign companies to locate production facilities in the United States.

Recognizing some of the dangers and contradictions inherent in this mix of policies, some American leaders began to perceive limits to Reaganomics. Elements within the second Reagan administration began to pay more attention to international economic co-operation. The major figure behind the new thinking was the new Treasury Secretary, James Baker, who replaced the former Secretary, Donald Regan. Regan, the ex-chief executive at financial services giant Merrill-Lynch, was a believer in the relatively unfettered market. Baker's view suggested that intervention of some kind, co-ordinated with the other major economic powers, was needed to save the market from itself. In September 1985, Baker launched the first of his 'initiatives' in a meeting with the Group of Five finance ministers, resulting in the so-called Plaza Agreement. This was followed up in 1987 with a second initiative, resulting in the Louvre Accord (Law 1989).

The initiatives reflected a new American perception of the need for international co-ordination and co-operation in the sphere of macro-economic management. Specifically, the first initiative involved measures to reduce the overvaluation of the dollar (and thus to help reduce the trade deficit and defuse protectionist pressures in Congress), to find a way out of a potential world-wide deflationary spiral and regenerate global economic growth and to get to grips with the 'debt crisis'. The major domestic stumbling block continued to be United States fiscal policy, which was having depressive economic effects outside the United States. The Pentagon initially resisted cuts in military expenditures, whilst there was also strong resistance to further reductions in domestic welfare expenditures. Outside the United States, the strategy involved attempts to force a demand stimulus in other major economies, especially in Germany and Japan.

To keep the American side of the bargain required curbing of the Pentagon's ceaseless appetite for vast expenditures. In the longer term, it meant some internationalization of the perspective of the American military–industrial complex, such that its leaders redefined their concepts of security to include international economic co-operation and stability. In the late 1980s the Pentagon launched its system of competitive tendering, cutting procurement costs, and embarking on transnational co-production ventures to extend scale economies (Halliday 1986: 235). The real growth in American military expenditures in fact stopped in 1986, and there developed a widespread political consensus not to increase its levels. The final nail in the coffin for Pentagon big spenders was the resignation of Caspar Weinberger as Secretary of Defense in 1987, to be replaced by Frank Carlucci, who set about making spending cuts before Congress applied the axe.

In addition, by early 1988, there was substantial evidence that Japan had attempted to boost domestic demand, as had Britain, although this was less true for West Germany. Moreover, the value of the dollar fell dramatically against a range of major currencies, by something in the region of 40 per cent in the nine months following the 1985 Plaza Agreement, partly as a result of the co-ordinated actions of the Group of Five. The United States backed a shift in International Monetary Fund policies, away from harsh conditionality, towards policies which were more likely to promote some long-term economic expansion in at least some of the larger recipient countries. Overall, these changes represented substantial movement towards policies favoured by most Trilateral Commissioners.

With respect to United States' security policies *vis-à-vis* its major alliance partners, the Reagan Administration, much like its predecessor, trod a thin line between exploiting their allegiance and destroying European confidence in, and loyalty to, the United States by doing so. The risks of undermining alliance consensus were also highlighted in the sphere of nuclear weapons negotiations, when the United States effectively proposed massive cuts in arsenals, and endorsed the prospect of a nuclear-free Europe. Such proposals produced a political crisis in the NATO alliance because, between 1979 and 1983, European member governments had attempted to convince their publics of the need for more, not less, nuclear weapons to counter Soviet potential.

However, it may be asserted that these moves, whilst significant, did little fundamentally to undermine the forces which create the common interests which sustain alliance unity over most basic principles. In the last analysis, this may indicate a strong sense of confidence on the part of the United States based on the knowledge that neither Western Europe nor Japan could provide a real alternative to United States military leadership.

However, United States economic policies during the late 1970s and 1980s did have far-reaching effects. The recession of the early 1980s debilitated the power of labour, both inside and outside the United

States. It contributed to a deterioration in the terms of trade for developing nations, and to a weakening of OPEC's influence on oil prices. Shortage of foreign exchange led many countries to establish export processing zones, and adopt a more 'welcoming' attitude to foreign enterprises. Shortage of tax revenue, with which to sustain government spending, made governments more willing to consider privatization of public sector assets. Doubtless many of these tendencies reflected factors other than United States economic policy, but the latter was clearly influential. These developments were in contrast to the defensiveness towards OPEC and the Third World which prevailed for much of the early and mid-1970s, and which was reflected in a number of Trilateral Commission and Council on Foreign Relations publications, arguing for 'partnership' and 'accommodation' with Third World countries, the strongest of which had begun to use their resource and commodity power to substantial effect (see Gardner *et al.* 1974; ibid. 1975; Beigie *et al.* 1976).

Reagan's policy can thus be interpreted as an intensification of the push towards the post-war United States goal of liberalizing the more dynamic sectors of the international economy, as well as liberalizing labour and capital markets within the United States, in ways which benefited the strongest American corporations. A range of countries moved in the same direction, although a great deal of statist mercantilism still persisted. The 'liberalization' of the Chinese economy is but one example, although the Chinese had other reasons for their changes in policy (the Soviet Union and Vietnam also opened the door to foreign direct investment, the latter offering 100 per cent repatriation of profits from 1987). The traditionally mercantilist Japanese also moved, albeit slowly, towards the liberalization of their capital markets. Moreover, the fact that such 'liberal' policies were still being pursued by the United States, whilst calls for protectionism were mounting in Congress, reflected the influence of American transnational factions of capital in the determination of American foreign economic policy. Notwithstanding rhetoric concerning the 'threat' or 'virulence' of protectionism expressed consistently in Trilateral Commission literature, it can be argued that protectionism in certain sectors (or its threat) may promote an increase in foreign direct investment and greater transnationalization of production. Some American and European protectionism may, for example, help to undermine Japanese insularity, and reduce the comparatively 'national' and corporatist orientation of Japanese enterprises, making them more transnational. It can be argued therefore that Reaganomics involved a reconstruction of the post-war hegemonic settlement, with the United States at the centre of structural changes liberalizing important aspects of the global political economy.

The future role of the United States: 'bound to lead' or 'bound to the mast'?

The turn of the decade fundamentally transformed the global economic, political and military landscape. The collapse of the Soviet Union, the unification of Germany, the Gulf War, and finally the intensification of European integration: these changes were crucial components of an unprecedented redrawing of the geopolitical map of the globe.

Like European politicians, US leaders are now asking how to develop a strategy for the 1990s and beyond that can come to terms with the new conditions being created by these historic transformations. In my view, because the United States is still the world's leading power, and will continue to be so for some time to come, it is important to look at the way these questions are being discussed in leading US political circles. Thus, although we have not explicitly defined hegemony in terms of the primacy of one state within the world order, clearly what the US leaders choose as a framework for action is crucial to the balance of social forces and for the provision of a steering capability in the system. Moreover, because of the role of the dollar and the centrality of the US economy (e.g. the depth and flexibility of its financial markets, its role as the world's single largest market for consumer goods, etc.) for all other countries engaged in international economic activity, the policies and actions/inactions of the US government are crucial.

An influential argument concerning the necessity of US primacy has been made recently in the best-selling book by the Harvard academic Joseph S. Nye Jr., *Bound to Lead*. It is part of a long tradition in US social thought claiming that the US and its citizens have a mission, a Manifest Destiny, to save the world from itself. Some economists would add that the US acts as a 'consumer of last resort', thus sustaining global aggregate demand and avoiding global deflation. Whilst there may be something to this argument it nevertheless rests upon the unsustainability of a system which allows approximately 256 million US citizens collectively to consume about 60 per cent of the world's annual consumable resources. From the viewpoint of the rest of the world, or at least from that of the European Community and Japan, like Ulysses forgoing the lure of the Sirens, then, in order to lead, the

US needs to be 'bound to the mast'. In this sense, at least from a world order perspective, the US government and its citizens should be persuaded to forgo the temptations of military adventures, perverse consumption patterns and fiscally-irresponsible tax-cutting (especially when this mainly benefits the wealthy) in order to reconstitute a less atavistic global order, with ecological and global macroeconomic responsibilities built into the construction and implementation of US policies.

In this context, the role of Japan will be crucial in the next twenty years. US policies in the 1980s would not have been possible without financing from Japan: perhaps as much as 40 per cent of annual funding of US budget deficits in this period has come from Japanese sources. The financing of the US intervention in the Gulf was made possible by payments from allies, notably Germany, Japan, Kuwait and Saudi Arabia. Indeed, indications are that the Pentagon has made a profit of about $15 billion on the deal.[5] The US government may be moving to an overt system of collecting tribute from its allies in order to sustain, at least in the short-term, its military–industrial capacity.

This reflects, roughly speaking, the fact that the struggle between 'transnational' and 'national' blocs of socio–political forces is crucial to understanding the current policies of the US government. Nationalist forces are associated with the security complex, declining, protectionist industries, and geopolitical thinkers of the realist persuasion, and they seem to have, perhaps temporarily, the upper hand. The evidence for this would include aggressive trade policies and the increased influence of concepts of 'strategic trade policy', a growth in US interventionism (Grenada, Panama, the Gulf War), and the attempts to scapegoat foreigners, notably Japanese, for any US economic ills.

On the other hand, while concerned with the competitiveness of US industry, transnationalists have corporate interests which are more global, and need continued access to the markets and capital of other countries. They have forged strategic alliances with foreign firms, and the identity of their interests with the territorial US is less clear-cut. They are concerned with opening the world to the freer movement of capital, goods and services: they are liberal economic internationalists. Thus they advocate that the US government co-operate more with its key allies in providing a steering and stabilizing capability for the global economy, as well as helping to underpin its systemic integrity. Included in these ranks are the big US financial corporations and banks who benefit from anti-inflationary policies and demand greater macroeconomic stability. The persistent US budget deficits are viewed by this grouping as a key cause of the huge balance of payments deficits, the rise of protectionism and the gyrations in, and weakness of the US dollar. In this context we can expect any future, long, drawn-out and costly war to begin to place the nationalist bloc on the defensive, and for elements in the transnationalist flank to become more assertive.

Nevertheless, President Bush's decision to send US forces into the Gulf has to be understood in this context and in terms of a widespread questioning of both the ability and the destiny of the US to lead, reflected in the popular appeal of the best-selling thesis of Paul Kennedy's 1988 book, *The Rise and Fall of the Great Powers*. This debate has produced a form of social pathology in the political classes in the United States concerning the future stability of the world order and the place of the US system within it. This debate has been sharpened by new US nationalism originating, at least in its recent manifestations, in President Nixon's policies of the early 1970s, and today represented in the rising salience of Realist thinking, which equates hegemony with the mobilization of force and emphasizes relative rather than absolute 'national' gains in economic welfare as the goal of policy: this issue is at the heart of the way that the 'competitiveness' debate has been framed in the United States. These tendencies have now to find a new focus for foreign policy after the apparent defeat of 'actually existing communism', because a central justification for US globalism has been eliminated.

What can be perceived now in US economic debates is a problematic which suggests an intensification of inter-imperialist rivalry and the break-up of the world economy into antagonistic blocs, now that the glue of the Cold War and US primacy and dominance seems to have dissolved. Developments in US policy (e.g. the US–Canada Free Trade Agreement and the Omnibus Trade Act of 1988) might be interpreted in this light. These debates suggest a new schizophrenia in the political consciousness of US opinion leaders. The eclipse of the Cold War has brought with it the search for a new enemy. Will this be Japan (the prime candidate according to recent public opinion polls), Islam perhaps, or the US rivals in a greater Europe? Here, remembering the pseudo-Leninist theories of imperial rivalry, it is highly significant that US theoreticians have begun to debate the question: are there one or many (competing) capitalisms?

This question is linked to the revisionist debates over the nature of the Japanese system and its influence in East Asia (e.g. Karel van Wolferen's *The Enigma of Japanese Power*, and Clyde Prestowitz's *Trading Places*) and to the broader US–Japanese relationship. In this sense, one of the aspects of the Strategic Impediments Initiative (SII) talks should be understood as a means of trying to make Japanese capitalism more open to the penetration of, and thus more like, an ideal–typical image of US liberal, 'competitive' corporate capitalism. Similar goals characterized earlier skirmishes in the Yen–Dollar Committee in the mid-1980s over Japanese financial liberalization (spearheaded by US financial services companies like Merrill-Lynch, indicating that a key issue was US firms' penetration of the Japanese market). The chances of the US strategy succeeding are, in my view, slim, and even if it were to succeed it would not necessarily bring about the desired result of subordinating Japanese economic development to that of the United States. Coupled to the 'Japan problem', for many political leaders in the US (and *vice versa* for the Japanese), is a fear of the implications of a united Western Europe, particularly when, as a result of the elimination of the 'Soviet Threat', Europe has become much less dependent on the US for its security on the continent.

It is perhaps partly for this reason that the US government launched its diplomatic and military offensive in the Middle East, resulting in the Gulf War to liberate Kuwait (not only an important oil supplier but also the key financial centre in the region for recycling petro-dollars) from Iraqi control. In this sense the US government re-enforced global private property rights and reasserted state sovereignty as a principle of the international system, as well as using its military dominance to secure increased political control over one of the world's major productive assets: oil supplies. (Oil accounts for about 38 per cent of the world's primary energy consumption.)

This means that Japan and Western Europe (except perhaps Great Britain) and all countries who depend on Middle Eastern oil are subordinated anew to US policy in the region. In this regard it is worth noting that the biggest oil companies are still largely US-controlled, with British Petroleum and Anglo-Dutch Shell also major players in the region. President Bush was an entrepreneur in the Texas oil industry (one of the homes of the tradition of vigilantism in the US), and regarded himself as an 'oilman', as well as being a former Head of the CIA, an organization crucial to understanding the US role in the region. In addition, it is a truism that the US security apparatus and associated industrial interests are still very powerful in US domestic politics. The Pentagon needs to find a new role in the aftermath of the capitulation of the Soviet Union as a global military superpower.

For the European nations the political effects of the Gulf War at the leadership level have been to begin to open up long-standing divisions over their strategic alignments and future potential to develop an independent foreign policy and strategic capability. Although the Japanese leadership was politically blocked by domestic opposition to its policy of attempting to make a direct military contribution to the UN forces in the Gulf, as expected, the British became heavily involved and in line with post-war traditions unquestioningly supported the US position (the British aerial forces suffered the heaviest per capita casualties on the coalition side). France maintained its traditional independence from the US and sought to shape a generic Euro-response, essaying a number of diplomatic initiatives to avoid war. Germany remained mainly on the political sidelines. After the outbreak of war the French supported the US, causing a deep rift to open between different flanks in the Socialist Party (the Minister of Defence, J.-P. Chevènement, for example, opposed the war and resigned on this issue).

These developments may mean a wider politicization of the defence question across Europe, highlighting the lack of democratic accountability of pan-European defence planning, organization and leadership. In turn, this may place a brake on the momentum towards the future political integration of the European Community.

As yet there is very little to suggest that the US leadership is fully conscious of the need to reconstruct a more co-operative, consensual and co-ordinated form of international military leadership, at least with its key allies in Western Europe and Japan. The US seems determined to use its vast military power to sustain its global primacy, and shows a willingness to attempt to extract resources from its allies and clients to pay for it. Given the domestic inhibitions in Japan, limiting the scope and extension of the Self Defence Forces, Japan is perhaps the most vulnerable target for this type of strategy, along with, of course, the Saudis and Kuwaitis.

Thus, the prospect of the US government extending its military capabilities and reach are enhanced by the prospect of tribute from allies, a position that goes well beyond the arguments in favour of fairer burden-sharing and eliminating 'free-riding' which characterized US arguments with its allies in the 1970s and 1980s. This is because the fiscal position of the US Federal government is weak, with persistent and growing budget deficits for much of the 1980s. As has been noted, much of the supply of finance for US government operations has come from overseas (recycling German and Japanese balance of payments surpluses), so that the US federal government (to say nothing of the local and state governments in the Union) is in debt to the tune of approximately one trillion dollars by the end of 1992, with interest payments at about 70 billion dollars a year (Healey 1991: 11). Against this background, the need for financing by allies took on the force of necessity: even for the US government, the limits of the possible are changing, partly because of poor macroeconomic policies, partly because of the restructuring of global production and finance.

The new dynamics of international finance here should be compared to the era of haute finance in the nineteenth and early twentieth century, where co-operation could be swiftly organized through the good offices of the likes of the Morgans and the Rothchilds. The launch of any US Treasury War Loan would have needed the co-operation of the large pension funds, insurance companies, and other giant players in the global financial markets. Given that these interests wish to see US budget deficits reduced, inflation to be contained, and perhaps the dollar strengthened, we can assume that they will begin to behave, like the nineteenth century international financiers (who acted to help prevent general war among the Great Powers), as a type of peace interest in the US, if only for reasons of private gain.

The US dilemma concerning the financing of the Gulf War reflected a structural contradiction in the emerging global political economy: there is an as yet very incomplete process of the internationalization of authority, particularly highlighted by the use of military power in a political structure divided into different territories, sovereignties and thus constituted partly by political boundaries and national identities. Despite the growth of transnational networks of interests and identity, reflected in the activities of private international relations councils, cross-investments and alliances, and the impetus given to the activities of the UN, the global political superstructure is very underdeveloped. This stands in contrast with economic structures which are tending towards planetary reach.

CONCLUDING REFLECTIONS

The scope and nature of the transnational structures of power associated with the Pax Americana have undergone a transformation, driven principally by the restructuring of global production (involving the gradual supplanting of Fordism by flexible production and the peripheralization of economic development, both within and between countries) and the emergence of an apparently quasi-autonomous structure of global finance. These developments have been accelerated by a deepening and widening of international competition and innovation as the global economy has shifted to higher levels of knowledge-intensive activity. Nevertheless, this has occurred in a period of slowing economic growth, punctuated by recessions of increasing severity since the mid-1970s.

The globalization of world capitalism, apparently to be extended geographically and socially following the economic entropy and collapse and thus the political capitulation of 'existing socialism', has gone with economic polarization and deepening inequality. It now seems legitimate, however, to ask whether the system is sustainable on present economic and policy trends, particularly since the thrust of the prevailing market–monetarist policies of structural adjustment, macro- and microeconomic monetary and fiscal discipline, has been globally deflationary.

In the new international political and economic structure the role of the US state and of the socio–economic forces within the US have become more ambiguous and problematic. In the immediate aftermath of World War II, not only was the United States the unchallenged economic superpower of the capitalist world, but its economy was also relatively self-sufficient. The relative self-sufficiency and territorial security of the United States allowed for the development of a strategy premised upon the outward expansion of US economic, political and cultural forces, consistent with the internationalization of the New Deal Fordist model of development. The internationalists' vision of a new world order was, however, opposed by more inward-looking, continentalist or isolationist forces. In the 1980s, in a period when the US economy was becoming rapidly internationalized, the clash between the territorial and globalizing forces within the United States became more pronounced, reflected partly in the growth of US protectionism and the demonization of Japan.

This clash of interests reflects the fact that the United States has had, and still has, a contradictory position in the emerging global political economy. On the one hand, the US political economy has been central to post-war economic development world-wide – that is, it represents a universalizing moment in the historical development of capitalism. On the other hand, the US political system and political culture tend to be inward-looking and ethnocentric. This internal-external dialectic, reflecting a contradiction between territoriality and globality in the emerging world order, lies at the heart of the problematic role of the United States as embodying a 'universal contradiction' in the context of post-Cold War global politics. The United States is the political and military guarantor of disciplinary neo-liberalism, but is not subjected to the same levels of monetary and fiscal discipline as are other countries (reflected in the ability of the United States consistently to run balance of payments deficits and thus to transfer the real burden of economic adjustment on to the rest of the world). The US government is by far the world's biggest debtor and its policies for much of the last twenty years have been a primary source of international macroeconomic instability.

These issues can be related to the central fact of the economic and political history of the late 1980s and early 1990s: the cumulative, if uneven structural transformation of the political economy. In other words, the key change is not the 'end of the Cold War' and the collapse of the military-political superstructures associated with world communism as such (some might argue that Cold War politics is far from over in so far as it encompasses the struggle between labour and capital on a world scale). Indeed, the case of the economic and political restructuring of the former Soviet Union can be likened to a process of demobilizing the enemy under the supervision of the G7, the European Bank for Reconstruction and Development and the IMF, i.e. by the agencies of the transnational historic bloc which I have identified earlier in this essay. Transforming the successors to the former Soviet Union into functioning capitalist economies is a process which would appear to require many years to complete, if indeed it will be successful.

As I have noted, the United States is the military guarantor of neo-liberalism. Nevertheless, it is the least likely of all the major states to submit to its economic disciplines, in large part because of the structural limitations of its own political and constitutional system, and because US politicians refuse to accept limitations on US freedom of manoeuvre in the interests of global macroeconomic stability. Even within the United States itself the contradictions of the Reagan–Bush era are becoming more and more apparent, especially in major US cities (reflected in the riots of May 1992) and in the agricultural hinterlands.

More broadly, the economic logic of neo-liberal austerity can be regarded as contradictory in so far as it may be associated with global macroeconomic problems in the 1980s and 1990s. It relates to what Marxists call the realization problem and Keynesians call a shortfall in global aggregate demand. In other words there is the potential for an enduring global depression, or a long-term crisis of under-consumption. The economic crisis partly results from changes in production which tend to eliminate the quantity of labour and thus increase structural unemployment, and from the simultaneous application of market-monetarist deflationary policies which lower demand in an era of slower growth. Deflationary macroeconomic policies, and the emphasis in the dominant discourse on microeconomic rationality, are also bound up with concepts of economic development which are still associated with ecologically and socially insensitive thinking.

. The engine of post-1945 economic growth was partly fuelled by cheap energy, and partly by the pump-priming of global aggregate demand through Keynesian policies to mobilize the Fordist structures of mass consumption. The government expenditures used for these purposes included, in the US case, substantial military expenditures at home and overseas. In the context of the debt deflation of the late 1980s and early 1990s, comparable in some ways to that of the 1930s, and given the fact that much of the world has been in an economic depression for several years (involving the liquidation of capital and the destruction of institutional and physical infrastructure for economic development), there are good grounds for arguing that capitalism is entering or is already in a crisis of underconsumption. Workers are both producers and consumers, and if there is a sustained decline in their relative income shares then this is likely, at some point, to mean a shortfall in aggregate demand, or in Marx's terminology, a realization problem. This problem is accompanied by indebtedness, financial fragility, macroeconomic instability, to say nothing of the corruption in high places associated with the speculative bubble in the asset markets in the late 1980s, especially in Japan. Whilst there is no simple relationship between economic and political crisis, it seems clear that global politics in the 1990s will be highly unstable and the emerging world order will fall far short of the hegemonic congruence of social forces associated with the Pax Americana.

NOTES

1   This essay draws on Chapter 5 of my *American Hegemony and the Trilateral Commission* (Cambridge University Press, 1990), and on two earlier essays: 'Reflections on Global Order and Sociohistorical Time' (*Alternatives*, Vol. 16, No. 3, 1991, 275–314), and 'Economic Globalisation and the Internationalisation of Authority: Limits and Contradictions' (*Geoforum*, forthcoming, August 1992).

2   P. Cockburn, 'Oil Price Fall Forces Moscow to Cut Imports', *Financial Times*, 4 April 1986. Oil made up about 60 per cent of the Soviet Union's hard currency earnings.

3   As a matter of fact, the internationalization of capital intensified much faster than world trade. Between 1983 and 1989, world GDP grew by 7.8 per cent annually, world exports grew by 9.4 per cent, but world foreign direct investments flows grew by 28.9 per cent annually (UNCTC 1991: 4).

4   Paul A. Volcker, 'Economic Strategy', remarks made to Trilateral

Commission luncheon, 14 November 1985, Washington DC. The text is based on a verbatim transcript.

5   Lawrence Korb, a Pentagon official in the Reagan Administration and a fellow at the Brookings Institution, made this assessment from Congressional Budget Office estimates and from his own knowledge of Pentagon financing. See 'Padding the Gulf War Bill', *New York Times*, April 4, 1991, A4.

REFERENCES

Amen, M. M. (1985) 'Recurring influences on economic policy-making: Kennedy and Reagan compared', in P. M. Johnston and W. R. Thompson (eds) *Rhythms in Politics and Economics*, 181–200, New York: Praeger.

Arrighi, G. (1982) 'A crisis of hegemony', in S. Amin, G. Arrighi, A. G. Frank and I. Wallerstein, *Dynamics of Global Crisis*, 55–108, London: Macmillan.

Barraclough, G. (1967) *An Introduction to Contemporary History*, Harmondsworth: Penguin.

Beigie, C. E., Hager, W. and Sekiguchi, S. (1976) *Seeking a New Accommodation in World Commodity Markets*, New York: Trilateral Commission.

Bergsten, C. F. (1985) 'The problem?', *Foreign Policy*, 59: 132–44.

Calleo, D. P. (1982) *The Imperious Economy*, Cambridge, Mass: Harvard University Press.

Cline, W. R., (ed.) (1983) *Trade Policy in the 1980s* Washington DC: Institute for International Economics.

Cox, R. W. (1987) *Production, Power and World Order. Social Forces in the Making of History*, New York: Columbia University Press.

Frieden, J. (1987) *Banking on the World. The Politics of American International Finance*, New York: Harper & Row.

Gardner, R., Okita, S., and Udink, B. J. (1974) *A Turning Point in North–South Economic Relations*, New York: Trilateral Commission.

Gardner, R., S. Okita, B.J. Udink (1975) *OPEC, The Trilateral World, and the Developing Countries: New Arrangements for Cooperation*, New York: Trilateral Commission.

Gill, S., and D. Law (1988) *The Global Political Economy: Perspectives, Problems and Policies*, Brighton: Wheatsheaf; Baltimore: Johns Hopkins University Press.

Halliday, F. (1986) *The Making of the Second Cold War*, London: New Left Books.

Healey, D. (1991) 'A Bloody Shambles in the Wake of War', *The Guardian Weekly*, 31 March 1991, p. 11.

Hervey, J. L. (1986) 'The internationalization of Uncle Sam', *Economic Perspectives*, Federal Reserve Bank of Chicago, 10.

Hoogvelt, A. (1987) 'The new international division of labour', in R. G. Bush, G. Johnston and D. Coates (eds) *The World Order: Socialist Perspectives* Oxford: Polity Press.

Kennedy, P. (1988) *The Rise and Fall of the Great Powers. Economic Change and Military Conflict from 1500 to 2000*, London: Unwin Hyman.

Kudrle, R. T. (1986) 'The several faces of the multinational corporation', in Hollist and Tullis (eds) *An International Political Economy Yearbook*, vol. 1, 175–97.

Law, D. (1989) 'The Baker initiatives and macroeconomic co-operation', in S. Gill, (ed.) *Atlantic Relations: Beyond the Reagan Era*, Brighton: Wheatsheaf.

Nau, H. R. (1984–5) 'Where Reaganomics works', *Foreign Policy*, 57: 14–37.

Nau, H. R. (1985) 'Or the solution?', *Foreign Policy*, 59: 144–53.

Nye, J. S. (1990) *Bound to Lead. The Changing Nature of American Power*, New York: Basic Books.

Pijl, K. van der (1984) *The Making of an Atlantic Ruling Class*, London: Verso.

Prestowitz, C. (1988) *Trading Places*, New York: Basic Books.

Strange, S. (1976) 'International Monetary Relations', Vol. II of *International Monetary Relations of the Western World, 1959–1971*, A. Shonfield (ed.), London: Oxford University Press.

Strange, S. (1986) *Casino Capitalism* Oxford: Basil Blackwell.

United Nations Centre on Transnational Corporations (UNCTC) (1988) *Transnational Corporations in World Development: Trends and Prospects*, New York: United Nations.

United Nations Centre on Transnational Corporations (UNCTC) (1991) *World Investment Report 1991. The Triad in Foreign Direct Investment*, New York: United Nations.

Wolferen, K. van (1989) *The Enigma of Japanese Power: People and Politics in a Stateless Nation*, London: Macmillan.

INDEX